Lewine Mair is the first woman to have been given the golf correspondent's job on the *Daily Telegraph*. She has been in the post for nine years and, in that time, has been shortlisted for both British and American sports writing awards.

THE REAL MONTY

The Autobiography of
COLIN MONTGOMERIE

with Lewine Mair

*To my wonderful wife and children
Eimear, Olivia, Venetia and Cameron –
you are my inspiration
and thank you for everything.*

An Orion paperback

First published in Great Britain in 2002
by Orion
This paperback edition published in 2003
by Orion Books Ltd,
Orion House, 5 Upper St Martin's Lane,
London WC2H 9EA

3 5 7 9 10 8 6 4

A CIP catalogue record for this book is
available from the British Library.

ISBN-13 978-0-7528-4983-6
ISBN-10 0-7528-4983-2

Typeset at Selwood Systems
Midsomer Norton

Printed and bound in Great Britain by
Clays Ltd, St Ives plc

The Orion Publishing Group's policy is to use papers that
are natural, renewable and recyclable products and
made from wood grown in sustainable forests. The logging
and manufacturing processes are expected to conform to
the environmental regulations of the country of origin.

www.orionbooks.co.uk

CONTENTS

ACKNOWLEDGEMENTS

It would be remiss of me not to publicly thank those who have helped me and helped specifically with this book:

To all my family including my father and brother and his family.

To my caddies Alastair McLean, for ten great years, and more recently Andy Prodger.

To my coaches Bill Ferguson, Paul Marchand and Denis Pugh.

To Hugh Mantle.

To Guy Kinnings and Jane Brooks and the rest of my team at IMG – Brendan Taylor, Rachel Ward, Clare Glover and Michele Mair.

To my many sponsors who have supported me so well.

To everyone at the European Tour, the PGA and the R&A – my thanks to all of you for your help.

To all my friends and colleagues on the European Tour and PGA Tour and, in particular, to all my friends and colleagues on the Ryder Cup teams with whom I have had the privilege of playing.

To everyone at Orion who has been so helpful and to Lewine Mair who has worked so hard with me.

My thanks to all of you for helping me achieve all I have wanted to.

Finally, my thanks to the golfing public, without whose enthusiastic support it would have been difficult to do what I have done.

FOREWORD

Very rarely in sport can we say with something approaching near certainty that a record will never be equalled – far less beaten.

Sporting records are challenged every day – every year – that is why sport is huge box office.

Colin Montgomerie is the proud owner of a golfing record never likely to be matched. Consider: between 1993 and 1999 he won seven successive Vardon Trophies as European number one. During that time he competed in 139 official events – winning twenty times and finishing tenth or better in a further sixty tournaments. In five of the seven years his stroke average varied between 69.37 and 69.70. What is more Colin went into the final event of the 2000 season with a realistic chance of winning for an unbelievable eighth time – before Lee Westwood finally removed what is European golf's equivalent of the Premier League Championship from his grasp. During that period Montgomerie also tied both the United States Open and the United States PGA Championship, narrowly missing those titles only in play-offs to Ernie Els and Steve Elkington.

At the time of writing Colin Montgomerie has just completed his sixth Ryder Cup match by adding four-and-a-half points, thus taking his already impressive points haul to sixteen wins and five halved games from his twenty-eight matches. Both captains Sam Torrance and Curtis Strange, together with twenty-three of the game's very finest exponents, agreed 'Monty' to be clearly the Man of the Match at the Belfry. Not for the first time either. Montgomerie played key starring roles in Europe's other successes at Rochester and Valderrama in 1995 and 1997 respectively. At Brookline in 1999 he was magnificent and defiant in the heart-wrenching narrow defeat of Mark James's transitional side.

Quite simply Colin Montgomerie is the ultimate competitor, whether in team or individual play. His natural and uncomplicated style, with an unsurpassed rhythm at its very best, has helped him set those records which may never be equalled. His presence and support for the European Golf Tour and the Ryder Cup has been unequivocal and pivotal throughout all his successes to date. My privilege has been to be Executive Director during this period and to admire from the bench the remarkable achievements of a most remarkable man – with much more to come.

Kenneth D. Schofield CBE
(Executive Director, PGA European Tour)
October 2002

Chapter 1

TO HOUSTON
(VIA NEW MEXICO)

September 1983.

It was four o'clock in the morning at the New Mexico Military Institute in Roswell, the town where, back in July 1947, the US Air Force identified wreckage on a local field as that of a flying saucer from outer space. I had lain awake all night and now I was slipping silently out of bed. Before I went any further, I glanced anxiously at the roommate, who might well have been from Mars for all I knew of him. Mercifully, he was still asleep.

Having eased my golf clubs out of the open window, I dropped them on to the grass two storeys below. The thump outside had nothing on the one in my chest. I then did the same with my suitcases before climbing through the window and shinning down the drainpipe. At the bottom, I took a minute or two to draw breath. After that, I picked up my bags and crept out of the college grounds. Luckily for me, the New Mexico Military Institute, unlike many another American military institution I have heard about since, had enough faith in its students not to lock the gates at night. At least, it did then.

My destination was the Greyhound Bus station some fifteen minutes down the road. The bus I boarded when I got there was the one back to Albuquerque airport, where I had arrived only two days before. Not too many other citizens had the same trip in mind. Those who did might well have been among the most upright folk in the land, but to me, at that ungodly hour, they looked more than somewhat sinister. In my guilty state I spent the whole of the three-hour bus journey thinking that one of these people would put two and two together and ask for hush money. After all, going AWOL from any military academy was no minor offence.

When, at last, we pulled into Albuquerque airport, my first move was to dash for a phone and ring my father, James. 'I've had to get out of there,' I began, 'I couldn't stick it another minute.' Those first comments were greeted with silence. It was my father who had made the initial contact with the New Mexico Military Institute when it was decided that I should go to a university in America rather than one at home. Not many people on this side of the Atlantic knew too much about the American university scene back then, and when my father heard that the NMMI ran a good golf programme he wasted no time in following up on that lead. As the Managing Director for Fox's Biscuits, he did a lot of travelling abroad and, at the end of a week in San Francisco, he made a special detour to see the college. He talked with the coach, a thoroughly nice guy who was sufficiently taken with my place in the Scottish youth team to offer me a two-year scholarship. My father's feeling was that if my golf were to improve sufficiently over the two years at the NMMI, I could turn professional. If not, I could do a follow-on university course at home.

There was a golf course on the college campus and the coach explained that the team played every afternoon. As far as my father could tell, admittedly at a time when there were no students in residence, the place did not seem over-military. In fact, he had no reason to suppose there was anything wrong with it at all. However, as I would rapidly discover when I got there, it was more army than university. There seemed to be three types of students: those who knew enough about themselves to worry that they might abuse the freedom they would be given at an ordinary university; those whose parents demanded that they go somewhere strict; and those with military genes. Those in the last group were probably following in the footsteps of their fathers and grandfathers.

As my father had, I took an immediate liking to the golf coach, but I wasted no time in taking an avid dislike to everything else. But that was just me; other people were probably entirely happy with what was on offer. Within a matter of hours of our arrival, we had been issued with army uniforms and given a short back and sides. The very next day we had to be in our uniforms and on parade in the square at five o'clock. I find it tough enough to respond to the alarm in order to make the seven-thirty starting times that some tournament organisers subject me to. At the NMMI there was not just a bell to wake the dead but a subsequent spate of barked instructions. If you did not conform, you were punished. Severely.

Certainly, it was not what I was looking for from my American experience. I had had entirely enough in the way of discipline at home and at Strathallan, my Scottish public school. I had come to America predominantly to play golf and, despite the enthusiasm of the coach, the NMMI did not appear to see the game as one of the more important items on its agenda.

Following his mute response at the start of our trans-atlantic call, my father, who had an enviably distinguished army career behind him, made a rapid assessment of my disaster of a foray into the military world. In the certain knowledge that I had burned my boats at the NMMI, he issued instructions: namely, that I should use the credit card he had given me – for emergency use – to buy a ticket to a big city. I had a choice: Los Angeles, San Francisco, Dallas and Houston were all winking from the departures board.

On the grounds that Albuquerque–Houston was the first available flight, I chose Houston. There were no complications and, once I was safely ensconced on the two-hour flight, I began to breathe more easily.

When I got off the plane in Houston, I followed the paternal instruction to book in at an airport hotel and, presumably because it was the most obviously accessible, I opted for the Doubletree, which was just beyond the perimeter of Bush Airport. That done, I dialled home again. Like me, my father had been thinking things through. 'There's nothing for you back here in Troon,' he said. 'Stay put and I'll sort something out.'

The two days felt like weeks as I sat twiddling my thumbs in my hotel room. I ventured into downtown Houston at one point but was far too worried about possible repercussions from the NMMI to begin to enjoy myself. (In fact, they never did try to make contact, then or since.)

While I waited, my father got to work. One of his first moves was to ring a friend of his at Ilkley, a scratch-handicap vicar by the name of Paddy who played most of his golf at Sunningdale. Dad knew that Paddy had golfing relations in the States whom he visited from time to time and, as luck would have it, the news that I was in Houston struck a chord. Paddy happened to be on good terms with the Athletics Director at Houston Baptist University called Ed Billings. First Paddy and then Dad gave the director a call. Before too long, Dave Mannen, the golf coach at the university, turned up at the Double Tree.

He started by asking some questions about my golf. I filled him in on my place in the Scottish youth team and the fact that I was playing to a handicap of three. Though not unimpressed, he was unable to offer me an immediate scholarship because the term had started and all the scholarship places were taken. Instead, he said he would take me in a 'walk-on' capacity for the first year. I did not know what that was but he described it as the equivalent of a regular student suddenly reaching the point where he was good enough to fight it out with the golf scholarship holders for a place on the team.

My father, who had thought that his days of shelling out for my education were at an end, was going to have to pay for the first twelve months and, with me being an 'out of state student', that was going to come to about £12,000. I felt terrible about making such an expensive nuisance of myself but, on the other side of the coin, I knew that if things went according to plan, I would receive a full scholarship for the next three years, one which would cover everything bar my journeys to and from Scotland.

After we had talked that day at the Doubletree, Dave Mannen drove me up to the university to have a look round. I liked what I saw. Houston Baptist is an early 1960s building: big and grey but strikingly friendly. Everyone I met that day, from the man at the door to the admissions people, greeted me warmly and, even though all the other students had already started to settle in, I did not feel out of place. At the end of our meeting, Dave and I shook hands.

I was to start the next day.

Chapter 2

SETTING HOUSTON BAPTIST ALIGHT

One of my first tasks at Houston Baptist was to enrol in the right blend of classes. I was armed with seven 'O' levels and two and a half 'A' levels in economics, geography and general studies. I had failed the 'A' level in maths. To my amazement, they told me I could do medicine, which, with no science 'A' levels to my name, would never have been an option at home. Flattering though that sounded, the course that made the most sense, especially if I were ever to make the decision to turn professional, was business studies, which included company law.

For the first two years, the course was very general, and I chose typing from among the lighter, subsidiary classes that were on offer. I liked the sound of that because typing was something I wished I had done at school. It was not the kind of choice you could ever have made in front of friends back home because typing, at least at that stage, was strictly for girls. Houston, though, was a long way from Troon, and I decided to go for it. I am glad that I made that decision. Key-pads, like the notes on a piano, stay the same, and, even though my technique has never been exactly orthodox, I learned to type more than adequately. Back in 1983, I hadn't begun to realise the extent to which computers would take hold, but today I can rattle off e-mail messages with the best of them. I doubt whether there is a professional on tour who does not travel with a computer. Aside from using it to keep in touch with friends and family, there are a number of the more technically minded who get their caddies to video their swings in order that they can send the pictures back to their teaching professionals at home.

For the purposes of university golf at Houston, we were asked to meet up at Dave Mannen's office. The golfing scholars had been billeted together in the halls of residence but, because of the circumstances of my arrival, I was temporarily staying on my own. I didn't know a soul when I pitched up from my digs to meet the other nine golfers. Two of the students had cars and, after a brief talk from Dave, our two drivers ferried the rest of us up to the Bear Creek Country Club. The idea was that we would play a medal round to decide which of the ten would make the five-strong team for the first tournament.

I shot a 71, which was second or third and good enough to give me a spot. It also qualified me for the first open college tournament of the season at the University of Phoenix, where Billy Mayfair had already started to make something of a name for himself. Billy won that event and I finished in the top ten. I was the best of the Houston Baptist brigade and that performance catapulted me to the top of the university side. Thereafter, I almost always played at number one or two.

Where you played on the team was the big thing. Playing and staying at number one would be an ongoing goal throughout my university days, while the same applied to winning tournaments. All told, I won ten, though it has to be said that some boasted stronger fields than others.

Dave proved to be an excellent coach and there were things I learned from him that I still practise to this day, especially the 100-putt routine. Tiger Woods, I know, does the same exercise with six-footers, but Dave taught us to do it with two-footers. You have to hole each putt in turn and, if you miss, you have to go back to the beginning and start all over again. It is, of course, all about muscle memory.

Over the four years, I met and played against plenty of golfers I know today. Apart from Billy Mayfair, whom I once defeated in a play-off at the Beaumont College tournament, there was Davis Love, Steve Elkington, Duffy Waldorf and Scott Verplank, to name just a few. There were also a lot of players whose names I still see when I look at the results of the Buy.com tour. The standard was high and because there was never a day when you were not practising alongside good players or competing against them, you could not but get better.

At that point, as I have said, there were nowhere near as many British players choosing the American university option as there are today. Since Scottish and British selectors concentrated on British-based results when it came to choosing Walker Cup teams, it was a bit of a risky business cutting oneself off from the home scene, though I somehow managed to remain in favour. It still is a difficult decision to have to make – and could become more so now that the British hierarchy, both amateur and professional, is actively encouraging young golfers to combine the sport with further education at home.

What happened to Luke Donald, who turned professional in 2001, set the alarm bells ringing. Briefly, he did as I did in going to university out there, but, instead of returning to play on the European Tour, at the end of the day he decided to make his professional way in the States. Luke, who won the American Universities' 1999 NCAA individual title and the Jack Nicklaus Award as the Collegiate Men's Player of the Year, took that route partly because he felt the US Tour was the best there is and partly because he wanted to stay with the group of friends he had made on the college scene. He has made a good job of getting himself established over there, but it is not too difficult to understand why Ken Schofield, the executive director of the European Tour, would sooner he had chosen Europe. As the women professionals in Europe have discovered to their cost, the more the better players abscond to the States, the tougher it is to sustain a thriving tour at home.

Since the start of 2002, the R&A have been handing out annual grants of up to £5,000 a year to top young players prepared to juggle a British university or college education with international golf. Some of the students are very sensibly opting for golf-related courses like green-keeping, golf course architecture or golf club management. To my mind, that makes a lot of sense because that way, if they fail to make the grade as golfers, they can still enjoy careers in the game.

Meanwhile, in another encouraging move, the R&A have been issuing grants to individual universities towards the coaching of the golf squad. They could go further and expand this college programme to embrace the whole of Europe. That way, the students in colder climes could benefit from playing the odd winter match in warmer weather. It will take time before any European university set-up will have the same calibre of fixture list as is found in the States, but at least they have identified the huge potential of this area and the process is under way.

Of those British players who were in the States at the same time as myself, Paul Mayo and Phil Parkin were the ones I knew best. They were two former Amateur champions, both attending Texas A&M (Agricultural & Mechanical), not far from Houston. Paul was a fine player but I have always thought that Phil was the best amateur I ever saw. I had watched the Amateur Championship at Turnberry in 1983, where he won the qualifying and the championship itself. He beat America's Jim Holtgrieve in the final by a comfortable five and four margin. In fact, he beat everyone he played very easily. He had the best swing and his putting was fantastic. I don't think people realised just how good he was. I was convinced he would have a fantastic future, not least because of what he did on the college scene. Though he was there for no more than a year, he won six tournaments and finished second in four more. He won one by *nine* shots from a field that included Billy Ray Brown and Steve Elkington. There came a point when, on his own admission, he was no longer finding it a challenge. Outrageous though this might sound, he decided to see if he could still beat the Americans without using his woods. Phil arrived at the last hole just one shot behind the leader, Rick Gibson. He then holed a twenty-footer for a birdie to leave Gibson with an eighteen-footer to win. With Gibson's putt a nasty, downhill affair, we were all expecting the outcome to be a tie. It was something of an anticlimax when Gibson holed, but for Phil to have finished second in that company and in those circumstances was extraordinary. He was very, very talented and he knew it.

He went to Formby in 1984 to try to win a second Amateur Championship and, when we had a practice round together, he hit every green on his way to a 62. He won the qualifying event before making his way triumphantly through to the last sixteen of the match-play stages. Then, in the kind of exit to which even the very best can be susceptible in match-play, he lost on the sixteenth green to the Scot Colin Brooks. The match over, he did something I will never forget. Having shaken hands, he walked on to the tee of the seventeenth and unleashed one of the finest drives you could ever see. As the ball bounded down the fairway, he turned to the somewhat baffled onlookers and announced, 'That was my last shot as an amateur.'

Phil Parkin never made it as a professional because of his eyes. Though he did not have the condition properly diagnosed until long after his playing career was over, his optic muscles functioned erratically and, try as he might, he could not trust himself to hole a putt. He is now an up-and-coming television commentator, but what happened to his golf was still very sad. With the possible exception of Scott Verplank, who won the Western Open before he turned professional, I must reiterate that I never saw a better amateur.

My own performance at Formby furnished proof that my golf was progressing at Houston Baptist. While the top Americans come over to Britain to learn about what Peter Thomson, the quintuple Open champion, has referred to as 'golf's third dimension' – the element of bounce and roll – I was becoming increasingly consistent from playing on the Americans' more uniform courses. Above all, I was learning to win. The coaches instil a feeling of superiority and confidence in you. They tell you that you can do it and you find that you can. Whenever I returned to Britain, I used to feel a bit superior. You couldn't help it – it was the way the Americans trained you to think.

But it was not just the golf I enjoyed during my university days. A high percentage of sports scholarship holders at American universities never finish what they set out to do on the academic front, but, to my lingering relief, I managed to hang on in there and complete my course. The degree I was eventually awarded – in 1987 – was a BA with majors in management and recreation. Also, though I have still to find the time to attend a presentation ceremony, the university have since given me their Distinguished Alumnus Award, which is presented annually to a former student who has made 'a significant impact on his or her profession and personifies the qualities of excellence embraced by HBU'.

Almost certainly because of its Baptist traditions, the standard of behaviour at the college was particularly high or, if you like, formal. The students did not let their hair down as they might at other colleges, though they enjoyed themselves just the same. I don't think I did anything untoward during my university years unless, of course, you count that night I was left on dinner duty …

As I have said, I had reached the point where I did not have to qualify for a team place. Hence, when we were all staying in the one apartment and the others were having to go through the qualifying process, it made sense for me to cook the evening meal. It may not be a result of cosmic significance but, on the TV show *Can't Cook, Won't Cook* a few years ago, my scones were voted better than Darren Clarke's. Those doing the voting were Darren's wife Heather, and my wife Eimear. Heaven knows what made Heather choose my scones but, in Eimear's case, she admitted to having spotted something that told her whose were whose. That was the first time I had attempted anything so adventurous since the aforementioned day at Houston Baptist University. A lack of funds was obviously a factor in my decision to make American biscuits, a relative of the English scone. I thought they would go down a treat. I purchased some dough from the local supermarket and, having made a couple of calls to Troon to check with my mother that I was going about things in the right way, I kneaded the mixture and soon had a tray full of individual scones. So far so good. I then put them in the oven and sat back, complacently, as I thought of the good reception my efforts would receive from the hungry golfers. Long before the twenty minutes' cooking time was up, there was a smell of burning so intense that it was clear, even to me, that all was not as it should be within those oven walls. Tentatively, I opened the door and out leapt some mammoth flames that shot up the walls and darted across the ceiling. The fire alarm was activated and the speed with which the fire spread defied belief. I dialled 911 before escaping the heat and the thickening smoke. By then, alarms were ringing out across the campus as I and other students ran into the road outside.

The Houston Fire Brigade arrived within a matter of

minutes. They scaled ladders and shoved a hose through the apartment window before filling the place up with white foam. After the flames had finally subsided, they explained that my mistake had been one of putting the scones on a heavily oil-coated tray. Not since the Dark Ages, when King Alfred the Great was blamed for burning a peasant woman's cakes, can there have been such a culinary conflagration.

Thus passed one day when I thought I was doing everything right and it all went badly wrong. The foam did not disappear. The golf team had to move out of the apartment, as did the basketball players in the flat below. At an average height of six feet seven or more, the basketball fraternity were not the best group to choose to upset.

To my relief, no bills were passed on to me or, more pertinently, to my father.

As for the basketball players, they seemed to have loftier things on their minds than getting their revenge. In fact, it is probably fair to say that there was a certain empathy among all the sportsmen and women at the university, with everyone getting together for the days when we would wash people's cars for five dollars a go for university charities.

Fun though we had as we hosed down those vehicles, I could not help thinking that it was time I had a car of my own. As I said, two of the team had cars in which they had to ferry the rest of us around, and I was horribly conscious of being among the group who were always begging for a lift.

Eventually, my father said he was prepared to get me a second-hand – or, as the Americans say, a 'pre-owned' – car, provided I paid the insurance and the running costs for myself. I managed to find an old Mazda GLC and splashed out ten dollars on a personalised number-plate – MONTY. The cost of the insurance was astronomical because I was still only twenty and not a permanent resident. Somehow, I had to find three hundred dollars a year and, since I did not have a green card that would enable me to take a proper job, I had to think of something else. In my desperation, I thought of something pretty quick.

As students, we played on some pretty plush courses, including the Lochinvar Country Club, which was an early Jack Nicklaus design and an exclusive establishment boasting 110 or so male members. The Lochinvar had two or three gala dinners a year and, since I knew the professional, I asked if a couple of friends and I could do the valet parking. On the first of these nights, Alan Shepherd, the astronaut, was among those who asked me to park his car, a white Porsche 928. At the end of the evening, when I collected it for him, he handed me an absurdly generous hundred dollars. The other two lads and I put the money in a pot and, by the end of the night, we had 1,500 dollars to divide among us. Very quickly, we expanded our little business, taking on that same role at Sweetwater and at Houston Country Club, where Paul Marchand, who has helped to coach me for the last few years, is a member.

Valet parking is not the most taxing job in the world when the driver is arriving. Then, all you have to do is put the gear in drive and take the car away. It is at the other end of the evening that it can turn into a bit of a nightmare. Speed is of the essence when a man sends you to collect his prize Cadillac but, inevitably, you do not always remember where you parked the vehicle. Once you have located it, you hurry to make amends, only to find yourself in such a state that you cannot get to grips with the controls. Where is the handbrake? Where are the lights? As the seconds tick by, you picture an impatient guest returning some of his ten-dollar bills to his wallet.

Mostly, though, people were kind to the students of my era because they appreciated that we were strapped for cash. It helped, too, that they had no notion of how we would while away those evenings by taking some of the more fancy cars for a spin. Alan Shepherd and his fellow diners could have been on the moon for all they knew of what was going on outside.

Chapter 3

OPENING SHOTS

My four years at Houston Baptist University came to an end in May 1987 and I went back to Troon, the west coast town to which my parents had returned when my father was given the job as secretary of Royal Troon Golf Club. He had been a member of the club since the 1950s.

Like my older brother, Douglas, I had been born in Glasgow and spent my first three and a half years there. I was no Tiger Woods. At the age of two, Tiger appeared on *CBS News* and the *Mike Douglas Show* putting with Bob Hope. At three, he shot 48 for nine holes at the Navy Golf Club in Cypress, California. At that age I was merely pottering around on the little practice course next to the ladies' club and within earshot of its members. What particularly appealed to me were the little valleys crossing the second and eighth holes. You could probably step across them but, to me, they represented huge carries. I was obsessed with knocking my ball over these dips, and the personal challenge drew me back again and again. Other small children were similarly employed. No one, as I remember it, took too much notice of us. It was great that we were allowed to be there. And that, of course, is something that has never applied at enough British courses.

Douglas, my brother, was six and I was coming up for four when my father, by way of advancing his career, moved down to Yorkshire. He and my mother joined Ilkley Golf Club and it was there, a couple of years later, that I had my first lesson from Bill Ferguson, the club pro. I can remember it as if it were yesterday. Bill took one look at my grip and pronounced it 'very strong'. Like other small boys, I had adopted a strong left-hand hold on the club for the purposes of slogging the ball a long way.

Bill, or Mr Ferguson as he was to me, was the National Club Professional champion at the time. He was hugely respected at the club and beyond, and everyone listened to him. When he told me that I would have to change my grip if I wanted to be any good, I did precisely as he said. If you look at the pictures in the plate section you can see that the swing I have today and the swing I had as a nine-year-old are much the same. In many respects, the likeness is uncanny, particularly with regard to my leg action. The follow-through, too, is instantly recognisable, though it became higher and fuller as I picked up confidence.

Each weekend in Yorkshire there was a captain–professional challenge match, and there came a day when Bill asked if I would like to pull his trolley. I was thrilled to be asked and did the job on and off until I was eleven. As a learning experience, it was probably one of the best of my golfing life. Any youngster who is offered a similar opportunity should not hesitate to make the most of it. There were all sorts of little things I picked up that have served me well ever since. To give just one example, Bill told me how there is always less sand than you think in the face of a bunker, the reason being that people normally rake downwards rather than up. You have to watch for that. Bill's 'clover' tip was another that has often come in handy. If you are in clover, literally rather than metaphorically, your club will hit through it more quickly than it would through grass. As a result, the ball will take off at greater speed.

There are some players who boast that they have never had

a lesson in their lives. Sometimes, what they are saying will be 100 per cent true but, in most instances, they will have learned through watching good players, either in the flesh or on television. Televised golf has probably contributed more than anything to the way swings around the world have recently become so much more uniform, especially with respect to the proliferation of Tiger lookalikes. Today's youngsters are trying to copy everything about the world number one, with Adam Scott, though he has many admirable qualities of his own, one of the most successful of the so-called Tiger-chasers.

To be self-taught is commendable up to a point, but, to my way of thinking, the sooner a young golfer has some individual professional help the better. If your fundamentals are correct, you have a better chance of everything else falling into place. My father took me to a certain level – to a seven handicap to be precise – but he could never put things across as well as Bill did. Where the paternal assistance was invaluable was in matters to do with etiquette, telling me when to attend pins, where to stand, and so on. I know that there are some who will say that I have tended to get too upset for my own good and everyone else's, but that is hardly his fault. It's mine.

Apart from holiday and weekend golf with Douglas and my parents, I did not play much in my young days at Ilkley. I was a day boy at Ghyll Royd Preparatory School in the town and followed all the other boys in playing cricket, hockey and rugby. I enjoyed prep school rather more than my senior schooling at Strathallan in Perthshire. Great school though it is, and much though I enjoyed the sport, Strathallan was too far from home. To get there, Douglas and I had to take one train from York to Edinburgh and another from Edinburgh to Perth. It was only on the Edinburgh–Perth leg of the trip that we would change into the kilts we had to wear by way of a uniform. We would never have dreamed of setting off in them at York station.

At Strathallan, as at Ghyll Royd, the sports on offer were rugby, hockey and cricket: rugby for a term and a half, hockey for half a term and cricket in the summer. There was a rough golf course round the edge of the rugby pitch called Big Acre but the game was not encouraged as it is today. I was a centre-half at hockey, a game I really enjoyed. I was not quite quick enough, while my long swing – I found it impossible to keep it knee-high – was a danger to everyone. My main strength was that I could read a game well. My brother and I would often combine to good effect: at short corners, he would stop the ball and move out of the way in order that I could give it a whack. We scored a lot of goals and I injured a lot of goalkeepers.

Cricket was my favourite, the school sport in which I went the furthest. I opened the bowling for Strathallan and came in to bat at four or five, by which time there were usually spinners to face. I hated them. I either made very good contact and scored a boundary or a six or I was stumped. Back at home, I used to enjoy keeping score for Ilkley and, in time, I was on the fringe for Yorkshire at under-eighteen level. There was one memorable occasion when I bowled to Geoff Boycott in the nets. Another time, Chris Old, who opened the Yorkshire attack, bowled to me in the indoor facility at Headingley. They described him as medium fast but, to me, his bowling was as lightning. I have never been so frightened in all my days. The ball bounces and you are not sure quite how high it is going to rear. It also pitches on a testing length so you are caught on the hop as to whether to go forward or back. Which, of course, makes it the perfect length. Instead of going forward, I was too often on the right foot or, rather, the wrong one.

I suspect that Montgomerie the cricketer did not look too unlike the golfer. Years ago, in an old copy of the *Sunday Telegraph*, there was an article on Ted Dexter, the most lordly of stroke-players, which was accompanied by a wonderful pair of photographs. The first depicted him at the end of a tee-shot and the second at the end of what looked as if it had been a full-blooded straight six. Save for the difference in clothing, they were, to all intents and purposes, identical, not least in the exemplary weight transference.

At school, however, I ended up with enough in the way of exams to satisfy my father, though my reports all made a point of saying that I had not exactly pushed myself other than on the games field, while they also reflected some bad breaks on the discipline front. If, say, twelve of us were involved in a slipper fight, you could guarantee that a master would materialise at precisely that moment when it was my turn to throw the slipper. What I learned better than any-thing else during my time there was that you do better to start off the trouble before taking a back seat and leaving everyone else to take the flak. I think I would have preferred the new-style Strathallan to the Strathallan I knew. Then, it was all boys. Now, they have two girls' houses and it is all very different.

When I left Strathallan, where the pupils come from all over Britain and beyond, that was it. Occasionally, I will bump into someone at an airport and we will remember each other from schooldays, but that is as far as it goes.

On leaving Strathallan with a golf handicap of six but with the odd sub-70 round under my belt, I embarked on the two years of virtually full-time golf that my father felt were my due. He realised how easily the game came to me and was understandably intrigued to see how good I could be if I really worked. At the same time, he could see that I had the necessary dream for myself. The idea of playing for my country tickled my imagination. I was embarking on a great adventure.

Having missed out on the Scottish Boys side, I decided to target the Scottish Youth team. All of which meant that I had to play Scottish-based tournaments rather than those closer to our Ilkley home. These Scottish golfing forays were not always the merriest, the reason being that there was a section of the Scottish golfing community who saw me as something of an interloper. I was not obviously one of them. I saw this as being due to a combination of things, most notably my English accent and the fact that I was a public schoolboy. Also, it did not help that I was quite good and getting better. No one ever said anything to my face but I was conscious of a certain resentment, and of how I had to do that bit better than the regular Scots when it came to being chosen for a team. My father was no less aware of what was going on than I was. In fact, he probably noticed it more than I did.

It would have been easier by far for me to play for England and I cannot pretend that the thought did not cross my mind. For one thing, I would not have had to travel so far for all my amateur golf and, for another, there was none of the resentment in England that I felt when I went north. Yet there was no way I could have thrown in my lot with the English. I am Scottish through and through.

I did not have too much time to brood on this state of affairs because, between tournaments, I was complying with my father's suggestion that I should do something to earn my keep with a part-time job. His position at Fox's Biscuits enabled him to find me a job with the company going under the title of 'relief rep'. My patch was Yorkshire and the nature of the post was such that I was always in a hurry, which was not a good idea for a teenager who had only been driving for what seemed like five minutes. Within no time, I had three crashes. This did not go down well, not least because I was one of the bosses' sons. The first time it happened, I wedged the bonnet of the company Ford Escort under the top rim of one of those famous Yorkshire dry-stone dykes. That car was a write-off, as was the one I spun on the ice in York a few months later. Having done a full circle, the vehicle hit a traffic island, finishing upside down. I was pretty shaken, needless to say. The third incident involved nothing more than a wickedly harsh scrape along the length of both doors. The police were involved on all three occasions and, each time, they penned the words, 'No other vehicle involved.' In other words, the accidents were my fault. There was no getting away from it.

Those incidents apart, the intermingling of part-time job and golf went well. I was not without talent in the biscuit-selling department. My father had always brought the latest lines in Fox's biscuits home and Douglas and I would tuck into them with great gusto. I had no difficulty in recommending what was, after all, an award-winning product. On the golf front, my first award was the Scottish Youths cap I earned in 1983, probably on account of my third place behind Stephen Keppler in the 1982 British Youths Championship. The first of our matches that year was against England and played over the New Course, St Andrews. It may have been August, but the weather conditions were more winter than summer. To borrow from the Scottish Golf Union's account, 'The morning foursomes were eventually shared after the Scottish team seemed to be in danger of losing them.' In the singles, 'the Scottish Youths were on the verge of defeat but a gritty performance from the last player in, who halved the hole, the game and the match, ensured that the Alex Mackay Memorial Trophy remained in Scotland'. I won morning and afternoon, while it was one Steve McAllister who was responsible for the 'gritty' performance in the last game. Playing for the Scottish Youths team would be the first meaningful achievement to go down on my CV when it came to making my application to the New Mexico Military Institute.

In 1984, on my first summer vacation from Houston, I was the runner-up to Spain's José Maria Olazábal in that Amateur Championship at Formby where Phil Parkin hit his 'last shot as an amateur'. Ollie, eighteen years of age to my twenty as we embarked on what was the youngest ever final, was the first player to win the British Boys' Championship and the Amateur Championship in the same summer.

The description the late John Campbell gave of the Spaniard in the *Daily Telegraph* may not catch Olazábal's lovely sense of humour, but it does reflect some of his other qualities: 'He is a dark, almost sinister figure who plays his matches in fits and starts with his foot resting on the accelerator, content to freewheel until he feels threatened. One such occasion showed at the seventh hole of the second round – a fiendishly difficult new hole with trees everywhere you don't want them. Montgomerie was three down – as he had been at lunch – and faced a desperate putt of fully 45 feet down the steeply sloping green. He jumped for joy as he holed it, but Olazábal's cool response was to follow him in from 19 feet for a brilliant half in birdies.' Ollie was four ahead by the turn and delivered his killer punch at the eleventh, holing his second from some 120 yards for an unanswerable eagle. I was relieved to delay the inevitable by winning the twelfth but promptly lost the thirteenth, to another birdie, before being beaten five and four.

Patently, it was disappointing to lose that match. After all, the winner of the Amateur gets to play not just in the Open of that year but in the Masters the following spring. But there was some compensation as I earned a place in that year's Scottish team for the Home Internationals and in the British team for the Eisenhower Trophy, or World Team Championships.

Over the next three years, I would achieve every amateur's ambition of playing for Great Britain and Ireland in the Walker Cup against the Americans, with my first appearance in 1985 and the second in 1987. In 1985 we lost 11–13 and I picked up half a point, that miserable contribution being all that the team gleaned from the second foursomes series.

Paul Mayo and I were one down after seventeen against Scott Verplank and Jay Sigal, whom David White, writing in the *Golfer's Handbook*, described as 'the strongest pairing that America could muster'. White wrote that the match would be long remembered for 'the spectacular long iron struck by Montgomerie with such sweet venom at the 18th to within 10 feet of the cup; and for the never-say-die putt from Mayo that fell for a birdie'.

In 1987 I fared rather better as an individual though we lost the match rather more easily – 16½–7½. England's Jeremy Robertson, Ireland's John McHenry and I all performed well in the singles. I defeated Jim Sorensen on the first day and Billy Andrade on the second. Bruce Critchley, from the Sky TV commentary team, wrote the report in the *Golfer's Handbook* that year and said that I was one of only a couple of British players who looked to be enjoying himself. He added something about my 'intimidating presence' and 'an air of confidence which seemed to inhibit both of his opponents, neither of whom played well'.

I was a miles better match-player by then and had every reason to feel confident when, in the wake of that Walker Cup week, I headed for the Scottish Amateur Championship at Nairn. It was an event that would help to determine the course of my life.

Chapter 4
ROAD TO THE AISLE

As I drove through the highlands to the 1987 Scottish Amateur Championship at Nairn, I was thinking about winning. It was time I won this particular event. I had won the 1985 Scottish Stroke-Play Championship but I was without a national match-play title and so was conscious of my amateur record being less than complete. Until then, I had been able to put my relatively disappointing performances down to a lack of experience. Now, at twenty-four, I had more experience than most, what with my two years of full-time amateur golf followed by four years at Houston Baptist.

When I arrived in Nairn, I read a series of newspaper articles, all of them giving the impression that I was just waiting to grab this title by way of a stepping-stone to turning professional. The journalists in question knew more than I did. In any case, quite apart from the fact that I had not yet ruled out the possibility of another career, I did not want to get too far ahead of myself.

While most of the other competitors at Nairn were staying at the little bed-and-breakfast establishments dotted around the town, or in caravan sites on its outskirts, I had booked into the Newton Hotel. Some of the other players would no doubt have seen that as a perfect illustration of how I was not one of them, but, by that stage, I had accepted that there was no point in getting upset by what anyone thought. As it happened, I had a specific reason for going to the Newton. Years before, my parents had spent the second night of their honeymoon there on their way to the Kyle of Lochalsh, the place after which they would name all three of the houses they would have in England over the next fifteen years.

I, on the other hand, turned out to be so greatly taken with Nairn itself and my week at the Scottish Amateur as to employ the name not just for the three houses in which I have lived so far, but also for my various golf-related companies.

From the start of that championship week, I hit fairways and putted soundly. There have been times, recently, when I have struggled with my holing out but, in those days, I had no shortage of confidence on the greens and had a definite hit in my stroke. In my second round, against Chris Cowan, who is now on the R&A's Rules of Golf Committee, I holed three putts in a row of between five and seven feet to win by two and one. Elsewhere, my ball-striking was nowhere near as sound as it is today, but here again confidence played its part. In my four years in America, I had learned how to win. Also, thanks to the sameness of the conditions in America, my swing had become firmly grooved.

On the Wednesday night, I was relaxing in front of the television in my room at the Newton when Grampian TV did an item on the championship and focused on Paul Girvan from Prestwick St Nicholas. Paul had played in the Walker Cup at Sunningdale and he, like me, was through to the last thirty-two. The interviewer was asking if he could go on to win. At that, Paul shook his head in a bemused sort of way. 'There's only one winner of this tournament and that's Colin Montgomerie,' he said. I will never forget his comment. The golf psychologists would have been appalled at the negative nature of what he was saying, though I have known even the best golfers make the same mistake. Ernie Els once awarded me the Volvo PGA Championship at a stage when there was still a long way to go. Paul's comment worked as a positive for me. It gave me an extra dose of belief and maybe even served as the first seeds of the confidence that flowed increasingly through my veins as I won my seven Orders of Merit.

The following morning I was up against a big fellow by the name of Jim Milligan, who would win the championship the following year. He was a member of Barassie and clearly knew a thing or two about links golf. I managed to win on the last green and that took me into the last sixteen. Two days later, I was through to Saturday's thirty-six hole final, where I was to play a fellow Ayrshire county player in Alasdair Watt. He was twenty to my twenty-four.

My parents came up for the final, while John Wilson, who lived next door but one to us in Troon, was another to make the trip. As secretary of the Ayrshire Golf Union, he obviously felt duty-bound to be on hand, what with the all-Ayrshire nature of the final. He was accompanied by his wife, Dorothy, and his eighteen-year-old daughter, Eimear. In spite of the fact that we lived so close, I had never previously been introduced to either of them, the reason being that I had spent so much of my time in the States.

Presumably, Dorothy and Eimear had been instrumental in persuading John to stop for coffee at Aviemore on the way up. Either way, they did not arrive in Nairn until lunchtime, by which time the first eighteen holes were over. The front nine had been close. Alasdair was one up and would have been two up but for the eighteen-footer I holed across the tenth green. That was the start of a homeward 32 – mostly downwind – in which I won seven of the last eight holes to be a healthy six up. My mother, who was always nervous when she came to watch, was wishing it were seven.

After lunch, I tied things up in the space of ten holes, with the final score nine and eight. It was easy enough but I could not afford to let up because if you let one or two holes slip away at the start of an afternoon it can very quickly become a landslide. I think the general consensus of opinion was that I was much the more experienced of the finalists, what with my college golf and my Scottish Stroke-Play title of 1985. Alasdair, on the other hand, had come from nowhere to reach the final and had had a great week at Nairn before he so much as hit a shot on the Saturday.

When it came to the prize-giving, my eye lit on Eimear as she stood talking to her parents in the corner. My dad introduced us, telling me that she was a student at Edinburgh University. Eimear, who was looking 'very Edinburgh' in one of those waxed Barbour coats, said a shy hello and that was that. She was polite and demure but, at the same time, she possessed an easy confidence in the way she handled herself in what was an unfamiliar situation. As to the way she looked, she struck me as being no less beautiful than she was clever. I thought to myself that she must have a golden future ahead of her. In brief, I was hooked. Later in the evening, we talked a little more. Then, bravely ignoring the fact that she had mentioned that she had a boyfriend, I took courage in both hands and asked if I might phone her the following week. As I drove back to Troon that night my joy at having finally won the Scottish Amateur was punctuated by thoughts of this wonderful girl.

It was a day or so after the championship and I was still plucking up the courage to ring Eimear when my father suggested I should go down to the DHSS office in Troon. 'I've paid enough tax over the years and if a suitable job comes up while you're deciding what you are going to do next, you'd better take it,' he said. I parked the car some distance away from the relevant office for fear that someone would see where I was going. Then, having walked a good couple of hundred yards and melted furtively through the door of the DHSS offices, I had the surprise of my life. There was Eimear. Her father had had much the same conversation with her as mine had had with me. She was on holiday from university and, since she had nothing else to do, he felt she might as well collect her unemployment pay and, at the same time, see if there were any interesting holiday jobs on offer.

She looked pleased to see me but, as she would tell me later, she was more than somewhat alarmed by my attire. Up at Nairn, she had apparently taken one look at my red trousers and white belt and thought to herself that I looked 'uncool'. As I stood in the queue wearing a gold watch and a pair of tartan trousers, the kind that Americans like to wear in Scotland, she was not about to change her opinion. By the time I had signed on, Eimear had disappeared.

Outside, it was pouring with rain and she was still nowhere to be seen. It was only once I had turned the car into Bentinck Drive that I finally caught up with her. Thanks to the weather, I had a perfectly good excuse to stop and offer her a lift. That was it. We started dating almost straight away and, after a two-year courtship, we were married in Troon Old Parish Church on 27 June 1990. So now you will understand why Nairn means so much to me. It was there that I won my national championship and it was there that I met my wife.

Chapter 5

SOCIAL ORDER

The masters at Strathallan may not have been particularly impressed by my habit in the classroom of doing just enough to get by and no more – but, throughout my schooldays, I always had the feeling that I was going to make something of myself and that I would not end up doing a regular nine-to-five job. Oddly enough, Eimear similarly sensed that she was unlikely to mirror what was expected of her by turning from law student to full-time lawyer.

Even after I had completed my American university course and won the Scottish Amateur, the two achievements that my father felt I should have under my belt if I wanted to forge a career as a professional, I was not 100 per cent sure where my 'special future' lay. Though I have since come to believe that you have to be prepared to take risks if you want to get anywhere in this life, my parents were not risk-takers. Douglas had gone into banking and the family would almost certainly have been greatly relieved if I had decided to do something similar. However, now that I had graduated, they were altogether less twitchy about the professional route. To them, an academic qualification served as an insurance policy.

I was twenty-four and wanted to turn professional but there was still a small voice inside saying that I might do better to use my degree to find a golf-related job. The most coveted in the business were those with Mark McCormack's IMG, an organisation that had developed from McCormack's friendship with Arnold Palmer. McCormack, a lawyer, offered to manage Palmer's business affairs and, before long, other players were calling for the same degree of expertise.

It is a good feeling to apply for a job for which you have precisely the right qualifications and, when the chance arose, I seized the opportunity to have an interview with two of the company's top executives, Peter German and Ian Todd, for a post as a client manager. The interview was to take place at Turnberry, where I now have my Colin Montgomerie Links Academy, and it was to be conducted over a few holes of golf. Peter and Ian had already played the first nine when I arrived, but the two of them seemed entirely happy to switch to a three-ball for the homeward half.

Across my amateur career, I had played in two Walker Cups and won both the Scottish Stroke-Play and Scottish Match-Play. However, I don't suppose I had ever scored as well as I did that day. After nine holes, I was the little matter of seven under par.

Ian and Peter were taken aback, to say the least. Instead of offering me a job as a trainee client manager, they had something else in mind. 'Why work for us when we can work for you?' asked Ian.

That was the defining moment. It was what I wanted to do and now two people who knew precisely what they were talking about were giving me the final confirmation I needed. (I do not know who got the client manager job for which I applied, but IMG certainly came up trumps with the client manager they found for me in Guy Kinnings, a fully qualified lawyer and a man who has been a great ally during my professional career.)

In spite of the fact that every one of my father's friends would have been wondering what on earth he was doing in encouraging me to turn professional at a time when it was hardly the thing for a public schoolboy to do, Dad echoed my views. In the end, it was almost as if the two of us were conspiring together to prove that it was a good move.

My first task, once the decision had been made, was to disentangle myself from various amateur commitments. I had agreed to play in the Men's Home Internationals at Lahinch and now I had the unappetising task of having to ring Matt Lygate, the Scottish captain, to say that I was going to have to pull out. Scotland had won the Home Internationals only once in the previous seven years and Matt was understandably desperate to have his strongest team out. He was not happy at my news but nevertheless wished me luck. (I would have felt better about what I had done if Scotland had won at Lahinch, but Ireland were the victors that year, with their team including one Darren Clarke.)

My first week as a professional was one to leave me thinking that we had made a bad decision.

I started at the top, at least in terms of playing my first tournament at 5,000 feet up in the mountains of Crans-sur-Sierre.

I was by no means a naive traveller, having journeyed to and from Houston during my American university days and having represented Scotland and Britain and Ireland at home and abroad.

However, things started to go badly wrong long before I drove up the winding mountain road to the course. Though I flew into Geneva, my clubs never left Heathrow. I hung around at the airport filling in forms, all of which meant that I did not arrive in Crans until well after midnight. At which time, this little Alpine resort was very dark and ominously still.

I had arranged to stay in a small, reasonably priced hostelry. It was not on the main street and, with no one around – not even any professionals or caddies – to point me in the right direction, I had no idea where to look. Eventually, after an hour and more of searching along each of the streets in turn, I ended up walking into the Rhodania Hotel, a large and fashionable place that stands above the third tee. There, the lights were still ablaze and the front door was propped open.

To my relief, they had a room. To my dismay, it was going to be £150 a night. I did not have that kind of money to spend, but what else could I do?

The following day I waited, to no avail, for my clubs and my shoes so that I could have a practice round. If it had just been the clubs, I could have borrowed some, but borrowing shoes has never worked for me. Indeed, as a legacy of that first tournament, I now carry a pair of golf shoes in my hand luggage.

As it turned out, nothing arrived until the Wednesday evening, just twelve hours or so before I was due to embark on my professional career from Crans-sur-Sierre's tenth tee. I was hardly in the relaxed state I should have been for my first starting time on tour, but I was positively serene compared to what I would be like at the end of the first hole. No one had told me anything about balls flying ten per cent further through the mountain air, and my caddie, a local lad who knew nothing of golf other than how it was played up the mountain, was in no position to proffer any warnings. It was James Braid who went to bed a short hitter and woke up a long one, and, that morning, I felt as if much the same had happened to me. Although I had never been a short hitter, I suddenly hit the drive of a lifetime down the tenth fairway. It was as if I had added an extra twenty-five yards simply by turning professional.

I strode proudly down the fairway and weighed up my second. It was 145 yards to the pin, just the shot for an easy eight iron. To my utter bewilderment, the shot was still soaring as it carried the green and pitched among the trees beyond. I ran up a six and finished with a 77, which, on that course, was the equivalent of an 87.

My next round was a 70, but I missed the cut with room
to spare. It was a very disillusioned young man who drove
down the mountain on the Friday evening and, by the time
I arrived back in Troon, I was £1,000 the poorer.

I am not, as you might just have gauged, the most patient
of men, and I was quick to tell myself, 'I can forget this. I'm
wasting my time.' Yet it was not simply on account of the
Crans experience that I was feeling a little low.

No sooner had I turned professional than the captain of
Troon had asked me to come to see him at his home. He
congratulated me on turning professional and wished me
well but barely were those words out of his mouth than he
was explaining that I would have to resign from the club.
Professionals were not allowed as members. It was not, as he
was quick to point out, anything personal – just that the rule
was in the constitution laid down in 1890.

I was relieved to hear that I could continue to play and
practise, but the situation left me feeling thoroughly uneasy.
My father, who had just been made the secretary, had always
been acutely conscious of how bad it would look were he to
hang about the bar at the end of a round, and he had made
it clear that I should not overstep the mark in my role as
secretary's son. But where, previously, I had been able to enjoy
a post-round chat with friends, I now felt out of things: I
would finish my golf and make a quick exit.

The same applied at Turnberry and Western Gailes, two
other west coast courses where I had played occasional
amateur golf. As a low-handicap amateur, I had always been
made welcome at these places but once I made the switch I
was conscious of the stigma attached to being a professional.
I think it was one of the assistants at Turnberry who told me
the form: it was only if the members invited me for a drink
that I could go into the clubhouse.

Paradoxically, at the same time as I had gone down a few
notches on the social scale in the private club golf

environment, I was perceived as something of a middle-class lad in the professional game. A middle-class background does not always hit the right note. I have already explained the problems I had when playing in the Scottish amateur arena and, when I arrived on the pro tour, I sensed it would be best to keep a low profile. There were, however, plenty of top players who did not give a damn who I was or where I came from. Players like Seve Ballesteros, Nick Faldo, Bernhard Langer and Ian Woosnam would say hello to me and other new arrivals, which was great. I was grateful for that, though I always went out of my way to treat them with respect. If, say, Seve were on the practice putting green, I would make sure that I kept clear of any hole he might want to use. 'That's Seve's hole' is what I would tell myself.

I succeeded in keeping that low profile for the first year or so, but not to the extent that I did not want to gain recognition as a player. I was hell-bent on winning for a first time and nothing, absolutely nothing, was going to get in my way.

Chapter 6

SHOTS TO SPARE

In my first year on tour I played in just three events and banked less than £2,000. But, after winning my way through qualifying school at the end of that 1987 season, I made enough of a move in 1988 to win the Rookie of the Year Award, a trophy donated by the three-time Open champion Sir Henry Cotton and selected by the PGA European Tour, the R&A and the Golf Writers' Association.

The list of names on that trophy was one to set my heart racing. Tony Jacklin in 1963, Peter Oosterhuis in 1969, Nick Faldo in 1977 and José Maria Olazábal in 1986. Ollie was two years younger than me but now I had the feeling that I was beginning to catch up.

I had moved from 164th on the money-list to fifty-second, and collected winnings of £60,095, while my stroke average was 71.45 as against the 71.77 of 1987. To break down my tournament performances, I played in twenty-two events and made the cut in fifteen of them.

In the first leg of the 1989 season I had a chance to capture the Catalan Open in Pals, a magnificent old city some forty-five kilometres from Gerona. Though it is not something I like to remember, I was two ahead after the penultimate hole, only to sign off with the most ham-fisted of three-putt sixes to let England's Mark Roe sneak ahead. 'I hope I've learned from the experience' was all I could bring myself to say at the end of the day.

Following that bitter disappointment, I had a run of five missed cuts, though, as it would turn out, they were the only five cuts I missed all year. Hardest to bear was failing to qualify for the Open at my home course of Royal Troon. Almost certainly, I tried just too hard to make an impression on family and friends, what with my father being actively involved in proceedings in his role as the club secretary. My game was so erratic at that point that I took myself off to see Bill Ferguson, with whom I had worked so well as a child. Bill never needed long to analyse a problem and, seconds after we had walked on to the practice ground at Ilkley, he told me that I had the ball too far forward in my stance. I moved it back and, from that moment, I was up and running.

It was getting on for two years since I had turned professional and, back in 1987, when I had taken that giant step, I had made a pact with myself that if I failed to make the grade with the swing I had in the space of the next two years, I would effect major changes. As I headed for the Portuguese Open, I was beginning to wonder if that was going to have to happen.

Quinta do Lago was one of those courses I liked from my first practice round. It had been designed by America's William Mitchell and opened amid much acclaim in 1974. Though the whole estate suffered badly from lack of investment following the revolution, it has over the years been restored and refurbished to the point where it is one of the foremost resort courses in Europe. The location is out on its own. Faro airport is only fifteen minutes away and there is a host of little fish restaurants all around. It is one of those venues that makes a rich contribution to the patchwork quilt of courses and cultures that is the PGA European Tour.

When I went back for the Portuguese Open of 2001, which would be won by Phil Price, I was fascinated to see how well Quinta had stood up to the onslaught of modern technology, with the two dog-legs having more than played their part. It is always the long, straight holes that are the most severely ravaged by the new clubs and balls. The dog-legs, where you cannot always hit a a driver off the tee, tend to be survivors.

In the 1989 Portuguese Open, Rodger Davis, the senior Australian player who wears plus fours and has his name woven into his socks, took the first day lead with a 66. Luis Carbonetti, Mark Mouland and I were in a share of second place on 67, though, as far as the next day's papers were concerned, all our efforts were somewhat swallowed up by the hole at the sixteenth. Zimbabwe's Mark McNulty, who had threatened to share the first-round lead with Davis, had been standing to the twelve-footer he needed for what would have been his umpteenth birdie when he suspected that the hole was no longer the regulation four and a half inches in diameter. I am sure that most of us would have thought we were seeing things but Mark was sufficiently sure of himself to summon officials and ask for the hole to be measured. He turned out to be right and, before too long, the greenkeeper arrived with the relevant tools and an explanation. He said that the hole's metal rim had been inserted too low down and that the turf above had expanded. It was a good half an hour before Mark was able to return to his twelve-footer and, by then, the interest attaching to whether he would cash in on the bigger hole was such that he had absolutely no chance of making it. He missed and finished with a 68, two shots off the pace.

I moved into the lead on the Friday with a 65 in which I was negotiating the umbrella pines and the multifarious water hazards almost as if they did not exist. I was feeling great about my game, and my 132 aggregate gave me a four-stroke lead over Carbonetti, Mouland and Juan Quiros. In the third round, I returned a 69 to maintain the advantage.

On the Sunday afternoon I was playing with Gordon Brand Jnr and America's Mike Smith. The latter would prove

I am in the foreground with a somewhat flat-footed action, which compares badly with the way my brother, Douglas, has moved on to his left side.

With my older brother Douglas again, on the children's course at Royal Troon, which was next door to the ladies' clubhouse. Douglas was seven to my five.

New boy at Strathallan, aged 11.

First love. The Mazda GLC I had during my days at Houston Baptist University. Soon after I got it, I splashed out an extra $10 I barely had on the number plate MONTY.

I am fourth from the left, a would-be all-rounder who went on to open the bowling for Strathallan. I also batted at number 4 or 5, but I disliked facing spinners every bit as much as the nastiest of curling five-footers.

Nairn, 1987. Receiving the Scottish Amateur trophy from Denis J. Miller, the President of the Scottish Golf Union, on the same day as I met Eimear, who would become my wife. (Photo: Norrie Macleod)

27 June 1990. Left to right: James Montgomerie (Dad); Betty Montgomerie (Mum); Kathryn (Eimear's sister); me and Eimear; Douglas (my brother); Dorothy Wilson (Eimear's mum), John Wilson (Eimear's dad); plus Andrew and Sarah Dixon, page boy and bridesmaid.

Sealed with a kiss. Eimear and me on our wedding day.

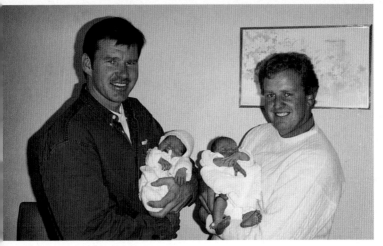

20 March 1993. Nick Faldo and me with our respective offspring, Georgia and Olivia, who were born on the same day at the Princess Margaret Hospital in Windsor. It was pure coincidence that we were at the same hospital.

Above Eimear with Olivia, our first-born, in 1993.

Left My father at the 1993 Masters. Having a son in the event is probably one of the easier ways of getting a ticket to the first major of the season.

Chapter 7

A GREAT MOTHER

On the morning of Tuesday, 17 April, 1990, I had been in the lounge at Heathrow and on the point of boarding the plane to go to the Madrid Open at Puerta de Hierro. Before leaving, I had time to put in a call to my father. He spoke first.

'Your mother's not well,' he said.

'What's wrong?' I asked, apprehensively.

Try as he might, he could not bring himself to tell me. He ducked and dived and I knew that he was in a hell of a state.

It was not one of those occasions when you have any trouble making a next move. I had a quiet word with my caddie and told him that I would not be going to Spain after all. Tiresome though it was going to be for him, he would have to go ahead with the trip and collect my clubs and cases at the airport in Madrid before coming back on the next plane. Obviously, I would pay him for his time.

In a state of total shock, I walked out of the lounge and turned towards Terminal 1, where I caught the next shuttle to Glasgow. The moment I was off the plane, I dialled home. This time, my brother picked up the phone.

I put the question to him: 'What's wrong with Mum?'

'Cancer,' said Douglas.

It was lung cancer.

Against a Spanish sky . . . (Photo: Getty Images)

Rocca makes light work of heaving me skywards in the 1995 Ryder Cup. (Photo: Getty Images)

Canon European Masters, Switzerland, 1996. Me with Olivia after I had returned record weekend scores of 61 and 63 to win in one of my favourite golfing places. (Photo: Getty Images)

Below Receiving honorary membership of Royal Troon with my dad and Douglas, my brother, on 14 July 1996. Few, if any, honours which have come my way have meant more.

to be the more tenacious. Even though I was ⟨...⟩ him, I was unhappily conscious of how he m⟨...⟩ did in making birdies at three of the first four h⟨...⟩ though, my birdies at the sixth and seventh went ⟨...⟩ and I was able to race away from him on my way ⟨...⟩ breaking 63.

I had won my first tournament on tour and I h⟨...⟩ by a massive eleven shots. In 1979, Bernhard Langer ⟨...⟩ the Cacharel Under-25 Championship at Nîmes by, b⟨...⟩ or not, seventeen shots while, way back in 1946, Henry ⟨...⟩ had annexed the French Open at St Cloud by a fiftee⟨...⟩ margin, which Peter Thomson would match in winni⟨...⟩ 1957 *Yorkshire Evening News* tournament at Sand Moor⟨...⟩ my eleven-shot triumph, the biggest of its kind since ⟨...⟩ Brown had won the 1984 Glasgow Open, was entirely g⟨...⟩ enough to make the 'Records' section of the *European T⟨...⟩ Handbook.* I will never forget the thrill of ringing home th⟨...⟩ evening and how my father and I agreed that I was probably ⟨...⟩ in the right job after all.

Having made that call, Eimear and I left Quinta do Lago⟨...⟩ and headed for Faro airport where I was able to drop off the rattling Fiat Panda (complete with exhaust hanging loose) I had hired for the week. That done, I never really look⟨...⟩ back.

At fifty-two, my mother had been smoking for thirty-five years. Until then, she had never seemed any the worse for it. She had been a fit, strong woman who made most of the family decisions, even though my father always seemed to be the one in charge. I know she would have loved to have had a daughter but, when none appeared she threw herself wholeheartedly into the all-male environment that had been thrust upon her. Mercifully, she did not find it difficult to love sport as much as the rest of us did. She started golf at much the same time as Douglas and me, playing alongside us on the children's course adjacent to Troon Portland. We all improved at roughly the same rate, not just then but when we moved to Ilkley and played throughout the prep-school holidays.

Mum was not remotely competitive but, perhaps because she spent so much time playing with two lads whose main aim was to thrash the ball farther than each other, she hit much harder than most of the women club golfers I have seen over the years. She had started off with a set of my grandfather's clubs but soon graduated to a set of women's clubs bearing the name of Jean Donald, a legendary Scottish champion and Curtis Cup golfer. The six iron from that set, a club she passed on to me, nowadays hangs in my study. It serves as a poignant reminder of the part she played in introducing us to golf.

As was the case with Douglas and myself, Mum benefited from playing on a lot of different courses. When we were a little older, my father would take us away on an annual golfing holiday. Sometimes we would return to Scotland for the two weeks, but there were years when we would head for France or Spain and the four of us would play every day. We did everything together. My father, at his best, had a handicap of five. I cannot remember the order in which the rest of the family broke into single figures but Mum became a pretty useful citizen off nine.

She loved the social side of the game as much as anything else and revelled in her role as lady captain at Ilkley in 1980, the year after my father had been the men's captain. But golf was by no means her only interest. She was similarly wrapped up in football, even to the point where she would turn on the radio to catch the Leeds result when she was in the house on her own. During our Ilkley years, the family made frequent trips to Elland Road. In those days, it was rare for women to be there on a regular basis, but Mum was always in the party. She loved the fact that she had been at Wembley when Leeds played Liverpool in the Charity Shield in 1973.

Mum understood sport and I always appreciated the fact that I was able to 'talk golf' with her as well as my father, not least when I was out on my own at Houston Baptist University. On my return, she was a good sounding board on the subject of what I should do with my life. Like my father, she felt that it was imperative that I should finish my degree before I turned professional because that way she thought I would be taking less of a risk. I have never doubted that my parents' advice was right on that score. Even today, there is a lingering sense of satisfaction at the way I completed my course at Houston Baptist.

My mother's pride added an extra dimension to my golf, both at amateur level and when I turned professional. For instance, when I won the 1989 Portuguese Open, she delighted in the way I had competed with all the guys she knew so well from following golf on television. I remember, too, how thrilled she was that I could at last go out and buy my own car, though I expect that a little of her elation was down to the fact that I would no longer be pinching hers.

Lung cancer was only the beginning of my mother's problems. The disease was spreading. No one outside the family was aware of what was going on when Eimear and I were married in June 1990, two months after the grim diagnosis. Dreadful though she must have been feeling, Mum made a huge effort for the wedding and that is something for which I could not admire her enough.

I set about trying to register a follow-up win to the one in Portugal. Apart from anything else, it would have been a fillip for my mother. No such luck. My concentration was hopeless. I had never had to deal with illness before and, wherever I was on the course, my thoughts would stray to what was happening back in Troon. Every day, I would ring my parents and, when I was not phoning them, I was on to my uncle, a doctor in Jedburgh who understood as well as anyone what was happening.

I popped back to Troon as often as possible and, each time, my mother was a little weaker. My father tried everything. He took her to see world experts in the lung cancer field, one in Switzerland and another in Munich. Both trips gave us a fresh infusion of hope but on neither occasion was there any lasting improvement. The writing was on the wall.

Eimear and I went to Troon for Christmas that year, arriving in early December from our new home in Walton-on-Thames. By then, Mum was spending most of her time in bed. She was hopelessly frail but she and I talked a lot, which was hugely important to me then and since. On 7 January, when we had been up north for a month, I left Eimear to spend a couple of days with her own family while I went back to Walton-on-Thames to get ready to go to Australia for the start of the 1991 PGA European Tour. Though my heart was not in it, I obviously had to return to work at some point.

On the morning of 10 January, I was woken by a 7 a.m. call. It was my father to say that Mum had died at home at 3.30 a.m. Not wanting to ring Douglas or myself at that hour, he had sat up all night waiting to make the call.

I went straight back to Glasgow to help prepare for the funeral. Everything stopped for a couple of months. My father and mother had been together for thirty years and Dad had had everything done for him. He had no idea how to look after himself and Douglas and I had to organise a rota of people who could help out in the weeks that followed. Since then we have been very proud of the way he has coped.

In the early stages of her illness, my mother had been given chemotherapy at the Western General in Glasgow and, following her death, I made the first of what has become a biennial donation to the hospital's cancer department via Professor Sir James Armour, a member of Troon and a golfing companion of my father's. They had not been able to save my mother, but I was full of admiration for the staff's caring approach. You would not go into nursing for the pay. It's a vocation and the rest of us should be eternally grateful that doctors and nurses are there for everyone. I know that I can only help in a minor way but I will always do everything I can for a section of the community which I feel to be ridiculously undervalued.

I have a full-time secretary who deals with little else other than my charitable foundation, which was founded back in 1993. I spend a lot of time signing old gloves, clubs, golf-bags and photos because these items can fetch a lot of money at auctions. It's a simple thing for me and other sportsmen to do, but it can make a difference.

As often as not, as I study the requests of another cancer charity, my thoughts will return to my mother. I can remember, as if it were yesterday, our last conversation. She wanted to talk to me about Eimear. Every mother whose son is getting married worries whether he is making the right choice, but gradually, in the six months since our wedding, my mother had come to see that I had chosen a wife in a million. She could sense that Eimear was able to take over from where she was leaving off in being as ambitious for me as I was for myself. She could see, too, that Eimear had an understanding of the game that went far beyond the sixteen handicap she had owned in her schoolgirl days. 'I don't want to tell you what to do and what not to do in life,' she said that day, 'but never, ever, lose that lovely girl.'

Chapter 8

A SARTORIAL DUFF

After winning my first tournament in 1989, I had to wait until August 1991, by which time I was twenty-eight, for a follow-up. I had added two runner-up spots to my CV in 1990, the Volvo Open de Firenze and the Lancôme Trophy, but in the spring of 1991 I missed five cuts in ten starts.

As I said, for the first couple of months after my mother died, my mind had not been on the job at all. I would suddenly find myself knocking a perfectly straightforward drive out of bounds or even four-putting. I shot a 78 in the third round of the Girona Open in February when I had been sharing the halfway lead with Steven Richardson.

Eimear helped to straighten me out at this period. 'Look,' she said, 'there's only one way we are going to get through this and that is to get out and play.' My father, meanwhile, explained that it was at times like these that you either walked away from what you were doing or became stronger because of it. All of which explains why, when I finished second in the Volvo PGA Championship in May 1991, I described it as 'a big stepping-stone for me'.

I had signed off birdie, birdie for what looked like an unanswerable aggregate of 271, seventeen under par, only for Seve Ballesteros to make a birdie at the par five eighteenth to catch me. He chipped up from short and left of the green before sinking an eight-footer. The play-off, as everyone agreed, was vintage Ballesteros. At the 471-yard first, he hit an incredible five iron second – it was all of 200 yards – to three feet for his winning three.

Because of the way things had gone, though, I felt as if I had won and lost at the same time. I had grown stronger, especially with regard to temperament. Whenever I thought about my mother, it occurred to me that it was pretty ridiculous to be fretting over missed five-footers. 'It never should mean that much, but it once did' is what I told Steve Muncy for an article in *Golf Monthly*, though, as we all know, I have had ongoing troubles in keeping golf's more fickle rebuttals in perspective.

Following the Volvo PGA, I had four top-ten finishes in my next six starts and was still in the same buoyant mood when it came to the Scandinavian Masters at Drottingholm in the first week of August.

Once again, Seve was to the fore. On this occasion, he was first back to base, with a fourth-round 64 that included an eagle and six birdies, three of which were at the sixteenth, seventeenth and eighteenth. He was lying on 271 and, like everyone else, this wiliest of competitors was waiting to see what would happen to me down the stretch.

In the first twelve holes I had had six birdies to shake off Ian Woosnam. Now my task was to stay ahead of Seve. Not least because of the aura of the man, it was a tough exercise, but I acquitted myself well, emerging with a five-under-par 67 and a winning tally of 270.

What a moment. I had beaten one of the men I admire most in this game. 'I'm proud I could come from behind and win under pressure,' I said to the press who, like myself, had been well aware that I had not been too severely tested with my eleven-shot win in Portugal two years before.

My Rookie of the Year title, along with those two tournament triumphs, gave me the 'credibility' I had craved on tour, but, at the same time, it was obvious that a few of my fellow professionals were a little miffed at the speed of my advance. I was particularly conscious of giving offence in 1992 after I had returned from what was a near miss in the US Open at Pebble Beach. We were at the Scottish Open at Gleneagles and, when it came to the last round, in which I was going out in the final pair with Paul Curry, I opened a new parcel of sweaters that had been provided by Pringle, my excellent sponsors at the time. There were three lovely cashmeres in the box, all of them in plain blue save for a striking white St Andrew's cross emblazoned across the chest. I liked what I saw and it never occurred to me that anyone would be reading anything into these garments. I changed my mind on the first tee.

As I took off my waterproof jacket I had a massive shock to the system. The Scottish crowd went wild. Such a reaction was great for Pringle but it was disconcerting for me and truly horrendous for Paul, who had shot a magnificent 60 on the Saturday for a one-stroke lead.

I have to say that I will never forget the moment when I appeared over the brow of the hill at the third. There were more and more cheers for this advancing, one-man army. Lawrence Donegan, who mentioned the incident in a feature in the *Guardian*, referred to the sweater as 'a ridiculous golf jumper emblazoned with a St Andrew's cross' and suggested that I had worn it 'in the expectation of winning'. Nothing against Donegan, but he could not have been more wrong. Would that I had possessed that kind of confidence.

I did and I didn't carry it off. I had a 65 but ended up two shots behind Peter O'Malley, who had shot a rip-roaring seven under par – two eagles and three birdies – for the last five holes of his 62. After seventeen holes he had been tied with Bernhard Langer and myself but he tossed the two of us aside at the 525-yard eighteenth with the second of his eagles – drive, six iron and a twenty-five-foot putt.

'Poor Montgomerie,' said one of the cuttings. 'The big Scot

was the huge home favourite and his 264 aggregate would have won five of the previous six Bell's Scottish Opens and tied for the other.'

The statisticians told me that no one in the history of the game had ever produced such scoring to win a tournament, though there were a couple of people who had come up with a 62 in making an unsuccessful, last-ditch attempt to catch a leader.

The St Andrew's cross sweater was still wet and fluffy from the day's rain when Pringle asked if they could have it back. They thought it would make money for the Princess Anne Trust, which it did. I heard later that they had auctioned it off for £5,000.

Later in the season the imitations were everywhere. In fact, there was a host of identikit Montys peppered throughout my crowd at that year's Dunhill Championship, all of them waving and enjoying lending support to a Scottish team that, as it turned out, ended up losing 3–0 to South Africa in the semi-final. David Frost, John Bland and Gary Player each opened with between two and four birdies.

I still have the other two sweaters in a cupboard at home and, at some point in the future, I will give them away for some good cause or another. I will not be wearing them. The feeling stirred up among the spectators was one thing, but the players' response, like Donegan's, was a big negative. The impression I got was that they were thinking, 'Who the hell does Colin Montgomerie think he is? He's only been around for three years…'

Chapter 9

THE MAGNIFICENT SEVEN

If you play well enough for long enough, you begin to earn respect. Ex-public schoolboy or not, I could feel that that was beginning to happen as I continued to make progress. By the close of 1991 I had moved up ten places from fourteenth to fourth on the Order of Merit, and by the end of 1992, my first full season with Alastair McLean, who would be my caddie throughout my seven years in a row at the top of the Order of Merit, I was up to third.

If I were to continue to improve every year, for that is what I had done in my first five seasons, there were only two possibilities for 1993: first or second. As it transpired, I leapfrogged the second slot and moved straight to the top.

When I came to research this book, the process of looking back over that period had a lot to do with my revival during the second quarter of 2002. It was only as I started sifting through the tournaments and the years that I realised how incredibly steady I used to be. I would win one week, finish fourth the next, third the next, eighth the next and so on. It looked as if it had all been pretty easy but, the more I thought about it, the more I realised that I never really gave myself credit for how well I played at that time.

'Uncomplicated' is a better word than 'easy' when it comes to describing why things worked out so well. When I was home between tournaments I never did what I do now in changing my golf-clubs and fretting about what the other players were up to and where they were on the money-list.

I had my own way of going about things socially, too. Early on, I had a particularly good friend in Steven Richardson. He was making much the same rate of progress as I was, winning the 1991 Girona Open and the 1993 Mercedes German Masters. We tended to play in the same events and were as likely as not to get similar starting times. But, as he started to struggle and I was lucky enough to remain on course, so we moved, almost imperceptibly, into different divisions.

These different divisions on the Tour are not something anyone talks about, but they exist just the same. The new arrivals are in a division of their own; then there are three or four more divisions until you arrive in what you could call the Premiership. In my case, I shot so quickly through the different ranks that I never made friends along the way. Then, when I got to the Premiership, I found that the top players do not want to mix anyway. Most of them are loners.

Paul Lawrie has talked of how, when he first went to play in America in 1999, he was amazed at how unfriendly it all was. He said he would come out of his hotel bedroom in the morning and see a long line of supper-trays down the corridor bearing witness to how each player had called for room service the night before. Though Paul is one who likes to socialise, things are not really that different in Europe. On those occasions when I find myself in the same hotel as players like Seve Ballesteros, José Maria Olazábal, Bernhard Langer and Nick Faldo, I seldom clap eyes on them other than in the hallway or at breakfast. Like me, they mostly prefer to have supper in their rooms and use the evening to chat to family on the phone. Spending so many evenings in a hotel room can be construed as antisocial but, in reality, it is as much a matter of welcoming a bit of space at the end of the day when you have been on show, as it were, from the moment you arrived at the course.

Heaven knows how many hours I spent on the phone to Eimear during my Order of Merit years. She was hugely supportive, talking me through all of my golfing insecurities at the same time as she was playing the major part in raising our three children. All three were born during my winning run, with Olivia arriving in 1993, Venetia in 1996 and Cameron in 1998. I have known tour wives who press their husbands not to go to tournaments during the week of an offspring's birthday or some other family occasion, but Eimear was never one of them. She understood that there were times when it would be madness to interrupt the momentum of a good golfing streak.

I started mixing more with my fellow professionals when I was chosen to captain the British team in the Seve Ballesteros Trophy and came to realise, from the other players' reaction to me, that I would love to captain a European Ryder Cup side. However, for most of my career, I have felt more relaxed among the caddies. When you are with the caddies, you can forget the competitive edge that is always there when you are fraternising with fellow players. If, say, you are out to dinner with someone who has had a better round than you have had that day, you are thinking – or at least I am – that you have to do better than him in the next round. As players, you are ranked every day according to your score and that preys on your mind. With a group of caddies, you can have a laugh, unwind. Believe me, that is vital if you are going to keep up the pace as I did over that seven-year stretch. As is well known, I am a regular customer at Caddyshack, the mobile restaurant that travels from tournament to tournament and serves up such delights as sausage and bacon sandwiches. If I have an early starting time, I will often breakfast with the caddies and join in the latest football banter before I go out to play.

Hugh Mantle, a lecturer in sports psychology at John

Moores University in Liverpool, and a man who has given me the benefit of his expertise since Julian Tutt, the broadcaster, first put us in touch eight years ago, has often spoken of the need for a stable base; of how the sportsman who is staying in yet another hotel does well to have the sensation that he is 'on home ground'. I may not hit as many shots on the practice ground as the next person but, as far as I am concerned, the day-to-day sameness of the range works for me in other ways. The informal air, the chat of the caddies and the smell of a good breakfast all contribute to what is the right backcloth for me for another competitive day.

1993

In 1993, Nick Faldo, who had won the Order of Merit in 1992, was handily placed to win it again. He had finished first, second and third in that order over the Carroll's Irish Open, the Open and the Scandinavian Masters, and, when it came to the last tournament of the year, the Volvo Masters at Valderrama, he was £104,000 ahead of the next person. Bernhard Langer was the man in second place, Ian Woosnam third and Sam Torrance fourth. I was fifth at that point and did not think for a minute that it would be possible to overhaul that little lot. Also, it has to be remembered that Nick, at that time, was number one on the Sony World Rankings and would stay there throughout 1993. It was not that I was short of belief ... My problem was that I believed I was going to finish second.

That had become a familiar spot. I had had eight second-place finishes in my first four years, and at the start of 1993 I had a ninth at the early season Johnnie Walker Classic at Singapore Island. That was the tournament where Nick, after he had holed an eight-footer to defeat me at the seventy-second, came up with that never-to-be-forgotten line concerning how ninety-nine per cent of putts that were short did not go in but this one of his had. I was second for a tenth time at the Volvo PGA Championship at Wentworth, this time to Bernhard Langer.

The first of my two wins in 1993 came in the Heineken Dutch Open at Noordwijkse, one of Holland's links courses. It has led to me opting for a Heineken ahead of any other beer ever since! It was an event I had not planned to enter but, having finished as low as fiftieth in the Scottish Open and having missed the cut in the Open at Royal St George's, I felt that I should not waste any time in starting to play my way out of the rut. I trailed David Russell – D.A. Russell as opposed to D.J. – by three shots after the first round and Ronan Rafferty by four at the end of the second. At the completion of the third round, it was José Coceres who held the lead, but when it came to the fourth round I overtook the lot of them, finishing a shot ahead of Coceres and Jean Van de Velde. The circumstances of that fourth round were totally unexpected. We had enjoyed three lovely summer days at the tournament but, on the Sunday morning, we were hit by a boisterous links wind. I remember hitting a three iron no more than 140 yards at the sixteenth into what the *European Tour Handbook* would call 'the teeth of a gale'. The *Handbook* also referred to the fact that lightning had struck as I strode on to the final green but that I was so concentrated on what I was doing that I never noticed. Because of my high ball flight, I have never been seen as a particularly good wind player. What worked for me that day was some great putting allied to a ruthless determination to hit the ball where I wanted. I had not won in nearly two years and it was important to me that I should turn the week into a victory. Even though it was at a stage in my career when the prize-money was still a thrill, what meant more was the way the result drove me forward. I finished seventh the following week, fourth a couple of weeks later and then eighth. It was amazing how the prize-money all mounted up.

In the previous year's Volvo Masters at Valderrama, the climactic tournament of the season, I had lost in a play-off to Sandy Lyle and sat on the podium and listened not just to Lyle's tournament victor's speech but to Faldo's Order of Merit speech. Faldo's was the first Order of Merit winner's speech I had heard and, as he delivered it, so I determined to be in his shoes in 1993.

I started out in the 1993 Volvo Masters, once again the last tournament of the year, with rounds of 69, 70 and 67, which left me at the top of the leaderboard, a shot ahead of Darren Clarke. By then, I was well aware of the fact that if I could win the tournament, I could wrap up the Order of Merit as well. The last round was a big one. Though Darren dropped shots at the first two holes, he came back with three birdies in a row from the fourth. The pressure was mounting.

I disappeared into sand at the fourteenth but managed to get up and down. Then, at the sixteenth, I hit into trees and left myself with a shot of 160 yards which had to be knocked under branches. My ball missed the tree and, having escaped that hazard, ran blithely through a bunker to pave the way for me to get down in a chip and a putt and hang on to the lead. I managed a 68 to beat Darren by a shot and, as I said at the time, considering everything that was hanging on the day, and considering how well Darren was playing, it was arguably the best round of my life. Mark McCormack's *World of Professional Golf* spoke of how I had withstood all the pressure 'without so much as a twitch'. Strictly speaking, that was a little out, especially with regard to the last hole. When Darren holed from twenty-five feet for a birdie, I had to get down in two from the same distance if I was going to win. I was almost too fraught to make it, and can remember thinking it was as well that I hit my first putt to nine inches to take the nerves out of the second one.

My father was more than a little impressed when I rang

him with the news that my 274 aggregate was six shots better than anyone else's in the five years the event had been played at Valderrama. However, we had not been talking too long when he had a question for me. Why had I not shaved before the last round? The answer was that it had completely slipped my mind. I was startled that I could have forgotten – and still more startled when I looked at the unshaven sight on the front cover of the next edition of *Golf Weekly*. But nothing was going to bother me too much at that stage.

Having won the Volvo bonus on top of the winner's cheque, I had a dollop of money in the bank. After I had won the Heineken, Eimear and I, who had been living with Olivia in a four-bedroomed flat in Oxshott by way of our second marital home, went to look at a new five-bedroomed house in Torland Drive along the road. At the time, it was only half built and had a price tag which was rather more than we could afford. By the end of the season, it was fully built and the price had become acceptable. We made arrangements to move in early 1994.

The money aside, there were other benefits: a ten-year exemption to the European Tour and guaranteed invitations to the following year's Masters, US Open and USPGA Championship.

The late Michael Williams, writing in the next day's *Daily Telegraph*, told of 'a remarkably steady climb by Montgomerie' before detailing how I had risen on the money-list from fifty-second to twenty-fifth to fourteenth, to fourth and to third in the five years before I landed the top spot. Ken Schofield, writing in his capacity as executive director of the tour, talked of 'a general consistency of performance that has elevated Colin Montgomerie to the very highest level'.

For all that I had told myself at the end of 1992 that I could be the winner in 1993, I was still in awe of Faldo and did not really think of myself as a number one. But, now that I had reached that position, I had no intention of relinquishing it. 'I've made progress every year since turning professional and I aim to keep doing that in 1994' was the remark with which I signed off from 1993.

1994

I have never pretended that I am anything I'm not. I have never yearned to be a cavalier golfer like Seve Ballesteros, one who has the spectators gasping in amazement as he cuts corners and attempts the impossible. Instead, I have always been happy to leave the heroics to others and concentrate on hitting fairways and greens and making putts. If you do that, you will always make money and that is what I set out to do in every tournament in 1994, and still do today.

That was my mindset, as they say, as I approached the 1994 Peugeot Open de España at Club de Campo, which I won by a shot.

I will never forget listening to a recording of Richard Boxall's observation on Eurosport shortly after I had finished. Boxall, for the record, was one of three, the others being Mark Roe and Mark McNulty, who were safely back at base at ten under par. 'What will Monty do now?' asked one of the commentators as I was standing on the eighteenth tee on the same ten-under mark and needing a birdie to win. 'Well,' returned Boxall, 'he'll hit the fairway because he hasn't missed one since 1987. Then he'll hit his sand wedge to three feet and he'll hole it.' He was right on every count, except that I was only left with a two-footer to win!

In 1994 at Turnberry I had had my best Open, finishing in eighth place following a third-round 65 in which I had played with Tommy Nakajima. He never said anything while we were playing but, when we finished, he volunteered, 'Monty, you best putter.' He then thought about it for a few seconds before adding the word 'ever'. R&A officials standing around the scorer's hut roared with laughter. It was a good moment but I knew that it was more a matter of Nakajima having coincided with one of my better putting days rather than my being a great putter through and through.

In August, I felt for Barry Lane when I defeated him in the Murphy's English Open at Forest of Arden. I birdied three out of the last four holes to beat him, with the shot I remember best – it was one of the finest shots I have ever hit – the four iron I knocked over the ravine at the 210-yard eighteenth to eight feet. Barry and Melanie, his first wife, were standing at the back of the green and I needed to hole my right-lip birdie putt to win. I've always liked Barry but that did not stop me from making my two. I pocketed £100,000 and shot to the top of that season's Order of Merit.

Then I consolidated my position by winning again the following week in Germany, the Volvo German Open at Hubbelrath. Beating Bernhard Langer in Germany was good news, not least because he is a different player in his native land. He feeds off the German support, and time after time others have folded in the face of it. In the knowledge that Bernhard had won the event five times overall, I had steeled myself to cope with the pressures of playing with him. Though I dropped two shots in the last five holes to waste the birdies at the twelfth and thirteenth – birdies that had taken me to twenty-one under par – I finished a shot ahead of him. It was a good win, and the first time I had won back-to-back titles in Europe. I felt so competitive that it was bordering on the scary.

It is all to do with a hatred of losing which would seem to go way beyond what others experience. I know of plenty of golfers who are happy with second- and third-place finishes, seeing them as representing a good week's work. Me, I am only pleased to finish second if I look like finishing third.

It affects me rather more than purely in a golf context. Most fathers, when they play chess or Monopoly with their children, are happy for the child to win. I cannot pretend that the same applies to me. The whole family laughs when, after Olivia and I have been playing one of these board games, she jumps up and announces, 'I've had to let Dad win again!' Eimear's response is usually a kindly but weary, 'Well, that's just the way he is.'

The reaction of Hugh Mantle, my sports psychologist, is not as damning as you might suppose. His feeling is that most British sportsmen and -women don't want to win enough. They are too happy to finish second.

The Order of Merit was a done deal when we arrived at the Volvo Masters that year, but I still wanted that extra title. On the last day at Valderrama, I was playing with Seve Ballesteros, who was in the lead on nine under par to the seven under of Bernhard Langer and myself. Langer, incidentally, had broken the course record with a 62 in the second round.

The first of the day's dramas had nothing to do with Seve as I hit some unsuspecting spectator on the head at the seventh and my ball richocheted out of bounds. I was blaming myself rather than the spectator who, thank heavens, was not badly hurt. The drive had been a particularly bad one and deserved to be in trouble, though I was maybe a little unlucky to end up with a double-bogey. I made birdies at the fifteenth and seventeenth to be on the same seven-under slot as Seve. If we were going to force a play-off with Bernhard, who had had a closing 70, we each needed to birdie the eighteenth.

Neither of us got what we wanted, for that last hole was the scene of a much-publicised rules incident involving Seve, who was tight up against a tree and in some sort of hollow. Guy Hunt, a rules official who had been a good enough player to have won the old Dunlop Masters tournament, came to give a ruling and was not prepared to go along with Seve's suggestion that the cavity was the work of a burrowing animal. Seve called for John Paramor, the head referee. John came as quickly as he could and it was clear that nothing was going to be resolved in a hurry. In the fullness of time, John went to work as might the most skilful of barristers. 'Do you think it could have been a dog?' he asked of the hole in the ground.

'You're right,' said Seve. 'That's what it was – a dog.'

At that, Paramor pointed out that a dog did not count as a burrowing animal and he could not, therefore, permit a free drop.

Seve took five and so did I. After the wait – it was around the twenty-minute mark and so long that the BBC went off air – I had ended up tugging my second from the right rough and making a bogey instead of the birdie that would have given me my play-off place. There is no question that I was thrown by the delay. It would have been a tall order for me to make a birdie from where I was, but I did have a sliver of a chance and that chance was taken away from me. I was upset. We all know the game was never meant to be fair but that was ridiculously unfair.

At the time, missing out on a possible play-off took a bit of the gloss off winning the Order of Merit. I had fully intended to celebrate and had organised a fine dinner for Eimear and myself on the private plane we took home. Instead, though I ate the dinner, I sat glumly on the plane thinking I was only as good as my last event while Eimear begged me to think about the year rather than the tournament. She reminded me how I was more under par than I had been the previous year and how my scoring average had improved, but to no avail. Nothing could cheer me up and, to my shame, I can picture to this day the hurt on Eimear's face on that return journey.

1995

The 1994 *European Tour Yearbook* finished with the suggestion that I was a major player in everyone's eyes save my
own. To my mind, it was important that I did not think of
myself as a major player, and I continue to think that way
today. It's what keeps me going, drives me to win tournaments. In Order of Merit terms, 1995 was the toughest year
of the lot as I ended up defeating my friend Sam Torrance at
the eleventh hour. Though Sam would not be aware of this,
it was a broadcast he did with Julian Tutt after winning the
British Masters at Collingtree, the fourth-last tournament of
the season, which aroused my competitive instincts as never
before. I was listening in on the car radio as I drove from
Collingtree to Troon to see my father, who had been ill. What
got me in that interview was Sam's semi-jocular reference to
how he had pinched my spot at the top of the Order of
Merit. 'Game on' is what I said to myself that day.

Of the two of us, I had made the better start to the season,
finishing second in the Dubai Desert Classic where Sam
missed the cut. That had been an important week for me
because I knew I was in danger of getting a bit of flak from
the media for taking the risk of changing my golf-club
manufacturer from Wilson to Callaway. Some of the press
were longing for me to get my come-uppance when my own
thoughts on the matter were that they were putting too
much emphasis on the tools, not enough on the workman.

After finishing second in Dubai three shots behind Freddie
Couples, I finished seventh in the Johnnie Walker Classic to
Sam's twenty-third before taking an elongated break. By the
time I returned, Sam had duplicated my second- and
seventh-place finishes, while he had also finished fifth in
Morocco. Then he went on to win the Italian Open and the
Murphy's Irish Open, in the latter of which he survived a
dramatic play-off with Howard Clark and Stuart Cage.

I replied with a couple of second-place finishes before
winning the Volvo German Open and the Lancôme at St
Nom-la-Bretèche. Each time, Sam was the runner-up. In the
Lancôme I was three ahead of Sam after three rounds but
only two ahead of him with one to play, and that is never
enough. Sam hit to eight feet and I accepted that he would
make his two before I teed up. In other words, I had to come
up with a three to beat him. My tee shot was not the most
promising: a six iron hooked under the Rolex clock tower.
But my thirty-yard downhill chip off hardened mud was out
of this world. Australia's Wayne Riley, who was playing
alongside Sam and myself in the last group and who is not
exactly given to Old World charm, stared at me in astonishment and said, 'Some fucking shot, that.' I was left with
nothing more than a tap-in for the win.

That was the season. One shot here, one shot there.

At the start of the Volvo Masters at Valderrama, I was
£3,000 behind Sam but I was having the better of this week
and, as I started on the homeward nine on the last day, I
thought I was home and dry. Sam had been among the
earlier starters that morning and there was no word of him
having staged anything in the way of a miraculous recovery.
It was only as I was playing the tenth that I had a nasty shock
to my system. There was a leaderboard behind the green and
they were inserting a new name at the top. It began with a T.
'It can't be,' I said to myself. Then the O went up followed by
a couple of Rs and I knew the worst. Sam had had a last-
round 68 and was the leader in the clubhouse on 285. He
must have felt quietly confident of winning the tournament
and the Order of Merit.

Having parred the tenth, I was hoping for a birdie at the
eleventh but left my six iron short of the green and failed to
get up and down. I thought I had blown my chance. But the
golfer I was then and hopefully will be again hit a five iron to
the heart of the twelfth green and holed for a birdie. Even

now, the memory of that two has me all but purring. It was that good, with Alastair McLean and I having one of those afternoons when we were as fine a team as player and caddie can ever be. Alastair was always quiet on the course. Unlike his player, he had neither ups nor downs but maintained the same attitude throughout. His concentration was excellent and, that afternoon, he did nothing to detract from mine. We were making sensible assessments and carrying them through. I am not saying I played sensational golf but I did what I had to do in the knowledge that Sam was watching every shot in the clubhouse. He had played the finest golf of his life over the season and, after twenty-five years on tour, it was his dream to win the Order of Merit.

I remember missing the sixteenth green on purpose so that I could chip up the hill and hole the putt. I did it perfectly. I laid up at the seventeenth, too, only this time I landed in the rough. I escaped with my five and then, on a day when I felt as if I moved into a new level in terms of the stress I was taking on board, I did what I had to do at the eighteenth. I drove a bit left, leaving us with a big decision as to whether we should take a seven or an eight for the second. On paper, it was a seven iron but, because of the adrenaline, I was fearful that I might hit through the back and that my chances of getting down in two would be more than somewhat remote. We went for the eight and I caught the front of the green, only to leave my first putt woefully short – a four-footer that looked more. Everything I had went into the holing of that putt. In fact, I could swear that that was the moment when my hair started to turn grey. The ball dropped in the left side of the cup and that was the most relieved I have ever felt on a final hole. My whole year hung on that putt. I had finished second behind Alex Cejka in the tournament but I had won the Order of Merit.

Sam, along with the rest of the European Tour, would have been sitting on the edge of his bar stool watching the denouement on television. He was one of the first people to appear on the green, which I appreciated hugely. 'Unbelievable!' he said. Later, when Cejka, Sam and myself were sitting on the podium, waiting for the prize-giving to start, Sam turned to me and said, 'I can't believe I'm sitting up here and that I haven't won the Order of Merit.' As he said, if it had been anyone else rather than me who had finished second, he would have been the Order of Merit man. I felt genuinely sorry for him. Half of me wished we had shared it; the other half was damned glad to have made my Order of Merit hat-trick. It was good for European golf and good for Scotland that two Scots had dominated the year.

My win was important, too, for Callaway. To have won the Order of Merit with Wilson clubs in my first two years and then to win it again with Callaway was a great career result.

1996

My start to the 1996 season had most to do with my finish. Over the winter I took three months off and, once we had enjoyed Christmas and celebrated the arrival of our second child, Venetia, on 21 January, I used the time to get fit. When I finally turned up on tour – at the Emirates in Dubai – I was a couple of stone lighter and feeling good about myself. According to the *PGA European Tour Guide*, 'It was a new, slimmer Colin that appeared for 1996.'

I had gone a couple of days early in order that Bill Ferguson, my original teacher, could help to get the rust out of my system. As we worked together, so word was going round that I was cutting things too fine and that I had given everyone else, particularly Ian Woosnam, too much of a head start if I had any intention of winning the Order of Merit for a fourth successive year. Woosie had captured the first two events, the Johnnie Walker and the Heineken Classic.

But the Friday morning headlines were all to do with how I had returned in style, with my opening score a 67 that left me in second place to Miguel Angel Jimenez, who had started with a 63. I proceeded with a second-round 68 and another 67. I was still one stroke behind the Spaniard but 100 per cent convinced that I would beat him. When it came to the last hole we were locked together at seventeen under par.

Miguel hit much the longer drive and promptly made an elementary match-play error, for match-play was what it was all about at that stage. I had been planning to lay up with a six iron but, when I saw him brandishing his three wood and realised that he was gearing himself up to carry the water with his second, I decided to put the six iron away and take my driver. Because the wind was left to right, I took aim on the hospitality tent on the left of the green. The ball landed on the green and stopped dead. It was my shot of the year and also maybe the best of my seven-year spell at the top of the Order of Merit. On my golfing travels I have seen plaques here and there telling of famous shots and, in the eyes of its proud owner, that shot was worthy of a memento. They probably never have inscriptions of such length but, if it were down to me, the words would tell of how I took my driver off the fairway, knocked it over the water on the last hole of the tournament and all at the end of a three-month break. At the risk of sounding a bit big-headed, I think I gave my fellow professionals something of a jolt that week. There is no question that they were thinking that I could not reel off a fourth Order of Merit but, after that start, they were not so sure.

I had two more wins that year, the first of them in the Murphy's Irish Open at Druid's Glen and the second in the Canon European Masters at Crans-sur-Sierre where, in what was a record European Tour scoring burst for the weekend, I had rounds of 61 and 63. Eimear was there and, with me playing so well and being in the best of humour because of it, this was one of the most fantastic weekends of our lives. When we were not on the course, we were lapping up the scenery, eating well and spending money in the children's clothing shops. The shops in Crans-sur-Sierre are quite an experience!

All in all, 1996 was a year in which, for the most part, I was consistency personified. That Swiss weekend apart, not too much was brilliant; I just performed well week after week to have the edge over Ian Woosnam, who had started the season with such a flourish.

To quote from Ken Schofield's reflections on the Tour's twenty-fifth anniversary season, 'What with three wins and three runner-up spots, Colin once again demonstrated his astonishing consistency … His achievements provided further evidence of his unique ability to maintain a level of play which will inspire others to raise their own standards.'

Following an operation at the end of August, my father had been recovering from a heart bypass that had become necessary when he suffered severe chest pains at a time when my brother Douglas was away on his honeymoon and I was on the point of going to the German Open in Stuttgart. Typical of my father, he had thought the pains were nothing more than a bout of indigestion and, as I would discover when I drove up to Scotland instead of flying out to Germany, he had answered them with a couple of Rennies. The packet was still lying on his bedside table. Only after they had failed to make a difference had he rung a neighbour, a chemist by the name of James Brodlie, to ask for advice. The bypass was a success and he subsequently followed his surgeon's orders to leave his car in the garage and walk everywhere. In November, after he had been given the all-clear to fly, he came with me to the Million Dollar tournament at Sun City.

The week before we left, there had been an interesting development as I realised that the time had come when I needed someone to keep tabs on my technique. I had heard good things about Denis Pugh, now the coach at Wisley, and asked Guy Kinnings at IMG if he would sound him out. Guy got in touch and asked Denis if he would be interested in working with an IMG client, but omitted to mention which one he had in mind. Denis thought Guy was joking when he eventually revealed that I was the client. As Denis pointed out, he had never even met me.

We got together at Leatherhead Golf Club when I was holding a golfing clinic on behalf of Callaway. Denis watched as I went through the lesson and then we had a long chat in which we exchanged thoughts on the swing. I liked the way he talked because nothing he was saying was too technical. I also liked the fact that he seemed to appreciate that mine was a natural swing and not one he would want to change. He made a couple of comments about what he had noticed in my alignment that day and, after taking his suggestions on board, I played some great golf in South Africa the following week. I won the million-dollar prize, holing a seven-footer at the third extra hole – the eighteenth – to defeat Ernie Els after he had pulled his second to the left of the green. Before I stood to that seven-footer, it entered my mind that the difference between finishing first and second was $750,000. Somehow, I had to put that thought on one side to be able to concentrate on the putt. Thanks to Hugh Mantle's breathing and focusing techniques, I just about managed to putt with a clear head.

It was great to be able to play so well in front of my father, albeit the play-off was hardly what the doctor would have ordered at that early stage in his recovery.

1997

The 1996 Order of Merit was my fourth in a row. But, with my restlessly competitive nature, I was not content to have equalled the record that Peter Oosterhuis had set in the

1970s. I yearned to beat it and move into fresh territory. In many eyes, I was attempting the impossible. As the press were to say, there were too many variables in the game, from the bounce of the ball to the weather to intrusive spike marks, to allow anyone to be so consistent. There was also the point that the other players had had enough of me. They were collectively determined to put an end to my run. Yet, once it started, 1997 was a still more consistent season than those which had gone before it because it was the first year in my career in which I never missed a cut, either in Europe or anywhere else.

I had three wins, with the first of them, the Compaq European Grand Prix at Slaley Hall, a particularly poignant affair in that my grandmother, who was coming up for ninety at the time, was in the stand behind the last green as I put the finishing touches to a 65 in which I had had seven birdies in my last eleven holes. I had no inkling that she was there and it was only after I had won that she came over. My uncle had driven her across from Sunderland and she has talked about it from that day to this.

After the US Open, where I began with a 65 but ended up losing by a shot to Ernie Els, I went to Druid's Glen to defend my title in the Murphy's Irish Open. I was three behind Lee Westwood heading into the final round but got off to the better start. I had a birdie to his three-putt bogey and went on to hand in a record 62 – yes, a 62! – to finish seven shots ahead of him and nine clear of Nick Faldo. It had been an interesting battle between Lee and myself. Before we went out on the Sunday, he had said that he feared no one. That, though, was precisely how I was feeling as I approached the round and, once I made that first birdie, there was no stopping me. It is not often that you cannot believe what you have done at the end of the day but, even now, I find it incredible that I should have reeled off as many as eight birdies and an eagle in the space of eighteen holes.

As we were walking from the seventeenth green to the eighteenth tee, I had to ask Alastair how many under par I was at the time. That was very unusual for me, because I almost always know not just how I stand in relation to par but how everyone else stands, too. The answer was nine.

Coming down to earth after that performance was never going to be easy. Everyone talked about how easily I would win the Scottish Open but I did not come close. I finished tenth there and twenty-fourth the following week in the Open at Troon. My last three rounds at Troon were 69, 69 and 70 but I had opened with a 76, and you cannot compete with that kind of start hanging round your neck.

Bernhard Langer threatened to win the Order of Merit when he picked up what was his third tournament of the year at the Czech Open, but I had a couple more second-place finishes and a third up my sleeve. My runner-up spot in the One2One British Masters was a 'good' second place. Though I was one shot away from missing the cut, I had weekend rounds of 67 and 63 to finish one behind New Zealand's Greg Turner. It had been described as a two-horse race as Greg set off on his final round with a two-shot lead over Thomas Björn. But I galloped into the picture with my 63 and, in the end, Greg did well to hang on. He made a great speech. In paying due tribute to One2One, the sponsors, he noted that his wife was pregnant and that that was also down to 'a one-to-one'! At the end of that week, I was £80,000 ahead of Bernhard, only for him to capture the German Masters in Berlin, where he came home in 29 on the last afternoon for a truly magnificent 60. No one, as they say, gives a damn who finishes second and least of all when it is second behind Bernhard in Germany. But if to no one else, where I finished that week was important to me. That was one of the most crucial aspects of my Order of Merit stretch. If someone were going to win, they would win, but if there was any chance of finishing second, I seized it. That day, I had a closing 68 that left me four adrift of Bernhard but one ahead of Thomas Björn.

The Volvo Masters was disappointing because it was cut to three days on account of the weather. My task that week was to finish ahead of Langer and, when he opened with a 66 to my 65, it was clear that I had my work cut out. His second round was a 70 to my 71 but, when it came to the third round, which turned out to be the last, I had a 71 to his 74. On the Saturday night, the heavens opened and we woke up to find flooding down the first fairway. They were trying to play but, two hours into the start of the fourth round, they called it a day, a decision which meant that I had finished eighth to Bernhard's fifteenth and the Order of Merit was mine for a fifth time.

Good Christian that he is, Langer congratulated me nicely. Had it been the other way round, I would have been furious that I had had the chance of winning snatched from my grasp.

1998

They talk about people being driven but it is hard to believe that anyone can ever have been more driven than I was as I set out to make it six in a row. I was on this conveyor belt and it was the start of my marriage going badly awry, only I could not see it. I was blind to everything bar the Order of Merit.

Once again, I made a late entrance and, when I teed up in the Volvo PGA Championship at Wentworth, I had competed in only three of the fourteen tournaments I could have entered. I was living dangerously but, in a way, that made me more motivated, if that were necessary. Having finished fifth in the Benson and Hedges, I was determined to win the Volvo PGA for the first time.

The signs were not good. I was about to miss the cut

when Andy Prodger, who had stepped in to carry my bag when Alastair McLean was injured, helped me to conjure up a birdie, birdie, birdie finish to my second round. It enabled me to stay above water and I proceeded to score a 65 and a 69 over the weekend to win. On the Sunday I was playing with Dean Robertson, a fellow Scot who was all set to take the trophy when, poor chap, he hooked out of bounds at the sixteenth. That one bad shot cost him dear. He had been one shot ahead going into that hole and he should have seized the event, which would have been a great result for him at that stage of his career. At the eighteenth I needed a birdie to avoid a play-off with Ernie Els, Gary Orr and Patrik Sjoland. With my record in play-offs – played three, lost three on the European Tour – I could not afford to let things get that far.

As was noted at the time, the orthodox way to achieve a birdie at the eighteenth is to hit a long, fading drive round the dog-leg and find the green with a mid- to long iron. The way I did it was to overdo the fade from the tee and hack out of a thick clump of rough before hitting a lob-wedge to nine feet. The putt was downhill and somehow I managed to hole it. I had willed home a lot of putts like that and, in this instance, 'willed' was the operative word because I did not have much of a putting stroke going for me at that point.

People go on about my not having won a Major but that Volvo PGA Championship felt like a Major to me. It was my fifteenth European Tour title and the £200,000 first prize was the biggest of my career. As I said in my speech, there was nothing more pleasing than seeing Ernie Els, who had had the better of me in two US Opens, sitting in the runner-up chair.

All told, I played seventeen tournaments in 1998 and of those I won three and had ten top-ten finishes, while my stroke average came down again and my winnings increased. Of the other four tournaments, I missed two cuts in a row, the first at the Smurfit European Open and the second at the BMW in Germany. After the second of these I was due to drive to Switzerland on the Monday and, with this unexpectedly free weekend, I stayed on in Germany and practised on the Saturday before playing a round as a marker when someone pulled out on the Sunday. As I was marking, I rediscovered some confidence in my putting. It would contribute to the two wins that were about to be mine – the One2One British Masters and the Linde German Masters. Winning the Linde German Masters was so important because Darren Clarke and Lee Westwood were catching me up fast on the Order of Merit. I was desperate to win that week and doubly so after something I had heard in the bar. It was all about Darren and Lee and how, if they finished first and second on the money-list, they would have the power to change a few things on the Tour, with particular reference to the perks-for-top-players situation. Appearance money is not called appearance money as such but, if a sponsor wants you at his tournament, he arranges a shoot-out, or some such thing, to make extra money available by way of an inducement to the top players. Like my management company, I was happy with the status quo, but Darren, Lee and their manager, Andrew Chandler, were not. I was perhaps being super-sensitive, but I had the feeling that they were planning ahead as if I were out of the picture. That, above all, was why I won the Linde German Masters, though I have to admit it was a close-run thing.

In shades of what had happened that day at Valderrama when I had to wait while Seve Ballesteros tried, unsuccessfully, to get a free drop on the eighteenth, I had a long wait at the last while Padraig Harrington needed a referee to ascertain whether his ball had crossed the hazard. It took ages and, at the end of it, I had to get down in two from forty-five feet to win the tournament from Robert Karlsson and Vijay Singh. You would not need to have been too good a lip-reader to get the gist of the relieved expletive that escaped my lips as my second putt – it was all of six feet – fell into the hole.

That result left me so far ahead of Lee that I took the Belgacom Open off. I thought I would enjoy the rest before the Volvo Masters at Montecastillo. Instead, I had a perfectly foul time and the rest of the family would have wished I were a million miles away. I watched on television as Lee holed his second shot at the tenth on the Saturday, and I kept watching as he went on to win in extra holes. Why, oh why, had I taken that week off? It almost killed me.

Lee was now well placed to catch me at Montecastillo. If he won the tournament, the Order of Merit was his. Meanwhile, if Darren won, I could not afford to finish outside the top eight. There were all kinds of complicated permutations but those were the most salient points.

In the press conferences on the Tuesday and Wednesday, both Lee and Darren once again made the mistake of talking of me in the past tense, albeit nicely enough. The last five years would be known as 'the Monty years', they said. That 'end of the era' script did it. I had to show them that I was not finished.

Darren won the tournament but I played safe, secure golf to finish in third place and to win my sixth Order of Merit. Yes, there was a certain amount of strain but I was still in that heady position where, on the European Tour, I could almost say what I was going to score when I went out: 'OK, I feel good today, I'll shoot a 68 … I feel very good today, I'll shoot a 65 … I don't feel so hot, I'll do a 71.'

1999

The last year of the seven and, in terms of the way I was striking the ball, probably the best. I won five regular tour events along with the Cisco World Match Play Championship in which I beat Mark O'Meara, who had won the Masters and the Open the previous year, in the thirty-six hole final.

Not for the first time, I made a slow start to the season but, when it came to May, I won the Benson and Hedges and the Volvo PGA Championship at Wentworth within the space of three weeks. I won the first by three shots from the vast-hitting Angel Cabrera, while at Wentworth I finished five shots clear of Mark James. With a last-round 64, my four-round aggregate that week was a record-equalling 270, eighteen under par. 'Monty's just great at the moment,' said Ernie Els, in a little aside to the golf writers that meant a lot to me.

Following that double, I captured the Scottish Open at Loch Lomond, where, as had also been the case at the Volvo PGA, my middle and shorter irons were accurate beyond all expectations, including my own. Time after time, I would leave myself single-putt distance from the hole. I would be a little right of the flag or a little left but I was seldom too short or too long. With a closing 64, I came from three shots behind to pass a sextet which included Lee Westwood, Sergio Garcia and Jesper Parnevik. That Sunday, I had nine birdies in a twelve-hole stretch in front of a crowd which contributed a huge amount to the tournament. Especially when the weather is fine, there is nothing to match playing down the seventeenth and eighteenth at Loch Lomond with pockets of spectators watching from the boats. 'The support I had today was unbelievable,' I told the press. 'I couldn't be feeling better about my game going into the Open.'

Alas, I think it was a case of having played so well that I had nothing left for the Open the following week. I was nowhere near the same player as I had been at Loch Lomond as I finished in a lacklustre share of fifteenth place. The only thing I did get right was to predict, very early on the last day, that Paul Lawrie would end up winning.

After the Open, Lee Westwood surfaced in the battle for the Order of Merit with back-to-back wins in the Dutch Open and the Smurfit European Open before I re-established myself with victories in the Scandinavian Masters and the BMW International Open. Paul Broadhurst held the first-round lead in Malmo but I led thereafter, winning by nine from Jesper Parnevik. In the BMW International Open, I won by three from Padraig Harrington, whose second place was of great significance to him in that it enabled him to clinch the tenth and last spot on that year's Ryder Cup team. Thanks to those two titles, my quest to win a seventh Order of Merit was virtually complete, though, because of the wealth of prize-money available at that year's end-of-season event at Valderrama, Lee, Sergio Garcia or Retief Goosen could have overtaken me had they picked up the winner's cheque. I have to admit that I'd have felt cheated if that had happened. As it turned out, Tiger Woods took care of things for me by defeating Miguel Angel Jimenez at the first extra hole. I finished in twentieth, which was neither here nor there.

After Tiger had given his winner's press conference, I was duly called to do the rounds of press and television inter-views about my seventh Order of Merit, or, to give the name of the silverware concerned, the Vardon Trophy. Much was made of my official earnings for the season being in excess of £1.8 million but, delighted though I was to be making that kind of money, the fact that our earnings are so public has often had the effect of making me cringe. In fact, if you were to ask me to name the thing I like least about our Tour it would be this eternal emphasis on how much money a man is making. I was brought up in a house where my father would never have dreamed of disclosing how much he earned. He would have thought it the height of vulgarity to put such figures about. Why on earth, you have to wonder, could the Tour not have opted for a more discreet points-based Order of Merit? In the media tent, Gordon Simpson, the press officer, made mention of the number of times over the year I had used the word 'stress'. Would I confirm that the pressure was more than it had been in the six previous seasons? The answer was in the affirmative, the reason being that I had turned winning the Order of Merit into something I *had* to do. Though I could not see it for myself at that juncture, there is no question that I was obsessed. On that very day, heaven help me, I even started talking of the possibility of winning it for an eighth time. 'I don't,' I said, 'have to tell you guys that I'm the most ambitious player out here, apart maybe from Tiger Woods. I want to achieve more and more from this game and provided I can stay healthy and fit, I feel I can improve again. If I've improved for this twelfth year in a row, there's no reason I can't make it thirteen.'

The press asked Ken Schofield, our executive director, if he thought that seven Orders of Merit could ever be beaten. Ken suggested that it could just happen before adding, 'I think we can safely say that if anybody is ever going to win the Order of Merit eight times, then that man will be Colin Montgomerie.'

I genuinely doubt that anyone could make it eight. All I can say is that if anyone did, he would not have a wife at his side at the end of it. I just survived and no more.

2000

The run ended in 2000, when I slipped to sixth place. Lee Westwood played great golf and finally did what he had threatened to do for a long time by coming out on top. I won the Novotel Perrier Open and the Volvo PGA Championship, but where, for example, I had had five second-place finishes in 1999, there were none of those in 2000 and only ten other finishes in the top ten out of my twenty-three tournament starts. On paper, it was hardly a bad year, but it felt bad to me.

When it came to the end of the 2001 season, the PGA European Tour held a dinner party for me at Wentworth on

6 November to celebrate my seven in a row. Strange though this might sound, that was precisely the right time for the function. If only temporarily, by then I had backed off a bit from my more obsessive days and had come to have a proper understanding of what I had achieved. There is no shortage of Waterford glass in our house, but the trophy I received that day to commemorate my Order of Merit run is one that stirs more pride every time I look at it.

Chapter 10

THE AMERICAN MAJORS

In the professional game, every tournament day is a test, with the results appearing oh-so-publicly in the next morning's papers. When it comes to the Majors, things are a million times more intense. Starting from the Sunday of the previous week, or even earlier, the sports sections will be full of how they expect you to play and to what extent they think the venue will suit your game. You are called upon to talk about how your preparation is going and, since the last thing you want to do is sound negative, you can often find yourself getting caught in the trap of sounding positive to the point of boastful. I have done it a few times.

In the days when the US Open was all about hitting fairways, I used to launch forth on the subject of how I felt one or even two up when standing on the first tee and how the event genuinely suited me. From time to time, a public declaration that I was up for the days ahead and playing well has worked in my favour. But on those occasions when I have got off on the wrong foot, the journalists have been quick to pounce. I dare say I would react the same if I were in their game. Nowadays, I tend to be a bit more circumspect.

Over the years, I have come to realise that a good starting time at a Major can play a key role in getting you off on the right foot. As a rule, I like to be up and away before the main traffic of the day. You almost have the feeling that you are sneaking round before the start of the championship and its hubbub. The only exception I would make here is for an Open at St Andrews, where my preferred first-round starting time would be around four o'clock in the afternoon. Quite often, the evening can be the best part of a St Andrews day, with a flat calm and a low sun to accentuate the rumpled fairways and their shadows. Some of the spectators will drift away for their dinner, but those who remain are apt to back you body and soul. The atmosphere can be as good as it gets. There are certain points where the people will be close enough to be within earshot of everything you say; others when they seem a million miles away – as, for example, when you are putting out on the second green. The same applies to the loop at the far end of the Old Course. That can be a very lonely affair but it gives you space to gather yourself before you come down the stretch.

Your playing companions can affect you no less than your starting time and, at this period in the game's history, you don't really want to be drawn alongside Tiger Woods for the first couple of days. Or, for that matter, to be in front of him or behind him. Though I myself have yet to play with Tiger in the first two days of a Major, I have made a close study of what has happened to people who have. Rarely do they score well, simply because there is so much going on around the world number one. It is not just tough for Tiger's playing companions. It is tough for the spectators, who can never see as much as they want, and tough for the marshals, whose job it is to maintain control.

Another point to ponder is when to arrive for a Major. Should you be there early? Or should you do a Freddie Couples and stay away until the very last moment? Of those who have made a success of arriving before the rest, Ben Hogan came a week in advance for the Open he won at Carnoustie in 1953. Jack Nicklaus's Open policy was much the same, though less because he wanted to play round and round the course than because he wanted to be in Europe to shake off the last vestiges of jet lag. I tried the early approach at the Masters in my first year, 1992, and it was a disaster. I barely scraped into the top forty. Like many another, I found it totally counter-productive. I played on the Sunday, Monday, Tuesday and Wednesday and, in so doing, managed to leave all my good shots behind in the practice rounds.

There is another reason why this approach is not one I would adopt again for Augusta. It has always seemed to me that they change the course on the Wednesday night. I have this picture, and I am sure it is not too far out, of green-keepers working through the night in a bid to stop anyone from tearing the course apart. The Augusta members are almost obsessed with protecting the place and, in many ways, you can understand why.

Like the greenkeepers at a Major, not too many contestants will get too much sleep on the night before the off. Whenever anyone talks of how we will have gone to bed early, someone will bring up the tale of Walter Hagen and the 1929 Open at Muirfield. Hagen was said to have been partying in the small hours of the morning before the final round when an official advised him, reproachfully, that Leo Diegel, who was two shots ahead of him at the time, had probably been in his bed for hours. 'Maybe so,' came Hagen's reply, 'but he's not sleeping.'

I can tell you, from my own tossing-and-turning experi-ences, that Hagen was 100 per cent right. My preference for the night before a Major is for Eimear and myself to go out with two or three other couples for a good meal where golf will not be the sole subject of conversation. I can also tell you that it does not do to have too good a breakfast the following morning, especially tempting though that can be at any one of the Major venues because the food in the locker room is invariably mouth-watering. If you eat a lot, it weighs heavily on your stomach and you know about it. The best idea is to eat lightly and have something packed in the golf-bag.

I have learned, through experience, that you do well in the week of a Major to control everything it is humanly possible to control. You may not have a say in too much else, but you can take charge of such things as the day you arrive and whether or not you succumb to that extra strip of bacon.

The Masters

My thoughts turn to the first of the Majors, the Masters, long before the turn of each year. I think about how long I should take for my winter break and where and when I should start up again. Then I decide how long I want to spend in America prior to Augusta.

The Players Championship is the one compulsory pre-Masters tournament. Many describe it as 'the fifth Major'. It is a brilliant event, one that boasts as good a field as you will see all year, and produces one great winner after another. (The nearest I have come to winning was in 1996 when I finished second to Freddie Couples, with an aggregate of 274 to his 270.)

In 2002, I went from the Players Championship to the Houston Open and from there to the BellSouth before heading for Augusta. In normal circumstances that would have been too much but, on this occasion, I felt I had no option. Having had to pull out of the Johnnie Walker Classic in Perth with a bad back, I was woefully short of competitive practice and needed a good run of events in order to shake off the cobwebs. Because my basic fitness was good after a winter programme of swimming and exercising, I managed to cope with all that play and improved each week before finishing fourteenth at Augusta.

Though I can hardly say I have hit on the right answer as

to how to prepare when I have yet to finish higher than my share of eighth place in 1998, I suspect that I do best when I use the previous week to relax. We have had a couple of family holidays in Florida, with my leaving the party to drive to Augusta on the Sunday. On the Monday, I take aim on being the twenty-third person to register. It is not just because my birthday is on 23 June that I see 23 as my lucky number. Things have always tended to go my way when my caddie has a No. 23 bib on his back.

More so than applies to any other course in the world, a round at Augusta is an emotional roller-coaster. There is a different set of circumstances on every hole, with the first tee coming as a shock in itself. I have known my hair to stand on end as I walk through the ropes – and that is just on the practice days! The Masters is Twickenham, Ascot and Wimbledon rolled into one. During the entire week, the crowd on the lawn beyond the clubhouse is a veritable *Who's Who* of the golfing world. Doug Sanders, that colourful character who came within a short putt of winning the 1970 Open at St Andrews, will always be among the first to catch the eye. Gary Player, who is so good at the PR side of the game, could be under the oak tree giving interviews to a succession of TV and radio people, while Sir Michael Bonallack, the former secretary of the R&A, and sundry other R&A and USGA officials are often based at one of the tables on the grass.

The first tee is not too many paces away from all this, and there, as on the lawn, you are keenly aware of the unchanging nature of the place. The Masters is not just about the top tier on the current money-list. It embraces everyone from Byron Nelson, that legendary old champion who in 2000 did his last stint as an honorary starter, to, say, Adam Scott, one of the more sensational new arrivals from the amateur ranks.

Once I have hit from the first, the next big gulp I am likely to take will be at the short fourth. This 205-yard, tree-girt par three is one of the toughest holes on the course, partly because of the swirling wind and partly because there is almost always a delay before you can hit. You try hard to keep your confidence intact during the waiting period, but it is almost impossible not to be aware of any mishaps that might be affecting the group in front. Maybe they are three-putting from the back. Maybe someone has fluffed a little chip from short and left of the green. You do not want to know but, somehow, the information seeps through.

One sign of a great hole is how it can start to prey on the mind long before you get there, and that certainly applies with the 155-yard twelfth. Even by this course's standards, it is an examination apart. For a start, you find yourself being applauded simply for arriving on the tee. It is a state of affairs to have you thinking, here we go, this is the shot. I can't mess it up. Of course, it is very easy to mess it up because there is absolutely no bail-out area. You cannot be too big and, by the same token, you cannot be too short. You just pray that you land between the front and back bunker and that your ball does not detonate all the 'oohs' and 'aahs' that accompany the ball that splashes into the depths of Rae's Creek. The shot, usually an eight iron but a nine if the flag is front left, needs a touch of luck apart from anything else because here, as at the fourth, the wind is apt to be at its most teasing. I've had twos, I've had fives and I've walked off that green being mighty grateful for a four. Like the seventeenth at Sawgrass or the Postage Stamp at Troon, the hole can make or break you.

Any feeling of relaxation once you have got your ball safely into the hole will be replaced by the strangest of sensations as you arrive on the tee of the 485-yard thirteenth. Where else in championship golf, other than on the loop at St Andrews, do you find yourself some 200 yards away from the paying public? You feel acutely isolated, disconcertingly cut off. There will be just you, your playing companion and the two caddies, along with two officials, one from the USGA or the R&A and the other from the professional game. Anyone who has followed golf for a few years will remember the lone figure of Freddie Couples as he dispatched his ball into the trees on the left in Mark O'Meara's Masters in 1998. Until then, everyone had thought that he would be that year's winner. Not until you have hit your tee shot and are halfway to your ball do you have the feeling of stepping back into the tournament. Always assuming your drive was truly middled, you are then looking at a second which, to me, is one of the most inviting shots that Augusta has to offer. Catch it well, and you can be safely on the putting surface and in with the chance of the birdie or eagle that could set you up for the rest of the round.

I would have a problem in naming my favourite hole because, when I think of Augusta, I see the view of Amen Corner from the eleventh fairway rather than any single hole. To my mind, it is the finest view in all golf and one which reminds me, every time, just how lucky I am to be playing the game at this level. Mind you, I must confess that the scene is more than a little enhanced if I happen to be a couple under par as opposed to a couple over.

Though I had my joint eighth place in 1998, I had my most exciting run in the Masters in 1997, the year I had been a runner-up at the Players Championship two weeks earlier. After rounds of 72 and 67, I was lying second. I was directly behind Tiger and was playing with him on the Saturday.

The story of how I found myself riveted to what he was doing rather than minding my own business is told later (see p. 193). Suffice to say here that I had a 74 to his 65 and was afterwards 100 per cent correct in my prediction that he would go on to win by more than the nine shots he was ahead on the Saturday night.

That year, I wasted my good start and finished thirtieth. In 2002, things worked the other way round. Having started with a 75, I was twelve holes into a rain-delayed second round when play was abandoned for the day. I was three over par for the tournament at that stage and could not afford to drop another shot when play was resumed first thing on the Saturday morning. I survived that exercise by the skin of my teeth and then had the satisfaction of hauling myself up through the field with rounds of 70 and 71.

The US Open

In contrast to the crisp spring sunshine of a vintage day at Augusta, the US Open is all too often a cauldron of heat and humidity. The mere mention of this event makes me think of shirts that can be wringing wet after a couple of holes. The other thing to come to mind is the noise. A US Open, and this applied more than ever before at the 2002 edition at Bethpage State Park in New York, is noisier by far than our Open, even before any serious drinking is under way. As everyone knows, I have had my spats with those members of a US Open crowd who have emerged the worse for wear from the beer tents, but more of that later.

People have always said that the US Open represents my best chance of winning a Major and, for a long time, that was definitely true, what with the long rough putting a premium on straight driving. But the emphasis has been a little different in the more recent instalments. Though Bethpage State Park was a case apart and almost everything a US Open venue ought to be, the USGA hierarchy started to depart from the old-style US Open set-up around 2000. Their courses were starting to look very like the courses you see week-in, week-out on the USGA Tour, which was not the most uplifting thing in the world because the last thing you want is for a Major championship to lose its character. In its former guise I loved the week and it maybe did no harm to my chances that others didn't.

It was in 1992 that I had what most see as my nearest of several near misses. Pebble Beach, which is sited on America's Pacific coast, is a course that gives me much the same sense of eager anticipation as I get when I pull into the car park at Wentworth during a tournament week. In many ways, the course itself reminds me of Scotland's west coast, what with the rugged rocks and that glorious bay around the eighteenth where, at the start of the 2000 Open, the late Payne Stewart's fellow professionals celebrated his life with the equivalent of a twenty-one-gun salute as they blasted drives into the sea. I fell for Pebble Beach when I arrived in 1992 and my feelings remained the same even after I had my hopes so rudely dashed on the last day.

I had returned a last-round 70 for a 288 aggregate. My playing companion, a left-hander by the name of Russ Cochran, said that I would find myself in a play-off situation at worst. After all, the weather was horrendous. Jack Nicklaus, meantime, congratulated me on winning, both to my face and on television. As for the British press corps, they were every bit as excited as you would expect, for no Briton had won the US Open since Tony Jacklin, twenty-two years earlier.

I suggested to Alastair McLean, my caddie, that he should check in to my hotel, the Pebble Beach Lodge, just in case it came to a play-off. It would be a sensible precaution and, if it turned out to be unnecessary because we had won out-right, we were hardly going to worry about the cost of the night's accommodation. We then sat back to watch the denouement on television.

To our amazement, for conditions were going from bad to worse, Tom Kite got better and better. Though, initially, Alastair and I told ourselves that it could not last, Kite continued to get up and down from off the green at virtually

1995. The titanic struggle with Sam Torrance is over. When we went to the last tournament of the year, the Volvo Masters at Valderrama, I was £3,000 behind Sam on the Order of Merit. I was having the better of the week but had a last-day fright as they put his name up, letter by letter, at the top of the leaderboard. He had had a last round 68 to be the leader in the clubhouse but I did what I had to do in finishing with a stretch of pars to win what was my third Order of Merit. Here I am with my caddie, Alastair McLean, after holing from four feet on the last green. (Photo: Popperfoto)

Left With Nick Faldo at the 1993 Ryder Cup. Nick had just holed his putt at the 18th in the first-day fourballs that ran over into Saturday morning. For the record, we halved with Paul Azinger and Freddie Couples. (Photo: Getty Images)

Bottom left 1997 Ryder Cup at Valderrama. With Eimear at the Welcome Dinner.

Middle Who says I never smile? At the opening ceremony of the Ryder Cup, 1995. (Photo: Getty Images)

Bottom right With HRH Prince Andrew after we had won the Ryder Cup at Valderrama in 1997.

With Tiger Woods at the Ryder Cup in 1997. Not a match that either of us wants to lose. For the record, Bernhard Langer and I lost to Mark O'Meara and Tiger Woods on the first morning, but had the better of them in the afternoon. (Photo: Getty Images)

Last day of the 1997 Ryder Cup. I admit to having felt nervous at the 17th. With a crowd of that size it was hardly surprising. (Photo: Getty Images)

1997 at Valderrama. My two minutes of fame with the trophy that means so much. (Photo: Getty Images)

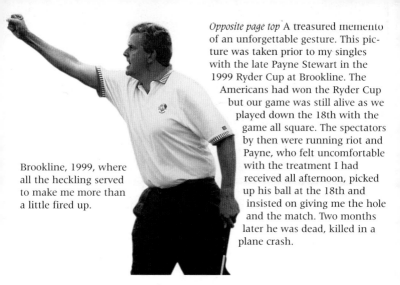

Opposite page top A treasured memento of an unforgettable gesture. This picture was taken prior to my singles with the late Payne Stewart in the 1999 Ryder Cup at Brookline. The Americans had won the Ryder Cup but our game was still alive as we played down the 18th with the game all square. The spectators by then were running riot and Payne, who felt uncomfortable with the treatment I had received all afternoon, picked up his ball at the 18th and insisted on giving me the hole and the match. Two months later he was dead, killed in a plane crash.

Brookline, 1999, where all the heckling served to make me more than a little fired up.

Below Eimear and I on Concorde with the Ryder Cup. We are taking it back to America for the start of the 1999 match at Brookline.

Opposite page bottom Loch Lomond 1999. Being toasted by the Pipe Major after winning the Scottish Open at Loch Lomond. There is nothing quite like winning in front of your own crowd. (Photo: Getty Images)

Celebrating holing a birdie to win the 1998 PGA at Wentworth. (Photo: Getty Images)

...ed one problem but caused another. The only trousers ...t went with it were navy blue: another 'wrong' colour for ...dsummer America.

...By the time I had started par, double bogey, double bogey, ...was not just hot but bothered, too. I had no chance. After ...at, I was trying to play catch-up with two great players and ...was never going to work. Not, mind you, that they played ...reat golf that day. They were round in 74 to my 78 before ...rnie went on to win at the second extra hole.

With hindsight, I should have gone to see the club professional, Colin Campbell, who had been one of Bob Jamieson's assistants at Turnberry. He would have found me a white, Oakmont shirt, which, like my tartan one, would not have upset anyone.

I surfaced for a third time in 1997 at Congressional. Rees Jones, the designer, had whetted my appetite for that particular US Open a couple of months earlier during the week of the Benson and Hedges at the Oxfordshire. He told me that he had redesigned the Congressional bunkers and the surrounds to the greens and that the place was made for me.

I was playing magnificently when I set out for that year's instalment. I had had a 62 in winning in Ireland, while I had just won the Great North Open at Slaley Hall by seven shots. My caddie Alastair was not the only one to say he had never seen golf like it.

On this occasion, though, I made my first mistake even before I left Britain. I had had a truly wonderful week at Slaley Hall. That was the tournament when my grandmother saw me win from the stands. So I was in a great frame of mind as I turned out of the Slaley Hall drive. I was going home for a night's sleep and to redo my packing before heading to the States on the Monday morning. The journey ...hould have taken no more than four hours. As it was, it took ...ight. I was in a state verging on panic when I arrived back at

Personally, I never like to compartmentalise my swing. I see it more as one fluid movement, which is heavily dependent on good timing.

every hole. Jeff Sluman similarly played out o͏̈ ͏̈as ͏̈sol͏̈
as the weather eased, so he came in second to͏̈ ͏̈tha͏̈
me in what was an anticlimactic third place. ͏̈mi͏̈

To be honest, I had lost that US Open on th͏̈
Playing alongside Anders Forsbrand in the thir͏̈ ͏̈I͏̈
group, I had returned a wind-racked 77 to Forsb͏̈ ͏̈t͏̈
That was when the damage was done. ͏̈i͏̈

I don't harbour any ill will towards Nicklaus for
said. He was pretty damned positive that I had w͏̈
thousands of others shared that view. Yet, looking ͏̈
don't think that winning a Major at that stage of my ͏̈
would necessarily have been the best thing. I doubt͏̈
much if I would have done so well in the intervening yea͏̈
things had come right that day. I would have been expe͏̈
to carry on competing at that level when, if the truth ͏̈
known, I was nowhere near ready to play that kind of golf ͏̈
a regular basis.

My next US Open performance to remember was at
Oakmont in 1994 when I finished in a share of second place
with Loren Roberts behind Ernie Els. I had putted as well as
I have ever done in stringing together the four steady
rounds which left me tied with Ernie and Loren on 279. I
was ready for the play-off but had a problem on my hands.
I had run out of shirts. I was with Pringle at the time and,
though they had given me six shirts at the start of the week,
the sticky heat was such that I had none left by the Sunday
night. Yes, I could have been sending them to the cleaner͏̈
but, when you are playing in high temperatures and eve͏̈
higher humidity, you sweat a lot and a salt mark appe͏̈
over the back of the shirt that nothing will remove. The o͏̈
acceptable shirt I could find for the Monday was͏̈
bearing a Black Watch tartan. I knew all about dark col͏̈
attracting heat but I also had to consider Pringle. ͏̈
imperative that if I were not going to wear one o͏̈
shirts, I should wear one that was logo-free. The tart͏̈

The trophies displayed on my study desk. (Photo: Getty Images)

Oxshott. I was worried about not getting any sleep at all and struggling to be organised in time to make it to Heathrow for a ten o'clock flight.

When we arrived in the States, I felt better than expected, and the following morning had nine holes of practice alongside Peter Mitchell, who was playing in his first American Major. I rested for the remainder of the day before playing another nine holes with Peter on the Wednesday. My golf was still in great shape and, maybe because I was feeling so good about it, I was not conscious of anything in the way of jet lag at that juncture. I could not wait for the start.

My first round was a 65 that Phil Mickelson described as 'the best Major round I've ever seen'. I had missed three four-foot putts on the first three greens but then started making the birdie putts. My only mistake, one I would make on all four days, was to bogey the seventeenth. At the end of that round, I was asked why I had not used my driver. The answer was that I had started off using a three wood and felt entirely comfortable with the way I was hitting it and the length I was achieving. I thought to myself, why change? As I went on to explain, accuracy counted for rather more than length on this course. Not, mind you, that I was exactly short with my three wood, because I could hit it anything from 265 to 285 yards.

It was on the Friday that my Newcastle–Oxshott journey caught up with me. I was conscious of feeling tired even before the rain delay that was called as I was playing the eleventh. I was still leading the tournament when play resumed. In fact, nothing had changed with the exception of the demeanour of some of those who were following our group. Where, earlier, they had all been behaving as a crowd should behave, they now had a few drinks inside them and were looking for trouble. By this stage, I was not using my legs as well as I had been using them and, when I missed a fairway from the sixteenth tee, something inside me snapped when a spectator yelled, 'Go home!' Because I was tired and fractious, I made the unforgivable mistake of answering him back and that, in turn, led to his drunken friends taking his side and hurling more insults in my direction.

Why did they pick on me? The fact that I responded as I did scarcely helped but, at that stage, Americans did not always feel very kindly disposed towards those Europeans meddling on their very lucrative patch. Besides having a good Ryder Cup record vis-à-vis the Americans, I had by then had three near misses in American Majors, with the 1995 PGA Championship at Riviera (of which more soon) ranking up there with my 1992 and 1994 achievements in the US Open. They saw me as a bit of an irritation, a threat.

The war of words did not continue but I ended up dropping a shot at the sixteenth and seventeenth and finishing with a 76.

The following day I did a lot to repair the damage. I hit back with a 67 which left me just the one shot behind Ernie Els going into the last round. The Sunday of any Major has a feel all its own and this one was no exception. At some point, Ernie and I learned that Bill Clinton had come to Congressional expecting to present the trophy to an American, only to disappear when he heard that the winner was more likely to be Ernie or myself. It may well have been a disappointing last day for an American audience but, between us, Ernie and I played some great golf.

There were two occasions in the final round when I held the lead but we were level after sixteen and I had a five-footer at the seventeenth to stay that way. At Congressional, the green of the short eighteenth was behind the seventeenth green, with the two separated by water. Jay Haas was putting out on the eighteenth as I was preparing to tackle my putt on the seventeenth, and such was the noise from his green that I decided to wait for a bit of peace and quiet. In retrospect, that was a big mistake. Just as Ernie would say later, the

American crowd were not too concerned as to whether we had any peace or not. By the time I felt ready to putt, the doubts you can feel over any length of putt if you wait long enough had caught up with me. I missed and lost by one.

How that hurt. It had been an emotionally charged week and, though Eimear did her best to comfort me at the end of the round, I was not about to recover in a hurry. I had played the best golf of the week and I had come away second.

USPGA Championship

Alongside the Masters, the US Open and the Open, the PGA has Major status. But, like it or not, the tournament does not have the special qualities of the other three. I have always inclined to the view that the Players Championship would make for a better fourth Major on the grounds that it attracts such a quality field.

My best PGA Championship to date was 1995 at Riviera when I lost to Steve Elkington at the first extra hole. The golf I played that week was the finest of my life. I was never in a bunker and hit sixty-nine greens in regulation. On top of that, I coped brilliantly with the pressure coming down the stretch. After sixty-nine holes I needed to finish birdie, birdie, birdie to tie Elkington, who was in the clubhouse at seventeen under. At the short sixteenth I hit an eight iron to four feet and made the putt. At the seventeeth, a par five, I chipped from eighty yards to eight feet and made that. Then, at the eighteenth, I hit a driver and seven iron below the hole to twenty-five feet. I don't think that Mark O'Meara, my playing companion that day, could believe what he was seeing as I rolled that one home to make the play-off.

I was tickled by what appeared in Mark McCormack's annual about the way I handled things down the stretch. 'Some people', it began, 'crack under this kind of pressure while others live for it. Here, Montgomerie showed he has the courage to play his best under trying conditions.'

Once that twenty-five footer had dropped, I was convinced that I would win, and, as we went back to the eighteenth tee, I said to myself, 'This is it.' What is more, since I had lost all five of the play-offs in which I had previously been involved in Europe and in the 1994 US Open, I felt the law of averages had to be on my side.

Elkington had the honour and pulled his drive into the left rough. I followed up with a drive so straight that it finished no more than an inch from the divot I had taken when playing the seventy-second twenty minutes or so earlier. Alastair and I joked about the yardage being identical but this time, instead of taking a seven iron, I took an eight. It went right at the flag and stopped twenty feet short. Elkington, meantime, had hit to the back of the green and had a putt of thirty feet. He holed and I missed from inside him.

It was tough flying home that night. I dwelt on how I had been seventeen under for the seventy-two holes and how that was the lowest total ever shot in a Major by someone who had not won. My golf from tee to green had been virtually faultless but, on average, I had had four putts more than Elkington per day. There was one particular putt, at the twelfth hole of my final round, which had stopped a millimetre from the lip and the commentator who said that that millimetre might cost me the championship probably got it right.

Elkington, who had been at the University of Houston at the same time I was at Houston Baptist, faxed me soon after. He said that although he was getting all the benefits of winning a Major, we had both deserved to win that day. It was a nice touch, but nothing was going to make up for my disappointment. That was when I began to wonder if I were ever going to win a Major.

As to what would have to happen for me to rate the PGA

as highly as the other Majors, I suppose I might be prevailed upon to change my mind if I were to get my name on the trophy.

Chapter 11

THE OPEN

Though they do not all feel the same way, there is no shortage of Americans to tell you that the Open is the jewel in the crown, the Major of Majors. It is the oldest championship of them all, dating back to 1860, and has been won, to name but five of the game's immortals, by Young Tom Morris, Harry Vardon, Bobby Jones, Jack Nicklaus and Tiger Woods.

Whenever I drive to Royal Birkdale, Lytham or Muirfield, or any of the other Open venues, for that matter, I am conscious of the fact that I could not be heading anywhere else. Links are almost always out on a limb and everything about them is out of the ordinary for the modern professional who spends ninety per cent of his golfing life playing inland. You can hear the gulls calling overhead and, at certain points on certain links, there is the smell of seaweed and the sea. A coastal wind is a different animal to its inland equivalent, while the turf, too, is a total contrast: it is dry and firm and you do not have to clean the grass cuttings from your spikes every few holes. In fact, when you get back to the clubhouse, there will be nothing on the soles of your golf shoes to suggest that you have played at all.

It is not just the sights and sounds on the links that tell you where you are. If you were to blindfold me and put me in the locker room at, for instance, Troon, Lytham or St Andrews, I would know precisely where I was from the smell of the lockers. It is a dry, wooden smell, possibly one of the most evocative in the game.

People are right when they say that Open links, coupled with half a gale, were not obviously made for me and my relatively high hitting, but the goodwill you get from the British crowd can be a stronger force than the most buffeting of seaside winds. That struck me as never before at Lytham in 2001, when the spectators got right behind me from the start and were still doing their best to will my ball into the hole on a last day when it was taking a mischievous pleasure in going anywhere but.

The first time I got myself in a good early position in the Open, though it was that and no more, was in 1991. One off the pace at the halfway stage after rounds of 71 and 69, I set out for what would be one of life's more extraordinary rounds in the company of Richard Boxall, nowadays one of our more entertaining commentators. I was still playing well but, fairly early on in the round, Richard started complaining about a pain in his leg. It reached the point where he was really suffering and, after he had shanked a shot at the eighth, he said that he would hit his drive at the ninth before deciding whether to stop. He went through his normal pre-shot routine on the tee and then, as he swung at the ball, there was an ominous crack which sounded like the snapping of a dry twig. He collapsed painfully on the ground with what was later diagnosed as a stress fracture at the base of his leg. Richard's wife, Jane, who was seven months pregnant, was in the gallery with his sister, Louise. The two of them were hugely distressed. Golf and the Open were hardly uppermost in any of our minds as the medics arrived to take the victim to hospital.

Suddenly, amid all the kerfuffle, I got with it. Not only had I lost my playing partner but Barry Lane and Vijay Singh, in front, were almost two holes ahead, while a series of players was backing up behind. Since Mark James and

Roger Chapman were the next up on the ninth tee, it seemed
to make sense for me to carry on with them. With this in mind,
I rescued my scorecard from Richard's back pocket and told an
approaching R&A official what I had in mind. He deemed it
the sensible option but, when he spoke to Mark and Roger,
he put it in such a way that they seemed to think they had a
choice. Because they were going well, they did not want to
take a third party on board. The official then suggested that
I should look to Barry and Vijay for help, even though they
were now three holes ahead. He radioed ahead and the pair of
them very decently agreed to wait on the thirteenth tee while
I played up with the R&A man in tow. By the time I reached
them, I had dropped two shots. It was a unique situation
playing those two holes on my own. The spectators would look
at me and then their starting sheets in a bid to ascertain what
on earth was going on. 'What have you done with Richard
Boxall?' came a query from the spectators on the right.

What had happened to Richard and the threat to his career
overshadowed the effect it had on my scorecard. Yet, for
some time afterwards, I wondered what might have been.
Given Ian Baker-Finch's remarkable closing rounds of 64
and 66, I would have been struggling to win, but I believe I
could have mounted a realistic challenge. For the record, I
finished with a couple of relatively uninspired 71s for a share
of twenty-sixth place.

Ten years on, at Lytham, I had not featured too much in
the pre-Open hype, but, after I had started birdie, birdie and
returned a 65, I was back in demand – and loving it. The score
left me three shots ahead of Brad Faxon, Chris DiMarco and
Finland's Mikko Ilonen. Still more pertinently, I was six ahead
of Tiger.

The club captain, Alan Halsall, had said that day that there
was nothing he would like more than to hand me the Claret
Jug at the end of the week, and it seemed to me that there
were not too many at Lytham who had any objections: the

crowd were behind me as never before. I think they felt I had been around for quite a while and that I deserved to win a Major. I also sensed, very keenly, that the fact that I had given an open, honest account about the problems in my marriage earlier in the year had struck a chord with a lot of them. I know that people with money can sire resentment in others, but that Open crowd gave the impression that they viewed me as a man who had much the same ups and downs in life as any of them. It did not seem to matter one jot that I was Scottish rather than English. 'Good luck to him' is what they seemed to be saying.

There is no question that Freddie Couples and Stuart Appleby suffered from playing alongside me over the first two days, as did Pierre Fulke at the weekend. I went so far as to apologise to him for all the 'Come on, Monty!' shrieks and explained that it was simply a matter of people getting a bit carried away on my behalf because I had been around for so long.

After the first round I explained to the press that that 65 was nothing more than a good beginning. 'I'm thinking of this Open as a twenty-eight-mile walk,' I told them. 'I've got another twenty-one miles to go and with a hundred and ninety-six bunkers out there I cannot afford to get ahead of myself.'

On the Friday I tacked a 70 to my 65, which left me with a one-shot lead over Fulke. On the way out, I had been no better than 36 but, coming home, I lifted the spirits of my loyal gallery with birdies at the eleventh and thirteenth. As was remarked on at the time, these spectators, who had seemed happy to let bygones be bygones in terms of my odd, angry outbursts, had become 'more like Monty than Monty'. For example, at the short fifth, when somebody inadvertently banged his umbrella into the spectator stand as I was about to hit, it seemed that the only person not to give him a filthy look was me.

When that round was over everyone felt I was going to hang in there and win the Open. Everyone, that is, except me. All day, my holing out had not been a patch on what it had been on the Thursday when I had ten single putts to set alongside a chip-in at the sixth. When it came to the eighteenth, I heard Ken Brown, the BBC commentator who was walking with us, say into his microphone, 'If he scores seventy, he'll be doing well.' At that, I was determined to do a 69 and it looked highly possible when my shot to the last green span back to five feet. When I missed that putt I knew, in my heart of hearts, that I was not putting well enough to win that Open. More than anything, it was the way I missed it – leaving the ball on the low, amateur side of the hole. I had hit it defensively and you can't win Majors by being defensive.

I did not admit to any doubts to Steve Ryder, when he interviewed me on a bench at the end of the round, but much of my early confidence had evaporated. I went out early the next day to practise my putting, but to no avail. My third round was a 73, which still left me up there with the leaders, but I needed to find an extra something from somewhere for the last round and it was not there. I had a 72 for 280, which left me in a share of thirteenth place. It was a bitter let-down but, against that, the warmth of the crowd left me thinking that I could not wait for Muirfield and 2002.

When that came round, I admitted at the start of the week that I had seen the 2001 Open at Lytham as an opportunity missed. 'With Tiger not performing, there was an opportunity for all of us. David Duval took it, I didn't,' I told the press, ruefully.

I was desperate to do better this time but, mindful of my back, which had been playing up on-and-off in the preceding weeks, I had no intention of overdoing things on the practice days over a course I knew pretty well.

Following what had been an erratic Scottish Open at Loch

Lomond in which I opened with rounds of 72 and 71 before handing in a 69 on Saturday and a vastly improved 66 on the Sunday, I had spent a weekend with the family at Gleneagles before having my first practice round on the Tuesday evening. It was a solitary and thorough affair in the evening drizzle. On the Wednesday I decided against a second practice round and elected instead to work on chipping, putting and the general pace of the greens. Also, I had another look at the 468-yard sixth, the one hole where I was not 100 per cent sure about where to land the tee shot. With nothing other than a bunch of hay out in front, it was difficult to take precise aim.

Where my putting was concerned, my main concern on the Wednesday was to get myself back on good terms with my belly putter, which, despite my closing 66, had opted out on the last day at Loch Lomond. There were four or five more putts that could have dropped that day. You do not have to practise with the belly putter as much as with a conventional implement because with the three points of contact – two hands and the body – everything is so much firmer. So all I had to do was check on posture and alignment. After that, it was all down to judging the pace of the greens.

I liked the way Muirfield had been set up, with the fairways narrow but not ridiculously so and the rough more than usually penal. As I would admit before the start, it was my type of golf-course on a links I liked above any other. When questioned, I said if everything were to come together for the next few days, I had every confidence that I could make an impression. 'Of course we can compete' is what I said. I was referring to myself and Andy Prodger, the caddie to whom I had switched in the week of the Volvo PGA Championship at Wentworth. I was feeling particularly blessed in having Andy on the bag at Muirfield, for he had been at Nick Faldo's side when he won at Muirfield in 1987. In our practice round he was able to tell me what Nick had done and there is no question that that extra dimension of knowledge played its part in my rising confidence. Andy's expertise is so respected that he was even called upon to do the hole-by-hole feature in the *Daily Telegraph*'s pre-Open supplement.

I had not played in the 1987 Open, but I had been there for the 1992 edition – at least for two days. The trouble then was that everyone was expecting a lot of me after my strong finish in that summer's US Open and my second place behind Peter O'Malley at the Scottish Open. In 2002, there was little or no weight of expectation. Just a quiet confidence based on ten years of experience. I said that if Tiger Woods played the way he could, the rest of us would not have too much of a chance. But that if he were to underperform and the door were to open as it had at Lytham, I was determined to be the man to seize the opportunity. Instead, you could say that I virtually slammed the door in my own face.

On the first day I opened with two birdies in the first three holes, only to sign off with a dismal 74 and a row with a perfectly decent radio reporter, Rob Nothman. He got to me when the steam was still coming out of my ears and when he began his interview by saying, 'Colin, I know it's been a difficult day, but just how difficult was it?' I snapped. I told him that it had not been remotely difficult before asking if his tape was off. Rob nodded and I suggested that if he were to ask 'a proper question' he might get a proper answer.

On the second day no one made a more significant move up the leaderboard than I did – from 106th to a share of ninth place, to be exact. In Thursday's 74, as one of the papers said, my swing, not to mention my temper, had been on the short side. 'Yesterday,' continued the article, 'there was a different Montgomerie, with nothing contributing more to the metamorphosis than the twenty-footer he holed across the first green on his way to a record 64.'

On Wednesday I had told people that one of the reasons I

liked the late/early starting times I had been given was because there was not too long a gap between the two. After my 64, I mentioned another benefit: because I was up so early, I had had no chance to get uptight about the contents of the morning papers, which, in this instance, and, I suppose, entirely understandably, included reports on my conflict with Nothman.

The crowd who had followed the 74 were waiting for me on the first tee on Friday morning. It struck me that they were prepared to forgive even my worst transgressions and it also struck me that I could not expect that to apply for all time. From what I could gather, they like the feeling that they can make a difference, which they certainly did that day. The whole lot of us felt triumphant after I holed from all of twelve feet for the birdie that took me to seven under for the day and four under for the championship.

With such a round under my belt, it was inevitable that there were questions as to whether I felt I could win. 'I think,' I replied, 'that my last hole today proved that I could if the chance were to arise. I wouldn't have holed that twelve-footer for a birdie if I'd been frightened.'

Eimear, Olivia and I enjoyed a great dinner that night and our plan was that Eimear would bring Olivia along to sit in the stand at the eighteenth the following day. It would have been pointless for Olivia to walk all the way because viewing at an Open is difficult enough for adults, let alone children, who cannot see anything unless they are prepared to peep through people's legs around the greens.

I remember looking out of the window from the Greywalls Hotel on the Saturday morning and seeing Bernhard Langer and Ian Woosnam. They had just completed a couple of rounds in the low seventies and were disappointed that they had not done better in the relatively favourable conditions. Andy Prodger and I started to prepare for our later starting time and, as we were walking from the putting green just beyond the hotel to the practice range, it started to rain. We told each other that it would not last but, as I practised, it grew colder.

Nor did things improve once Nick Price, one of my favourite playing companions, and I got started. After three holes, my circulation was playing up and I had no feeling in my hands whatsoever as I hit from the fourth tee. The ball shot from the toe of my three wood into the rough. At the fifth, I took the line down the left half of the fairway but, with the wind more menacing by the second, I failed to carry the 160 yards needed to clear the rough. I hit a shank with my wedge from the long grass, with my ball whizzing past Nick Price's ear before ending up in more rough. I hacked out before belting a drive under the wind to twelve feet. In normal circumstances I would have been delighted with the shot but not when it was wrapped up in a bogey six. The writing was on the wall.

What irked me most as I handed in an 84 was that I was suffering for having had that 64 in the second round. Had I had a more mundane 69, I would have been off much earlier on the Saturday and, like Langer and Woosnam, I would have missed the worst of the weather. That, though, is links golf, different in the morning, the afternoon, by day and by night.

When I handed in my 84, the press were talking to Tiger Woods about his 81. I did not hang around to talk to them – who would, in the circumstances? – and instead returned to Greywalls with Olivia, who had been dispatched to get me. Imagine my surprise, therefore, when I was accosted by someone in the doorway of the hotel the next morning who said, 'Are you going to be doing more of your storming off today?' I asked what he meant and he told me that the papers were full of how I had stormed off after the third round. There have been plenty of times when I have stormed off but this was not one of them and, ridiculous though this might sound, I felt more than a little peeved.

I was also irritated by allegations that I had caved in during that round. My body language lets me down time and time again and, just as I can look almost too confident as I stride down a fairway when all is going well, so, as I am the first to admit, I can look a miserable so-and-so when things start to go awry. I had tried to make what I could of the day, though I would not deny that if I had managed to keep my head up for longer, I might somehow have knocked a couple of shots off my total.

The ridiculous always happens to me, and it did not help that my 84 was a record twenty shots worse than my Friday 64. I must admit that Jim Black, a Scottish freelance writer, captured that aspect of events to perfection when he said that I had been 'in no mood to hang around and discuss my place in the record books'.

On the Sunday morning, Lee Janzen was out first, with a marker, with me and David Toms the first of the two balls. It was no place to be on the last day of the Open – a million miles from the cheers and the action. But who should make me see the funny side of things but Tiger, who had just blown his chance of winning the Grand Slam with the 81 that had been the second-worst score after mine. As I was practising my putting, he came up behind me and said, 'Morning, Monty … At least I kicked your ass yesterday!' To which I replied that it was just about the only one he had kicked.

Toms and I whipped round in two hours and forty-six minutes and someone cracked the joke that the only reason I was second last rather than last was because Toms, who was fourteen over to my thirteen over, had been hard pushed to keep up with me.

Complete rubbish!

After I had returned my 75, I had another go at the press, this time concerning their 'storming off' statements. The press – the wrong ones, as I would later learn, for it was the Sunday-paper boys who had been responsible for the story –

stood there looking a little nonplussed as I delivered what was, to them, an astonishing little homily concerning how I was fed up with their references to my attitude. 'I haven't,' I told them, 'shown any signs of temper in five years. I'm very, very disappointed.' Though I was far too fraught to stop and explain myself, my feeling was that there was no sense of balance in what they were writing. Why, when we knocked along pretty well together for most of the year, had they been picking on me exclusively when they could have latched on to a dozen or so other players who had been hurling clubs around the place and generally getting away with murder?

Before I left Muirfield that day, I furnished the press officer with the following addendum: 'I'm really hurt. I've pulled out of golf tournaments for the next two weeks. I can't handle it any more.'

The press returned to their computers to knock out stories on how I had finished with a 75 while Woods hit back after his Saturday spree in the eighties to close with a 65. I would be the first to say that his was by far the more impressive performance. He is miles better than I am when it comes to putting things behind him.

Meanwhile, I set off down the road with regrets mounting rather than receding. I should never have taken the press on as I did. It was crackers. Some hours later, Ernie Els would have driven away with the feeling that this was the climax of his career. He had won two US Opens but the Open was the championship he had craved above the rest.

Woods had done as he did in 2001 by giving everyone else an opening, and this time Ernie had been the one to take it. On the Saturday his easy swing had helped him to land a 72 in the worst of the weather. On the Sunday he wavered under the pressure of it all before finally winning at what was the fifth extra hole.

It was never going to be easy for me to put that up-and-down week behind me but, as everyone says, in a bid to help the recovery process, there is always next year. I will be forty when we tee up at Royal St George's, a year younger than Mark O'Meara when he won at Birkdale in 1998. Of course it is still possible. Not just for me but for my 'team' behind the ropes, I would love one day to hear my name when Peter Dawson, the R&A secretary, says those wonderful words, 'And the champion golfer for the year is …'

Chapter 12

THE UNREAL MONTY

O wad some Pow'r the giftie gie us
To see oursels as others see us!
Robert Burns

Sometimes when I turn on the golf on television in my hotel room I am appalled by what I see. The cameras could have captured a bad Montgomerie shot before panning in on the player looking hot and bothered. Minutes later, I will be on the screen again, this time plodding down the fairway with those unmistakable shoulders having slumped by at least forty degrees, if that were anatomically possible. Whenever I witness one of these scenes I say to myself, 'That can't be me.'

I can laugh at this character but I also feel an overriding sense of remorse every time the moody Montgomerie puts in an appearance. I am not remotely proud of him.

The explanation has a lot to do with the fact that I am a perfectionist. None of it would happen if I were happy to finish twenty-second every week, but, as everyone who has ever watched me knows only too well, I manifestly am not. Nothing bothers me when things are going well. I feel goodwill towards all men – even marshals, journalists and photographers. There is a grey area in the middle where I can play well in spite of myself, but when things take a real turn for the worse my alter ego can take hold. Not always, but sometimes.

If you were to ask what irritates me most on the golf-course, it would not be the rustle of sweet papers, the crunching of crisps or someone moving in the crowd. To me, nothing is more maddening than the marshal with the 'Silence Please!' board who holds the notice aloft only at the last moment. Though he would be raising it in plenty of time for those golfers who spend three or more seconds over the ball, it is too late in my case. Quite often, it goes up only a fraction of a second before I take the club away. Much the same applies to those photographers who are not used to my golfing ways. They will still be fidgeting around looking for the right angle when I am about to swing. No less than me, they are seeking the best shot they can get. If I carry on and everything goes according to plan, I will forgive the board-bearer or the cameraman. If, on the other hand, I hit the ball less than well, I have – to put it mildly – been known to snap.

To be ruthlessly honest, having a go at some innocent marshal, photographer or referee is hardly the most commendable way out. Instead of taking things on the chin, I am looking for someone to blame. Hugh Mantle, who is one of the highest-qualified sports psychologists in the business, says it is a means of projecting my anxieties on to someone else.

Though there have been plenty of times when I have thought I've got this weakness beaten, the tendency is one I have had to fight all my days. To my eternal shame, I once upset the lady captain at Wentworth in the Cisco World Match Play Championship. She was walking ahead of my game and, in conjunction with another lady member, was in charge of marking the position of the players' drives. When it came to the twelfth my lady held up her board in a stretch of rough, and when I got near enough to ask precisely where the ball was she pointed, a little gingerly, towards the bushes. 'If it's in the bushes, why are you standing in the rough?' I asked, menacingly. The answer was obvious: the poor woman was playing for time, trying to delay the delivery of the bad tidings. I chopped out of the trouble and went angrily on my way, but when the match was over Guy Kinnings passed on the message that the lady captain was distressed. I felt mortified. My mother had once been the lady captain of Ilkley and it occurred to me how furious I would have been had anyone treated her like that. There was the further point that the woman and her friend had been doing the job out of the goodness of their hearts when they could probably have been out playing themselves. I wrote a note of apology and, much to my relief, there was a forgiving reply.

Sam Torrance can never resist recalling an occasion in the World Cup at La Querce in Rome in which we were playing together and alongside Ian Woosnam and Phil Price, the Welsh pair who went on to finish in second place to Sweden's Anders Forsbrand and Per-Ulrik Johansson. An Italian gentleman had joined the party in some sort of official capacity and, as early as the third hole, he made his presence felt by accidentally kicking over a plastic cup as I was about to drive. Though I became absurdly conscious of him from that point, things proceeded smoothly enough until the ninth, a short hole with a narrow lane at the bottom where two cars were facing each other and had clearly reached a state of impasse. This being Italy, there was a spate of horn blowing and heated exchanges before the Italian gentleman was good enough to intervene. He was busy instructing the two parties that this was an international tournament and that they should sort things out quietly when, to his open-mouthed astonishment (and, retrospectively at least, to mine), I rounded on him. 'It's not them I'm worried about,' I hollered. 'It's you.' It was a cheap shot and you would have to suspect that no one had ever talked to the poor man like that before.

Denis Pugh was once on the receiving end from me at my irrational worst. It was on the occasion of the second round of the 1997 PGA Championship at Winged Foot and I was worrying about my driving. I asked Denis if he would make a point of standing behind me on the relevant tees and watching where I was aiming. I was keen that he should make notes and let me know what he thought after the round. Since everyone wants to watch the professionals from that position, this was not the easiest of briefs. Denis, though, made a point of ignoring what was happening on the greens in order to get himself in prime position for the next tee shot. In what was a noble effort, he succeeded in watching every drive from the optimum place. You would have hoped that I would have been suitably impressed. Far from it. Denis says that I went straight up to him at the end of my 71 and asked what he thought about my putting. And when Denis demurred and recalled the pre-round instruction, I apparently responded, 'It's putting I'm interested in. Who the hell gives a damn about my driving?' How, as Denis rightly asked, do you deal with a fellow like that?

Another story Denis has up his sleeve is of the time he recommended a slight adjustment to my stance during a practice session on the Friday night of a tournament. 'If what I'm doing is so wrong, why didn't you point it out at the start of the week?' came my peeved reaction. 'Because you weren't doing it at the start of the week,' said Denis, calmly.

In America, a few years ago, I used to waste no time in falling out with the official starter. Though I have always got on well with Ivor Robson, who has been Europe's number-one starter for as long as I can remember, things were apt to go wrong on the other side of the Atlantic where they do not pronounce 'Colin' as we pronounce it. 'Co-Lin Montgomerie' is what they call me. Padraig Harrington has said, very sensibly, that he does not mind how people pronounce his first name and is merely grateful when they have any kind of a shot at it. In contrast, the perfectionist in me could not bear hearing my seemingly straightforward name given out incorrectly. Trifling matter though it was, it bugged me like hell. Surely it wasn't asking too much for them to get it right.

At the 1997 US Open, I corrected the starter on the first day. Then, when I arrived on the tee the next morning, I was made to feel appallingly guilty as someone pointed out that I had just missed a ten-minute rehearsal in which the starter had been pacing up and down in front of the packed stands reciting, 'Colin Montgomerie, Colin Montgomerie, Colin Montgomerie.' I had it in mind to thank him if he got it right, but, after concentrating all my efforts on hitting a good tee short, I clean forgot.

I am probably not too different from anyone else when I say that a missed six-footer at the end of the day will ruffle me more than any other golfing mishap, especially if I have done everything pretty well until then. If I have stroked the putt nicely and the ball has been diverted via a spike-mark, the recovery period will be reasonably brief. But if I have pushed the putt or pulled it, you will find me tearing at my hair. There is more than one unfortunate press person who, with deadline looming, has had the unenviable task of having to approach me before I have had the time to calm down after one of those wasted six-footers or a similar mis- adventure. Sometimes I handle these interviews profession- ally enough, if through gritted teeth. On other occasions, I might leave without saying anything beyond a 'Not today, thank you,' which, to quote one of my press friends, sounds more as if I were having dealings with the milkman. Either that, or I blow up at some innocuous question.

In the 2000 Spanish Open, where I was sufficiently upset by a camera-snapping spectator behind the twelfth green to snatch his camera and hand it to a steward, a pressman called Mickey Britten volunteered that he had the answer as to why my putting was not so good. Now I do not know how he would have reacted had I criticised one of his carefully crafted sentences, but I could hardly have been said to sound grateful. 'You stick to your writing and I'll stick to the golf,' I advised.

Norman Dabell, who works for a handful of papers as well as the BBC, singles me out for a special mention in his recent book, *Natural Hazard*. Norman, who had just purchased a pair of sandals to counteract the extreme heat in Dubai, tells of how he had been asked by the Scottish papers to get a couple of quotes from me one Saturday, which, as it turned out, had been a bad Saturday. He was working out how to intercept me as I left the scorer's tent when I strode round the corner and inadvertently punctured his left foot with one of my metal-spiked shoes. He may have gone a bit over the top in what he wrote, but he vows that he still bears the scars.

Though press attention on the eve of Majors has died down a bit over the last couple of years, I used to find it tough to handle the many conflicting demands. Instead of saying 'no' straight out to requests which I was never going to be able to fufil, I would often make the mistake of procrastinating, or even agreeing to do something before turning it down at the last moment. Not good. Mind you, I think I can safely say that I am much better now than I was then. Increasingly, I have learned to put myself in the writers' and broadcasters' shoes though I could not, for the life of me, understand why they picked on me to the extent they did at the 2002 Open when others could be seen thrashing their clubs about in the Muirfield hay. Yes, I deserved some stick for my attitude but not as much as I got.

Though Muirfield was not the best of weeks for the regular golf writers and myself, we get along famously for much of the time. The relationship is an interesting one, my feeling being – and I hope they would agree – that the good times mostly make up for the bad. There has been more than the occasional quiet day when they have called for me in the press room and I have gone in there and pre-empted what is about to happen by saying, 'Right, I know you don't give a damn about my score so what do you want to talk about?'

They might want me to launch into my thoughts on the Ryder Cup selection process and how I have always wanted more wildcards. Alternatively, they might be looking for some of my more forthright opinions on the pace of play. Too slow, will be the gist of my message. Overall, I find few things more therapeutic than the banter and the laughter at a press room interview, though I have to be on guard against the pinless grenade that can come in the form of a seemingly innocently couched question.

In spite of its flaws, it has to be remembered that my temperament has not served me too badly over the years. It is in refusing to accept the mediocre that I manage to push myself and keep pushing until I am in a state where I am fit to burst. As I have indicated earlier, the seven Orders of Merit were not exactly handed over on the proverbial plate. There were years when I had the devil of a job to hang on as bold young men such as Lee Westwood and Darren Clarke decided that the time had come to topple me from my number-one spot.

If I had to pinpoint the area in which my temperament lets me down the most it would be the way it hastens any decline from bad to worse. There have been several occasions when I have finished eighth when I should have finished fourth; twentieth when I should have finished tenth. All of which is unacceptable and unprofessional, and, in my heart of hearts, I know full well that people have every right to say as much.

There are sports in which people are almost expected to be temperamental and can get away with my kinds of outburst with no questions asked. Golf, though, is not one of them. It is a game in which gentlemanly conduct is expected at all times, while a public-school background, whatever else it does for you, always seems to heighten those expectations in some quarters. Hugh Mantle maintains that a golf crowd is the least likely of the lot to condone poor behaviour. Since as

many as ninety per cent of the gallery will be golfers themselves who would give their right arms to be tournament-
playing professionals, they are always going to disapprove
when someone like me throws a fit at relatively little. They
ask themselves why on earth it should matter so much.
Sometimes I can see them mouthing an exasperated, 'It's
only a game.' I try to tell myself that, but it is not a message
that sinks in. Hugh, who can be hard on me in many areas,
has no trouble in sympathising with me on this score. A
person's career, whatever it might be, is serious to him or her.
If, say, a surgeon makes a mistake, it can be life-threatening.
I recognise that missing the cut is hardly the same as a slip of
the knife in the operating theatre, but golf is my job and if I
make a hash of it, I care. I really care.

Hugh believes that at least some of this intense craving for
success is down to what he sees as my relatively low self-
esteem. People used to think I was being big-headed when I
made one of my comments along the lines that I was going
to win two out of the next three tournaments, as I did before
the Benson and Hedges a few years ago. (That I managed to
do so was beside the point.) Hugh contends that if I were
half as confident as people think, I would not have needed to
say anything. As for my highs and lows, the pattern of which
have been such as to set people wondering if I am making
myself ill, Hugh maintains that these are not uncommon in
high-performance athletes. To capture a typical high, Steve
Beddow, from the Sky commentary team, not too long ago
painted this cheerful picture of how I was not content merely
to be playing my golf but was busy marshalling the crowd
and keeping tabs on the small boy who did not know where
to stand with his mobile scoreboard.

Beddow's observation reminds me of an occasion at Jerez
in Spain when, to the astonishment of Dave Cannon, one of
the finest golf photographers in the business, I suddenly
took his side in a row he was having with a steward. The

latter had told him that he was too close to the green and that he would need to take his pictures from outside the ropes. 'He's only doing his job,' I said, before returning to mine.

To reiterate, Hugh, Denis, Alastair and Andy have all been hugely helpful in working with me on the mental approach. They are always encouraging but tell me the truth about how others see me on a bad day.

My father, quite rightly, is hard on me for some of my on-course behaviour, and always has been. Eimear, who has lived with me for fourteen years, is a little more comprehending. However, she loathes the fall-out from some of the more notorious 'Monty incidents', and who can blame her? The day she got through to me was when she asked what I thought it was like for her to have to go and pick up the children from school on a day when I was all over the papers for having done or said something daft. As she said, if the boot were on the other foot and she were making the wrong kind of news, I would be feeling mortified.

Chapter 13

HECKLERS

The heckling I have had in the States cannot be divorced from the fact that I find it hard to keep my emotions to myself. Any heckling element in a crowd has always seemed to see me as an easy target, and that is why they come back for more, or at least have done until now.

It started in earnest on the Friday of the 1997 US Open at Congressional. David Pepper, who has been chairman of the R&A's Rules Committee and is currently chairman of the Championship Committee, was officiating in the match behind mine. He has a clear memory of three well-groomed but clearly intoxicated women in their early thirties swaying out of a hospitality tent after the rain delay. They homed in on my match and started to regale me with wolf whistles. You would have thought I would remember it, but I do not. Before too long, a few men joined in the fun, only their contribution was to yell abuse. 'Go home,' said one. 'Piss off,' said another. They were looking for a reaction from me and, before too long, they got it. 'Why don't you save that for the Ryder Cup,' I said, stupidly. When the heckling failed to subside, I made the further mistake of calling one of them a 'pillock'. I returned a 76. I had started to feel jet-lagged and fractious even before the hecklers had come into the picture, but there is no question that they did not do anything to help my fitful concentration.

It does not take much for things to ignite on the eve of a

Ryder Cup, and on the occasion of the 1997 match at Valderrama I found myself involved in a wholly unexpected furore following an interview with two Scottish journalists. The journalists in question were Gordon Simpson, who now works for the Tour, and John Huggan, then with the *Glasgow Herald*. In what was a pretty comprehensive interview about all aspects of the match, they had asked me to run through the list of Americans. What did I think of their individual games going into the match? I had plenty of respect for the US players, but when it came to Brad Faxon I noted that this might be a tough time for him since he was in the throes of a divorce. When it came to Phil Mickelson, who can still be wayward but who is straighter off the tee now than he was then, I said he might be hitting all over the place. And then there was Tiger Woods. My feeling there was that the course might not suit him as well as it might suit others. Someone with his length and strength could find it a little fiddly.

In context, the quotes were pretty harmless, but by the time they had been plucked from the *Scotsman*'s website I was in deep trouble. CBS flashed up each remark in turn and somehow managed to convey that I had been running down the opposition as a whole. In the end I had to write letters of apology to the players concerned. They said they understood that my comments had been taken out of context and were fine about it. But, as you would expect, CBS and some of the tabloid papers were never going to let bygones be bygones in a hurry.

There were no problems in Spain but things had taken a definite turn for the worse by the time the press had given my remarks a fresh airing before the following year's US Open at the Olympic Club in San Francisco. To give just one instance, a local radio station man called Jim Rome had encouraged his listeners to come to the course to bait me. 'Enjoy your day,' he told them. In the wake of Rome's recommendations, the Friday was particularly bad as I played alongside David Duval and Jim Furyk. 'It wasn't like it was a lot of people,' said Duval, afterwards, 'but some of them were brutal. I mean, it's a little embarrassing because as an American you don't like seeing someone from another country treated that way. It was way out of line.'

It was at the 1999 Ryder Cup at Brookline that the heckling became nothing less than vitriolic. Paul Lawrie, who was playing alongside me in the fourballs and foursomes, could not believe some of the insults he was hearing. Previously, he wondered if it were all more mischievous than anything else. Now, he realised that the hecklers' only aim was to put me off.

The Sunday singles at that Ryder Cup were even more extreme. The trouble had its origins on the first tee where some of the American players started whipping up the crowds before they drove off. Payne Stewart, my opponent, was not among them. He was the perfect gentleman from the start and could not have done more to try to protect me from the afternoon's events. To the irritation of the mob, I was three up after six holes though back to two by the time we arrived on the ninth tee. After Payne had hit, I teed up my ball and, for once, though it was never going to last, there was complete silence as I shaped to the ball. I managed to get as far as the top of my backswing when a man standing a couple of rows behind the tee could contain himself no longer. 'You ****,' he cried, with the key word so coarse and so alien to anything I had ever heard before on a golf course as to be unrepeatable. I stopped and had to readdress the shot. Prince Andrew (a keen golfer with whom I've become friendly over the years), my brother Douglas and Eimear all swooped on the culprit, an overweight fellow in shorts who was apparently reeking of beer. As the marshals helped to subdue him and led him away I turned to the crowd and said, 'First to go. If anyone else says that, they'll go as well.' My legs were now shaking.

Payne, who had just won the US Open at Pinehurst, was brilliant. He knew that there was more than one trouble-maker out there and, from that moment, he kept going into the crowd himself and saying to the security men, 'Get rid of him, him and him.' It sickened Payne only slightly less than it sickened my father. In Dad's eyes, it was as if the very game had been defiled. I looked for him after the incident but he had walked back to the clubhouse, his lifelong love of the game having taken an irreparable blow.

Years ago, David Feherty did me no favours when he christened me Mrs Doubtfire. David is a friend and a gifted commentator, but I hated the name and could not disguise that fact. Everywhere I went there would be a couple of people who would yell, 'Hey, Mrs Doubtfire!' from behind the ropes, perpetuating the label and making my blood boil. I complained to David's face at the end of the Brookline match because the goings-on of that day had revived the feeling that many of my problems in the States were down to him. The match was not long over when he and I bumped into each other in the team room. Though a former Ryder Cup player, he should not have been in there in the first place and, though I am not usually one to bother about such things, I said that either he would need to leave or I would. When he took no notice, Eimear and I left. David followed and asked, 'What's the problem?'

'What's the problem?' I repeated incredulously. I suggested that he should sit down in order that I could spell it out.

Eimear and I both proceeded to give him a piece of our minds, with both of us wanting to know why he should have made so much trouble for someone who had been a team-mate at the 1991 Ryder Cup at Kiawah Island. He accepted what we were saying, but only up to a point.

The atmosphere between us remained less than cordial until we came face to face at the 2000 PGA Championship at Valhalla. In one of those circumstances where someone has to say something, I spoke first. 'You have got a job to do and I've got a job to do,' I began. 'You hurt me a lot at Brookline but the time has come to put this behind us.' We shook hands, though the indifferent grunt that came with the handshake suggested that he did not care overmuch either way.

Outside of the Ryder Cup, the heckling never got to me more than it did at the 2002 Accenture Match Play Championship at Carlsbad. I suppose I was not expecting anything in this start-of-season event, but when I was playing Scott McCarron a group of T-shirted louts appeared with beer cans in hand. I spotted them a mile away. They applauded a couple of my missed putts and threw in the odd comment about my weight – even though I had shed most of it at the time.

After I had lost to McCarron and was on my way back to the clubhouse, a group whom I felt to be well aware of my defeat made a cheerful enquiry as to how I was getting on. My oblique and heated response was that the only thing worse than losing was having to spend another day in their midst. Later that evening, when I was still simmering, I said that I was seriously considering cutting back on my American schedule. I was over-reacting. Of course I was. I retracted those comments pretty swiftly, because there are plenty of things I love about playing in the States and have done since my days at Houston Baptist.

The USPGA Tour went out of their way to help after that Carlsbad incident. They started taking a much tougher approach towards hecklers in general, and when I returned to America for the Players Championship at Sawgrass they asked if I wanted an armed policeman to walk with my group. The officials felt it might help to dissuade potential trouble-makers from letting rip. I turned the offer down on the grounds that an armed officer might prove something of a distraction, not so much to me perhaps as to the other players in my group. Also, I knew that there were plenty of strategically placed guards on every hole.

That week, I received heartening reassurance that 99.9 per cent of Americans wish me well. One person after another had a quiet word, mostly when I was walking from the green to the next tee. They were saying everything from 'Nice to have you here!' to 'I'm Scotch.' They wanted me to feel at home.

There was one local radio chap at the Players Championship who, in shades of what had happened at the Olympic Club in 1998, told his listeners to turn their backs as I approached the green, but if that happened at all, it was wasted on me. I was following Hugh Mantle's instruction to ignore everything save what I was doing. There were still a handful of hecklers out and about, one of whom, after I had used a three wood from the sixteenth tee on the second day and come up well short of my playing companions, delivered that old joke as to how I should try removing the head cover before I hit. Then, on the following hole, someone gave a deliberate snort as I was halfway up my backswing. I carried on regardless and managed to catch that elusive little green, but I gather that one of my playing companions told the media that it was the rudest thing he had ever heard from a spectator.

When the press asked for my comments at Sawgrass, I explained that I did not want to talk about heckling in any shape or form. With so much having been made of what had happened in California earlier in the year, I knew that the time had come to keep a low profile on the subject if it were ever to go away. As Jesper Parnevik said, it had reached the point where people were shouting for the sake of it. 'Even if Colin doesn't do anything, someone has read about the heckling or heard about it and think that it's the way to go. They scream something even though they don't even mean it and probably don't have a clue about Colin anyway.'

For the purposes of the 2002 US Open, *Golf Digest* arranged a 'Be Nice to Monty' campaign/stunt in which they distributed 25,000 'Be Nice to Monty' badges to spectators arriving at Bethpage State Park. It was an amusing exercise on their part, and, though there were those who worried that it could have an adverse effect, it worked well enough. The New York crowd, a vociferous bunch if ever there was one, seemed happy to get involved and, when I started out from the tenth tee at 7.35 on the Thursday morning, it was fun to see people with badges in place. As I said earlier, the only person who had not been nice to Monty that day was Monty: my putting was desperately disappointing.

Hugh Mantle, who has been over to my American tournaments several times now, was with me that week. He did as he always does, walking round in the gallery, and was able to confirm that most of the comments were wholly complimentary and that it was only the tiniest handful of spectators who would have stirred things up, given half a chance. Hugh's reading of the heckling situation, when it applies, is that I should accept that hecklers go with the patch and that I should draw consolation from the fact that the people doing the heckling see me as someone worth bothering about. As he has said, for someone like myself who is not averse to a bit of attention, the only thing worse than being heckled is not having anyone take any notice of you.

Eimear's advice was similarly first-class. When I arrived home after the uproar at the World Match Play, she wanted me to look at myself from the outside. 'How would you react,' she asked, 'if it were Langer or Olazábal who were getting heckled?' She said I would reply, 'That's terrible,' before going on to say that the player concerned should do his utmost to put it behind him and not let the hecklers think they had got a result.

Though most of the players are agreed I have had more than my share of heckling, Butch Harmon was not wrong when he said that I hear more of what goes on around me than most: 'Rabbit Ears' is what he has called me. He points to Tiger Woods as the player from whom I should take my lead. Tiger, he says, has had to put up with 'all sorts' from the crowd. The first Masters he won in 1997 would have been particularly bad, especially if the number of spectators who poured out of the grounds was anything to go by. The last thing they wanted was to see a black player win.

I envy Tiger his putting stroke and not a few other aspects of his play, but, above all, I envy him his ability to turn the other cheek when people make their remarks. I have tried to be Tiger-like and was making little progress until I managed to get through the whole of that 2002 Players Championship without reneging on my good intentions. That was a start.

I doubt whether it will be possible to eliminate hecklers, just as I doubt that I will ever reach the stage where I can follow the instructions of those who have exhorted me to laugh off their comments. I'll win my first Major before that happens.

Chapter 14

RYDER CUP

If I tell you that I can remember virtually every shot I have hit in a Ryder Cup, it will go some way towards explaining how much this biennial contest means to me. In a Ryder Cup year, Guy Kinnings and I put a mark up against the relevant week on the office calendar in the knowledge that it is sacrosanct. Nothing can get in the way of it: no company days, no individual press interviews, nothing. Guy and I refer to it as 'a week off' even though we both appreciate that it is a week that is ten times more demanding than any other in the golfing year. You know you are going to go through hell during the course of the three days but, however tough it gets, there is nowhere you would rather be.

That we all tend to feel much the same way is a great tribute to Samuel Ryder, a prosperous seed merchant and the Mayor of St Albans who presented the trophy in the 1920s. Ryder did not start playing golf until the age of fifty-two, but donated the Ryder Cup trophy after having been impressed by the chivalry and camaraderie of the American and British teams who met in an unofficial match at Wentworth in 1926. On that occasion the British won by $13^{1}/_{2}$ points to $1^{1}/_{2}$. 'We must do this again,' he declared.

From 1927 to 1983 the Americans dominated the contest, but in the last twenty years all that has changed. Europe, as the British team became in 1979, won in 1985 and 1987, and retained the trophy when the match was shared at the Belfry in 1989. In the nineties America won in 1991 and 1993 but Europe came out on top in 1995 at Oak Hill and again at Valderrama in 1997, before losing the trophy at one of the match's more controversial instalments at the Country Club, Brookline, Massachusetts, in 1999.

It was when my mother died at the start of 1991 that I set my heart on winning a place in that year's Ryder Cup side in her memory. Mum had always followed the Ryder Cup and it would have meant the world to her to see me playing alongside men like Seve Ballesteros, Nick Faldo and Ian Woosnam, all players for whom she had a healthy respect.

Having been there or thereabouts in the Ryder Cup points list, I made myself a certainty for the team when I won the 1991 Scandinavian Masters at Drottningholm. Seve finished second that week and Woosnam third, and my abiding memory is of standing on the podium with Seve to one side and Ian to the other. Since Seve was not far away from being the world number one at that time, it was quite a moment.

I qualified in second place for the match behind Seve. The news meant much to the family, particularly to my father, for whom it had been such a sad and lonely few months.

1991

With Kiawah Island the venue, we were to travel out to America by Concorde. My father, who had been to Washington on the plane on a business trip in 1974, told me that that would be an event in itself, and he was right.

Whenever the match is in America, the butterflies begin to make themselves felt when you arrive at Heathrow. The press and television people are there en masse and the sight of them is always going to faze the rookies more than anyone else. I can remember saying to Eimear, 'Bloody hell! We haven't even left the country yet.' The men wear suits for the trip and the wives are dressed up correspondingly, because that is how it is when you travel on Concorde, an arrangement that began when Tony Jacklin was captain. He insisted on the best of everything for his team because he wanted them to feel good about themselves.

The official party took the front ten rows on the plane and the remaining sixty seats were taken up by European team supporters, all of whom had paid a healthy whack to be on the Concorde trip.

It was not just the golfers who had had to play for their places. The pilots and the stewards had drawn lots to man this special flight. Yet there would come a moment when they must have wondered if they had been as lucky as they thought. We had refuelled in New York and were flying down the coast towards Kiawah Island when the pilot responded to a suggestion from our captain, Bernard Gallacher, that he should do a fly-over of the course. We banked one way and then the other over the sandy terrain and were expecting to land shortly after that manoeuvre. Instead, we carried on flying. As the pilot had to inform us, one of the wheels could not be lowered. In what was more Heath Robinson than Concorde, the carpet had to be lifted and the back wheel freed manually.

Meanwhile, the crowds in and around the South Carolina airbase where we were due to land were becoming ever more impatient. Around 30,000 people had set up camp in the area, some with a view to seeing the golfers but many more in anticipation of seeing Concorde for the first time. They had pulled up on the highways and you could see them sitting on their car roof-tops.

Once we had signed in at the Kiawah Island resort, each of us was allocated his own forty-five-foot limo, and never mind that one such vehicle could probably have accommodated everyone. The chauffeurs dropped us off at a row of villas along the beach, all of them part of the resort. Eimear and I, each as anxious to do the right thing as the other, unpacked before meeting the rest of the team. We were introduced to the team cook, who was named Colin. *She* surprised us with the news that it was not an uncommon name for a girl in those parts.

The clubhouse on Kiawah Island had still to be finished, and with no locker rooms as such, each team was given its own air-conditioned trailer. We had our first look inside the following morning. There was a shoe-rack in the corner and, to my relief, I spotted that the Stylo shoes I had ordered were among the pairs that had been laid out – a reassuring sight. They felt a little on the small side but it did not take me long to work out that that was probably down to the previous day's flight. My feet were almost certainly swollen and, if they were not, I could have been imagining things. After all, I was already in a bit of a state at the thought of what lay ahead. I put the shoes on and went out to practise before my first reconnaissance round.

I was working away quite happily and my concern about the footwear had almost totally subsided when suddenly I noticed Nick Faldo, a veteran of seven Ryder Cups and very much the kingpin, striding towards me. He was dangling a pair of shoes from the second and third fingers of his right hand. 'Monty,' he called, making it clear that I should stop whatever I was doing. 'What size shoes do you take?' My heart sank. He did not need to say any more: the shoes I had taken belonged to him. Even though he was laughing, I felt about two feet tall. I changed on the spot, apologising all the while.

You notice things on your first Ryder Cup. There is nothing you do not take in, and I would have to say that I was positively wide-eyed on the Wednesday night at the gala dinner.

We travelled in our lengthy limos to the conference centre in Charleston and, on the way, Steve Pate's car was hit. With no seat belts, he flew into the television and ended up in hospital with an injured hip and ribs. By the time they had seen to their ailing team member, the Americans wanted nothing so much as to extricate themselves from the engagement, but, after an endless delay, things finally went ahead.

Earlier, when our side had arrived, we had been schooled in how we should enter the banqueting hall. We would walk into the room together before dividing into two parties of six. One party would go round one side of the room before finishing up at the end of a team table on the right, while the other would go round the opposite side before sitting down at the far end of the team table on the left. When the time came, we did what was expected of us and waited for the Americans to make their entry. There was no going round the side of the room for them. They walked down the middle to rapturous applause and took their places on the two near ends of the tables. They were in the thick of things. We were on the outskirts and feeling like outsiders. Needless to say, there were some discontented mutterings.

Before too long, attention focused on two massive screens that were showing what was announced as 'A History of the Ryder Cup'. The title could not have been more misleading. It was a history of American teams at the Ryder Cup. The entire twenty minutes was devoted to great US shots and victories. We saw Arnold Palmer, Jack Nicklaus, Lee Trevino, Tom Watson and Ray Floyd but nowhere was there any sign of the opposition.

By now Ken Schofield was in the mood to leave. But Bernard Gallacher prevailed upon him to stay. Michael Bonallack, or Sir Michael Bonallack as he is now, was another who could not believe what he was seeing. For myself, I remember whispering to Eimear, 'Is this really what goes on at a Ryder Cup?'

We were driven back to Kiawah in those daft limos and went to bed, only to be woken at four-thirty by a phone call. Someone on the island had given out our room numbers to the broadcaster on the local radio station and he clearly felt that it would be a bit of a laugh to disrupt the Europeans' sleep.

I began to understand how much this match meant to the Americans. They'd lost in 1985 and 1987 and even though they'd tied with the Europeans at the Belfry in 1989, we were still the holders of the trophy. Now the match was back in their own country, winning was the only option. The tension was everywhere.

When Corey Pavin and Steve Pate emerged in Desert Storm hats, that was the end. Were they completely oblivious to the fact that we had troops over in the Gulf, too? And, as Bernhard Langer was to say, did they not know that the Americans had been heavily reliant on German air bases?

The first tee experience was not what I had expected. In fact, the first tee at Kiawah is a poor one as it is a couple of hundred yards away from the clubhouse and correspondingly short of atmosphere. Because of this, I did not feel the expected surge of adrenaline. Also, with David Gilford and I not experiencing any of the usual vibes you get when two players are made for each other, my expectations were low. Though we had played well enough in practice, we could not make anything happen against the experienced combination of Lanny Wadkins and Hale Irwin. They were too good for us and we lost by four and two. Bernard Gallacher had taken a risk in putting two rookies together and it had not paid off. Europe picked up just one point to the Americans' three in that opening series.

I was then dropped from the fourballs and from the following morning's foursomes before returning to the fray on Saturday afternoon, by which time the score was $7^1/_2$–$4^1/_2$ to the Americans. We were now on to the second fourball series and I was to partner Langer. I have played with him several times since and he is the best partner anyone could wish to have. He has a great caddie in Pete Coleman and I had the feeling I was in safe hands with the two of them. I also felt good about the fact that Bernard Gallacher had had enough confidence in my ability to put me with such a senior player. Our opponents were Corey Pavin and Steve Pate, the latter of whom had not been in action before because of his injuries. 'I'll hit first and take the pressure off you,' said Langer, as we discussed our plan of action.

When the tee-off time came, Bernhard took the honour and knocked one out of bounds over the crowd and over the dunes. 'Thank you, Bernhard,' I said, laughing. Mercifully, I managed to hit mine down the fairway. Langer went to have a quick look for his ball before returning to my side as I was considering how to play my second. He had a question for me. 'How far is this?' he began.

'126 yards to the green plus twenty-four yards to the pin. In other words, 150,' I said. I was pleased to be able to give this meticulous man the kind of details he would want.

Alas, he was not remotely impressed. 'Where have you taken that yardage from?' he demanded.

'From the sprinkler head,' I said, pointing to the device.

Langer had the look of one whose patience was being sorely stretched. 'Are we talking about the back of the sprinkler or the front of the sprinkler head?' he asked.

For a second, I wondered if he were joking but it soon became clear that he was awaiting a sensible answer as opposed to a peal of laughter. The news that the sprinkler head measured only nine inches pacified him somewhat, but only for as long as it took me to hit the shot.

The moment the ball had left the club, he introduced a new set of rules. From then on, all the yardages would be done by Coleman rather than by my caddie, Kevin Laffey. Bernhard did not trust us. It made Kevin very nervous and it had the same effect on me.

Yet it would turn into a brilliant afternoon. Langer and I won by three and one, and with another 2½ points coming from the other three matches we bedded down that night with the score tantalisingly poised at 8–8.

After breakfast on the Sunday, the Americans said that Steve Pate was not able to play in the singles because of his injury. This meant that Gallacher had a horrible decision on his hands: he had to pull one of his players out of the last series by way of a reply. He decided on Gilford.

Faldo was chosen to top the singles line-up, with David Feherty going out second and me third. I was glad to be in that position because I felt safely tucked away. You are not going to win the Ryder Cup for Europe from that position but, equally so, you are not going to be the one to lose it.

The warnings I had about playing Mark Calcavecchia all amounted to the same thing: namely, don't let him get any kind of early lead. Unfortunately, there was not too much I could do to stop him. By the turn, he was four under par and five up. I had no answer to what was going on. Yet, whatever the overall merits and demerits of having two so very separate halves at Kiawah, the set-up worked in my favour that day. On the long buggy ride between the ninth green and the tenth tee I had some tough words with myself. I was not going to let Calcavecchia walk all over me any longer.

I had a stroke of luck at the tenth, where I went from one stretch of sand to another before holing from forty yards for the hole. That's better, I thought. Now, the margin won't be quite so dire. I then made a birdie at the eleventh to get back to three down, only to fail to make any further headway at the next two holes. I halved them both before making a hash of the short fourteenth to be four down with four to play. The end was nigh.

As we boarded the fifteenth tee, I was conscious of the wind having turned. All of a sudden, we were in a robust left-to-right breeze, which was a problem for Calcavecchia. A huge problem. He carved his ball miles right on to the beach. He found it and carried on but ended up losing the hole with a seven to my less-than-textbook six. Back to three down. At the sixteenth he hit miles right again and I won the hole with a par. Two down.

This particular wind was not my favourite either and, when it came to the seventeenth, I belted a two iron into the reeds. What with the whole of South Carolina on my left, it was a crazy thing to do. I deserved to lose. Yet, to my utter astonishment, Calcavecchia followed me into the water. The two of us repaired to the dropping zone, which, as it happened, was the ladies' tee. 'How far is it over the water from here?' I asked my caddie. 'I don't know,' he replied, with an honesty for which I was not prepared to give him too many marks at the time. It had to be down to guesswork and, with water apt to foreshorten distance, I elected to take a six iron rather than a seven and finished on the back of the green. Calcavecchia, when it was his turn, hit thirty feet left of the hole.

I putted up to 'gimme' distance and handed my glove and my marker to Kevin before thanking him for his help. Calcaveccia had two putts for the match and I could not see him making a hash of things this time. His first finished two and a half feet away and I was about to give it to him when I thought again. This was a team event and the more senior members of the European side would not approve of one of their rookies taking things into his own hands to that degree. Thank God for those second thoughts. Calcavecchia's two-and-a-half-footer never even touched the hole. One down.

Calcavecchia can get quite heated, but at this stage he was almost eerily calm. I was standing on the eighteenth tee when Tony Jacklin came up and whispered something I will never forget: 'If you can stay standing, you'll win this hole.' I did a bit better than that, hitting a drive and two iron to forty feet. Calcavecchia was way right again before catching the green in three. When I putted up close enough for my four, he had a ten-footer to halve the hole and win the match. He left it on the lip. The game was halved. I had finished double-bogey, par, double-bogey, par and won every hole.

Across the years, that result has served as a constant reminder to me – and to others – that no game is ever over until the last putt drops.

Up ahead, Faldo and Feherty had won and the latter and his opponent, Payne Stewart, had stayed put to see the denouement of our game. When Calcavecchia left the last green, Stewart put his arm round his shoulder and walked him towards the beach. By all accounts, Calcavecchia ended up needing medical attention for breathing problems. He felt that he could have cost America the Ryder Cup.

Though Seve Ballesteros and Paul Broadhust won a point apiece, the Americans had six singles points to our five by the time that Langer was coming down the last with Hale Irwin. We could no longer win the Ryder Cup outright but, if Langer could grab his point, it would be good enough for us to retain the trophy we had held since 1985. He had made a birdie to draw level at the seventeeth and now, with the eyes of the golfing world upon him, he was facing up to the six-footer on the home green that could save the day. Michael Bonallack has since called it 'the greatest pressure putt in the history of golf'. Langer missed and the whole of America broke into a triumphant cheer. Irwin, meantime, walked slowly towards his opponent and embraced him. As Mark McCormack would write in his *World of Professional Golf*, it was a gesture which 'spoke volumes' for their mutual respect and sportsmanship.

We returned to the team trailer while an exuberant American side celebrated on the beach. Ballesteros and Langer were hugging each other and crying openly. Everyone knows that Ballesteros is among the most emotional of men, but the memory of him and Langer in that tearful embrace is one that hits me every time anyone starts talking of how we should get paid to play in the Ryder Cup. Money would detract from emotion and the match would never be quite the same again.

Eimear and I were sitting in the corner watching the two of them when our attention turned to Langer's wife, Vicki, who is American. Doing her best to cope with the disappointment in her own way, she asked the family nanny to fetch the children from the crèche. In the meantime, she turned on the television. The cameras were focusing on the victorious Americans, all of whom were splashing about in the sea. Sam Torrance turned it off. 'We can be doing without that,' he grunted. Vicki turned it on again. Now Woosnam pressed the off switch. The sight of the Americans whooping it up was more than he could bear. Vicki turned it on again.

Eimear and I were still in our corner for the final instalment. With an almighty thump, one of our number made bloody sure that the television was finished for good.

1993

A month of so before the next Ryder Cup, Eimear was with me at Crans-sur-Sierre for the European Masters. Nick Faldo was staying in our hotel and before we left he told Eimear that when we got home, we should expect a parcel. Eimear and I discussed what might be in that parcel but drew a blank. We would have to wait and see. It turned out to be a massive box of Rextar Bridgestone golf balls, all of them No. 11s, because the eleventh hole is where almost everything major has happened for Faldo in a golfing context. Not only must Faldo have spoken to Bernard Gallacher and said that he would like to partner me in the fourballs and foursomes in the forthcoming Ryder Cup at the Belfry, but he had also decided what ball we would use as we played together in the foursomes. It was mind-boggling. The Titleist I used day-in, day-out did not get a look in.

Though Nick, with all his Majors, was clearly the senior partner, it came as a surprise that he should still be treating me as the office junior. On the other hand, I was hugely flattered that he would want me as his partner. So I did what I was meant to do by practising and putting with the ball, though, to be absolutely honest, if I had shut my eyes, I would not have had a clue which ball I was hitting.

Faldo has always been a loner, but he and I had a bit of something in common even before he introduced me to his golf balls. At the start of that year, our respective wives – he was married to Gill at the time – had given birth on the same day in the Princess Margaret Hospital in Windsor. For the Faldos, it was their third baby; for us it was our first.

Nick and I were in the waiting room together. He read copies of *Golf Monthly* and *Golf World*, and, from time to time, we both watched the England–Ireland rugby game. Georgia, so called after Nick's first win at Augusta, was the first to appear, with Olivia following soon afterwards. They were two lovely babies, and even now there is a picture in the hospital's entrance hall of the two of them together.

When it came to the Ryder Cup, Nick and I prepared virtually in unison, an arrangement which started as we were driving up the M40 and he drew alongside us in his S500 Mercedes and Gill gestured for us to open our window.

'Do you know the way to the Belfry?' Nick called.

On hearing that we did, he said he would follow us.

For the next three days we had the same alarm calls in the morning, played together over the day and ate together in the evening with our wives. Not only did the wives get on well, but our caddies, Alastair McLean and Fanny Sunesson, hit if off, which is always a good sign.

Yet, for all that we were doing everything in tandem, I was still very much the assistant pro. When, for example, Faldo decided that the pink cashmere uniform sweaters were too long in the sleeve, I was the one dispatched to the professionals' shop to buy a couple of replacements. I don't know quite what he expected, but the best I could come up with were a couple of lambswool sweaters in a darker shade of pink. If you look at the match photographs, you can see that they are not the same colour as the rest. Also, the official team logo was missing. When it came to discussing tactics, it was decided, or rather Faldo decided, that I would play the odd holes. I slept on it for three days and was having good vibes as to where I would hit my first shot. In truth, I was positively looking forward to it.

On the first morning Faldo was not 100 per cent happy with the way he was hitting the ball and had a quick session with David Leadbetter. We were due to play Freddie Couples and Ray Floyd in the fourth foursome and, like everyone else, we had our pictures taken on the first tee with the two captains. We also informed Ivor Robson, the official starter, that Floyd and I were the two who would be teeing up first. Floyd, when he was called, hit a good drive down the middle. I then had a couple of swings and waited with eager antici-pation for Ivor to introduce me. As I fidgeted, I was suddenly aware of Faldo walking forward with ball and tee-peg in hand. Ivor, who could not believe what he was seeing, was as astonished as I was. 'You're OK?' I queried, in the manner of one who had been taken completely off guard. 'Don't worry, Monty,' Nick replied. 'I'm going to go first. I'm not drawing the ball any more. Everything's fine.' His drive was a good one, but it was a weird feeling for me to have to face up to a second shot for which I was not remotely prepared. Disconcerting start though that was, we went on to win our first match by four and three.

I would not dream of knocking Nick, for there are plenty of champions whose supremacy owes much to the way they see themselves. He felt as if he were in a league of his own at that stage of his career and his golf was correspondingly brilliant.

The afternoon fourballs took for ever, and when Nick birdied the seventeenth to have us level with Couples and Azinger, we took one look down a gloomy eighteenth fairway and realised that we had no option but to leave the hole until the following morning.

We started up again at eight o'clock and were joined by an amazing number of early risers. I dispatched my ball into the bunker and Nick hit straight. Freddie, meantime, went into the water and Paul joined Nick on the fairway. Freddie being Freddie, he decided to leave things to his partner. I went for the green, only to hear an ominous splash. The end for me. Nick's second finished short of the green, and in his anxiety not to leave himself with a downhill putt he was still a good ten feet below the flag with his third. Paul, meantime, had caught the green in two and was around thirty feet to the right of the flag. He putted up stiff. Now Nick had to hole his ten-footer for us to halve hole and match.

'What do you think?' he said, by way of inviting me to have a look at the line.

'It's got to be right lip,' I answered.

'It's straight,' he said, contradicting me outright.

He and Fanny had another look before he repeated his opinion and I was brave enough to repeat mine. Then he knocked the putt in and the place erupted.

'Where did you hit it?' I asked, casually, after all the handshaking.

'I'll never tell you,' he returned.

With the score Europe 4$\frac{1}{2}$–America 3$\frac{1}{2}$, we now embarked on our third match together, with our opponents Lanny Wadkins and Corey Pavin. Because of what happened just a few minutes before, with Nick holing his putt, they did not have a chance. Faldo and I were brilliant in those foursomes, the perfect pairing.

On to our fourth outing, where we found ourselves out top against Chip Beck and John Cook. The feeling was that the US captain had put Beck and Cook in that position more on the off chance than anything else. Nothing was expected of them. Yet I was uneasy about this match from the start. All along, we had both been wearing white shoes, but Faldo had suddenly changed into blue. Ridiculously superstitious as I can sometimes be, I did not feel comfortable. Why on earth would he alter anything when we were going along so well? I asked him why he had changed and he said that his feet were damp. We lost by two holes, and even though Europe picked up just one point out of four that afternoon, we bedded down on the Saturday night with $8^1/_2$ points to the opposition's $7^1/_2$ and the feeling that we were on the point of another famous win.

Ian Woosnam halved the top single with Couples before Barry Lane lost to Chip Beck. I was next in the line-up and playing against Lee Janzen. We had a thrilling match, one which could have gone either way. Lee had just won that year's US Open at Baltusrol and was putting as if he were still there. I managed to eagle the fifteenth to go one up and I held on to that lead until all that remained was for me to hole a two-and-a-half-footer on the home green. It was eminently missable, and the more I looked at it, the more I thought as much. But, while the negative thoughts were stirring in earnest, Lee picked up my ball and congratulated me. It was an extraordinary moment, because if I was thinking the putt could be easily missed, he must have been thinking the same. Either way, his gesture left me full of admiration for a man who is one of the most unassuming champions of them all.

Peter Baker and Joakim Haeggman were our only other winners on what would turn into a bitterly disappointing afternoon. Faldo, with whom I had been linked all week, halved his match with Azinger down at the bottom, but the five Europeans in front of him – Mark James, Costantino Rocca, Seve Ballesteros, José Maria Olazábal and Langer – all lost.

In his winning speech, Tom Watson, the US captain, would refer back to the Saturday afternoon fourball in which Beck and Cook had the better of Nick and myself. 'John and Chip's win was at the heart of our victory,' were his words. I still find it tough to look back on that match, though there is one particular Faldo memory that will stay with me. Nick and I made our fourth successive two at the fourteenth. As we left the green, Nick said we were due an ace. He got it as he played Azinger in the singles, and it remains only one of four in the history of the Ryder Cup. Peter Butler made one in the 1973 match at Muirfield, while the others belonged to Howard Clark and Costantino Rocca in the 1995 instalment.

Mention of Rocca reminds me of something which made a profound impression on me at the very start of our week at the Belfry. The Italian, who was playing in his first Ryder Cup, had arrived to find that his name had been incorrectly spelled on both his locker and his Ryder Cup golf-bag. He was apoplectic and I remain convinced that it affected him for the entire week as he played just the two games and lost both. It was an occurrence that taught me how important it is to get little things right on the big occasion, for they can loom so large in the eyes of an individual.

At the end of the week, there was an official party that everyone was supposed to attend. Alastair, my caddie, asked if I minded if he did not come. He had to get back to Scotland because his father had died.

'Died,' I repeated, horrified. 'When?'

'On Tuesday,' he said.

It had been Alastair's dream to caddie at a Ryder Cup but,

far more than that, he had not wanted to let me down and that is why he had said nothing until that moment. I listened to what he had to say with a mixture of sadness and gratitude. Ebel had made watches for the players. I gave mine to Alastair as a memento of a week he would never forget. It was the least I could do.

1995

Bernard Gallacher, who had captained the European team in 1991 and 1993, was thrilled to have a third chance to try to win the Ryder Cup when the match was played at Oak Hill, New York, in 1995. He pored over his partnerships as never before and decided that he would do best to link Faldo and myself again. After all, we had won three points out of four in 1993. Faldo was playing well but, as he would be the first to say, he was not as focused as he had been in previous matches. He has since referred to the middle and later nineties as a period in his life when there was just too much happening.

On the first day, we lost by a hole to Corey Pavin and Tom Lehman in the opening foursomes and by three and two to Freddie Couples and Davis Love in the afternoon fourballs. Our afternoon match was nearing its end when Bernard Gallacher arrived on the scene. 'Lightning has just struck twice,' he said in a reference to our two losses. 'It won't strike again, so I'm going to leave you together tomorrow morning.'

It was a good decision on Gallacher's part. Faldo and I got back on track with a four and two win over Curtis Strange and Jay Haas. Only then did Bernard decide that the time was right to split the partnership. He put me with Sam Torrance, who had just won the British Masters, and paired Faldo with Bernhard Langer. Faldo and I both lost with our new partners, but I have to say that playing with Torrance was no less of a positive experience than playing with Faldo. We were two Scots who laughed at the same things and generally hit it off.

At the end of three days, Europe were trailing 9–7. It was a disappointing state of affairs but, given the circumstances, the scene was set for what has to be one of the best days that Europe has ever known.

Though Seve Ballesteros was still a great bet for fourballs, he was way too wild for foursomes and singles. Yet, as Bernard Gallacher recognised, he remained a deliciously disconcerting opponent, what with his ability to get down in a chip and a putt from anywhere. Gallacher sent him out top and I have always felt that if he had been up against anyone other than the endlessly stoic Tom Lehman, he would probably have won. (As one who has twice lost to Ballesteros in his Seve Trophy match, I can speak with a certain authority on the subject.) Everyone was intrigued as to what would happen in the Ballesteros–Lehman game and, as Faldo and I were walking down towards the practice ground to prepare for our games, we stopped to look at the giant screen that was showing their early holes. The cameras were focusing on Ballesteros, only he was so far off the beaten track with his tee shots that we could not, for the life of us, recognise which hole he was playing. Was this the third or the fifth? We did not have a clue. He chipped in at the second and had no more than six putts in his first seven holes on his way to extending the match to the fifteenth green.

It was our numbers two and three, Howard Clark and Mark James, who won us that Ryder Cup. Though a number of people feared they were being sacrificed in those lofty positions, Gallacher knew that they had it in them to get the job done. Neither had had more than one game over the first two days but they both got stuck in straight away, with Howard defeating Peter Jacobsen on the home green and Mark beating Jeff Maggert by four and three.

At a time when Ian Woosnam was heading for a halved game with Freddie Couples and David Gilford was shaping to beat Brad Faxon, I was walking off the thirteenth green with my match with Ben Crenshaw all square. I then reeled off four successive threes, only one of which was not a birdie. My win was rather tucked away as others bagged the more timely points, but it meant a lot to me. Though Crenshaw is one of the best putters there has ever been, I never gave him a look-in over those last four holes.

David Gilford's win over Faxon and mine over Crenshaw went up on the board at much the same time to make the score 11$\frac{1}{2}$–11$\frac{1}{2}$. Faldo was in the match behind. He had been one down to Curtis Strange leaving the fifteenth green, but when Strange missed the penultimate green with his second they were level mounting the eighteenth tee. It was a big match for both of them, but particularly for Strange, as he would have been well aware that Lee Janzen was no less deserving of the wild card than he was. As you would expect, Faldo was at his most positive after having been on the losing side in three of his first four matches.

He had the honour at the eighteenth but drove into so bad a position in the left rough that he had no option but to hack out on to the fairway, a pitching wedge away from the green. Strange, meantime, hit a wonderful drive, only to haul his second, a three iron, into the left rough. It was Faldo to play first and he did not disappoint his watching team-mates. His ball finished six feet away from the flag. Strange hit to eight feet. He missed and Faldo holed for what he would call 'the greatest scrambling par of my life'.

With Sam Torrance having won his match against Loren Roberts and Bernhard Langer having lost to Corey Pavin, Faldo's point gave Europe the lead at 13$\frac{1}{2}$–12$\frac{1}{2}$.

Europe needed another point from the last two matches. Per-Ulrik Johansson was on the point of losing to Phil Mickelson. Philip Walton, for his part, was three up with three to play against Jay Haas but nerves had started to kick in. He lost the sixteenth and seventeenth and everyone feared that the eighteenth might go the same way and that America would retain the Cup. Instead, Haas drove into the trees and our ashen-faced Irishman was able to finish things off. We felt so proud of him.

Europe 14^1/$_2$–USA 13^1/$_2$.

There are sights and sounds I will associate with the end of that match to my dying day. First, there was Bernard Gallacher's jump for joy halfway up the eighteenth fairway. Then there was the thud of seats springing back into position as thousands upon thousands of crestfallen American spectators upped and left in a hurry. Following that, there was silence.

The European Open was being held at the K Club the week after and Concorde was to drop off some of the party in Dublin on the journey back to London. The plane had not been to Ireland before and, as had been the case at the Kiawah Island match in 1991, the crowds waiting to see the Ryder Cup team were swelled by the ranks of those who were no less interested to watch Concorde land. The scenes at Dublin airport were incredible. I remember the pilot making contact with Prince Andrew, who was sitting among us, to ask if he minded if Philip Walton disembarked first when we had touched down. HRH had no objections. It was a moment Philip would never forget. Armed with the Ryder Cup, he walked down those steps to thunderous applause. Not even one of the Beatles would have been better received.

We then had a team press conference at the airport at which all the questions were addressed to Philip. None of us minded. This was his moment.

1997

It doesn't take much for things to ignite on the eve of a Ryder

Cup, and on the occasion of the 1997 match at Valderrama the interview I gave to the Scottish journalists Gordon Simpson and John Huggan (see p. 116) certainly kindled the flames. The tournament itself would be no less intense.

We had flown to Malaga in a 757 and I was detailed to take the trophy down the steps and hand it over to Jimmy Patino, the owner of Valderrama. Patino is no spring chicken but he had been working through the night to help to get his course in perfect condition for the match.

Seve Ballesteros, who'd taken over from Bernard Gallacher as captain, was another night-owl that week. At three o'clock on the Wednesday morning he was to be seen walking round the swimming pool at San Roque as he worked on his pairings. When he could not come to a decision, he roused Miguel Angel Jimenez, his deputy, from his slumbers and demanded that he come down for a discussion. I was happy enough with the outcome of their deliberations because I was back with my old comrade-in-arms, Bernhard Langer.

It rained torrentially on the first morning: the worst September storm they had known in those parts in eight years. Patino, who could see grass turning to mud on the lawns outside the clubhouse, stopped people from coming in at the gates. The green plastic bin-bags around the course were weighed down by a good six inches of water by the time play started, but the course drained magnificently. In fact, I can't think of any other course in the world that would have been ready for play so quickly.

In the fourballs, which Seve had decreed would be played first, Bernhard and I were three down after eleven holes against Mark O'Meara and Tiger Woods. Though most would assume that that was all down to Tiger, nothing could have been further from the truth. Most of the damage was being done by Mark, who holed a thirty-six-footer to close us out at the sixteenth. He was playing fantastic golf and Seve's plan of attack was going down the drain. Seve talked it over with us towards the end of the match but Bernhard told him, 'Don't worry, we'll beat them in foursomes. This course was made for us.' I learned afterwards that Tiger's response to the news that he would be playing us again hardly concurred with Bernhard's comments: 'Perfect,' he said. In this instance, Langer was the one who got it right. Having lost by three and two in the morning, we won by five and three in the afternoon.

Because the morning rain had delayed proceedings by ninety minutes, two of the afternoon foursomes had to be left over until the following morning. When they were completed, we had $4^1/_2$ points to the Americans' $3^1/_2$.

Langer wanted to sit out the second fourball series and this opened the door for Darren Clarke. Like Ian Woosnam and Thomas Björn, Darren had been more than a little peeved at the way in which Seve had not included him in the first day's activities. We were playing Freddie Couples and Davis Love, and, because Darren was nervous, I tried to boost his confidence by suggesting he hit first. It was maybe not the best move: his drive shot into a no-go area in the woods and he finished behind a cork tree. The tree split into two a couple of feet off the ground, forming a V which measured no more than a couple of feet across. Darren had this idea that he could hit through it on to the green. Billy Foster, Darren's caddie, shared my view that the shot was out of the question and that he would do better to punch the ball back safely on to the fairway. On that occasion, we had our way.

But we had no chance when Seve came along as we were all square playing the seventeeth. From the moment the thirty-second Ryder Cup had started, our captain had been everywhere. One moment he would be pulling up in his buggy to tell us how the other matches were standing and the next he would hove to in time to tell us how to play this shot or that. It was clear that the Ryder Cup meant everything to him. I was in the left rough at the seventeenth and Darren was on the right, and here was Seve, who had redesigned the hole and made it more alarming than ever, instructing my partner to go for the green. I was the captain of this fourball pairing and I resented his interference. After all, we were doing fine as we were. Darren listened to Seve and hit a three iron into the water. I then played safe but left myself with a shot of fifty-eight yards, a foul distance that was neither a full lob-wedge nor a half lob-wedge. I was on the point of getting the image of how I should play the shot when Seve arrived and wanted to tell me what to do.

'Are you OK?' he began.

In the circumstances I don't suppose I could have told him what I had to say more diplomatically than I did: 'Seve, I'm nervous as hell, here. Just leave me alone!' I said.

For once, he seemed to get the message.

Left to myself, I managed to hit to eight feet, and with one of the Americans having been in the water and the other over the green, I holed the putt and went on to win.

Darren had a potentially lucrative arrangement with his sponsors that week. If he won all of his matches, he was going to be given a new Ferrari worth around £110,000. He was halfway there with our result, but when it came to the singles he lost to Phil Mickelson.

It had been a tiring start to the Ryder Cup, what with the rain delays, and I remember feeling absolutely spent as I walked in to lunch with the overall score now a pleasing 8–4. But before I could sit down, Langer intercepted me.

'We're playing together this afternoon,' he said.

'When are we off?' I asked, startled.

'Ten minutes ago,' he answered.

We were the first pair.

'I'll have to change and have a bite to eat,' I protested.

After a frenzied rush, I ended up meeting Langer, Lee Janzen and Jim Furyk on the tee. The Americans birdied the first and I thought to myself, What in the hell am I doing here? Ours was always likely to be the only match to finish that evening and it was getting darker by the minute when we arrived at the last with a one-hole lead. It was my tee shot and I hit a bad one, cutting it into the trees on the right. When we got there, our ubiquitous captain was lurking in the shadows. From the way he was putting his head first to one side and then to the other, you could see that he was planning our escape. He then spelled out his plan to Langer: 'If you keep it over this branch and under that one, you could hit a low draw on to the green,' he said. He turned to me for approval and I was on the point of telling him that it all sounded a tad ambitious when Langer, with Teutonic common sense, went behind his back and chopped out sideways. My contribution was to chip to six feet.

The Americans, meantime, were on in two and thinking that they might escape with a halved match. It was their putt, and they, like us, were completely oblivious to the fact that the green had been double-cut. Apparently, the officials had told the green staff that they might as well go ahead and cut it for the next morning since none of the foursomes was going to get that far. We put it down to the bad light as much as anything else when Janzen sent his putt flying off the back of the green. Furyk missed the return, which meant that we now had two putts from six feet for the match. There were no more mishaps and we won.

We were ahead $10\frac{1}{2}$–$5\frac{1}{2}$ when those foursomes were completed. No side had ever come back from more than two points to the bad and the Americans needed to win nine of the twelve singles if they were going to defy the odds.

Back in the team room, Seve was working on the singles line-up. 'Who wants to go out first?' he asked. Ian Woosnam volunteered.

'Who wants to go out last?' he asked. Ignacio Garrido put up his hand.

At that, Faldo looked at me, Langer and José Maria

Olazábal as only he can. His brow was furrowed and he was clearly questioning the wisdom of this haphazard selection process. In the certain knowledge that Tom Kite would be loading the top of his line-up with his best men, we conveyed to each other that we would need to play at eight, nine, ten and eleven. It was as well we were on our toes.

The afternoon could scarcely have been more fraught. There were great scenes when Rocca, in a result with which he will no doubt regale his children and his children's children, defeated Tiger, and, having done so, carried his wife round and round the green by way of a celebration. But Freddie Couples had triggered an amazing American revival when he blew Ian Woosnam away in the top match. He was seven under par in winning by eight and seven. Per-Ulrik Johansson defeated Davis Love and Thomas Björn halved his game with Justin Leonard but, thereafter, there was a rush of American wins, interrupted only by Langer, who had the better of Brad Faxon. Tom Lehman hammered Ignacio Garrido, Mickelson beat Darren Clarke, O'Meara birdied five of the first eight holes on his way to finishing off Jesper Parnevik, and Janzen, though he had been two down with three to play, accounted for José Maria. Jeff Maggert beat Lee Westwood and Jim Furyk beat Faldo. To give just an inkling of what went on in that match, Faldo, who was two down at the time, hit a seven iron to three inches at the fourteenth and seemed set to get one back. Instead, Furyk chipped in for the half. At the next hole Faldo knocked a four iron to three feet. 'Pick it up,' said Furyk, when he reached the green. He then matched the birdie by holing from sand.

Langer's win had ensured that we would retain the trophy, but a tie was no good from our point of view. The Americans would have seen it as a moral victory. We had to win and now I was the only person out there who could bring that about. I was one up with two to play against Scott Hoch when he birdied the seventeenth to draw level.

He had the honour at the final hole and hit a little too far left. I then unfurled the best three wood of my life before catching the green with a nine iron. Hoch, who had had to circumnavigate a tree with his second, was short in two and on in three, about fifteen feet from the flag to my eighteen feet. I putted up dead and he conceded the remaining tiddler. As the best Hoch could do now by holing his putt was to halve the hole and the match, Europe had won the Ryder Cup. It was a glorious feeling, but since I had been out on the course for four hours, I dearly wanted to finish on a winning note myself. No chance. Along comes Seve. He walks on to the green and picks up the American ball, thereby leaving me with a halved match rather than a win. At the time, I felt cheated, but in the greater scheme of things it did not matter a damn. I had got the job done.

We have a painting at home of Scott and me shaking hands on that dark evening. Even now, it sends shivers up my spine.

I don't think I had ever felt as good a golfer as I did that afternoon. There were Scottish flags everywhere proclaiming, 'Monty No. 1', while the whole of European golf seemed to descend on the green to proffer their congratulations. Jimmy Patino's delight was tempered only by his anxiety at what these people were doing to his beloved putting surface.

I was still leading the Order of Merit, and for the Ryder Cup to come in the middle of that run of success with me hitting the last putt was an unbelievable highlight.

When I got home, I received hundreds of letters, one of them addressed to 'Colin Montgomerie, Golf, England', and another to 'Colin Montgomerie, c/o St Andrews'. Some were purely congratulatory affairs but many more concerned the result of my match with Scott Hoch. They had had good money on the result being 15–13 and Ballesteros's inter-ference made it $14^1/_2$–$13^1/_2$. I should have asked Seve to tender the replies. Instead, in a letter of apology which went out via IMG, I merely heaped the blame on him.

Just as we had won the 1995 match for Gallacher, we won this one for Seve. We knew how much he cared. There were several points about his captaincy, notably the lack of early communication with some of his players, which needed questioning. The only reason such things were not addressed was because the captain in question was Seve. He is a one-off, and just about the most charismatic figure the game has ever known, and the main reason why the European tour has flourished over the last twenty years.

Tom Kite continued to be a great American captain in defeat. He said he had brought his 'A' team with him and it had not been good enough. On the Sunday night he came into the European locker room and shook all the players by the hand. Scott Hoch and Mark O'Meara followed him.

All week, I had wondered whether the Americans were inclined to put almost too much pressure on themselves. The feeling had been prompted by a mistake I had made on the first morning when I had gone into their locker room rather than ours. There, on the wall, was this huge ten-foot by two-foot banner reading, 'LOSING IS WORSE THAN DEATH. YOU HAVE TO LIVE WITH LOSING.'

1999

In 1997, for the first time, I had felt as if I were a senior member of the side. In 1999, with the average age of the team still younger, I felt very senior, even though I was only thirty-six – still relatively young in golfing terms. In my first American Ryder Cup, I had been in the sixth row on Concorde. Now I had arrived in Row 1.

That was Mark James's doing. Our new captain knew how to make everyone feel good. All week at Brookline, he treated me as the number one, asking whom I wanted to partner and where I wanted to play on the team. Mark also had a

great way with the press, his answers going down particularly well with the American golf-writing fraternity, most of
whom had never heard such quirky retorts in their lives. On
one occasion we stopped everything we were doing in the
locker room to listen to a captains' press conference on the
closed-circuit TV.

'Where were you going when you left that match halfway
down the fourteenth fairway?' asked one earnest American
scribe who was trying to get to the root of James's tactical
acumen.

'To get a beefburger,' returned James.

If there was one error Mark made that week, it was failing
to appreciate just how much the Americans wanted to win.
They had lost in 1995 and 1997 and could not afford to lose
in 1999, especially on their own soil.

The other point I would make is that I felt desperately
sorry for Andrew Coltart who, like Jarmo Sandelin and Jean
Van de Velde, was not played at all over the first two days. It
is probably fair to say that James had intended to play Paul
Lawrie and me together in the fourballs and Andrew and me
in the foursomes. Because Paul and I were working out so
well in practice, he decided that he would keep us together
for all four of the opening matches. To be fair, it worked well.
We picked up two and a half points.

On the first morning, we had arranged that Paul would
take the odd holes. He had just won the Open, with his three,
three end to the play-off being nothing short of remarkable.
I felt I had no need to worry about how he would handle the
pressure. We were just getting ready to go to the tee when a
lovely old man in a USPGA blazer introduced himself first to
Paul and then to me. He would be our referee. He clearly
thought I was good for a chat, which I usually am, and
started to regale me with details of how his family had come
from Scotland. I listened for as long as I could but was soon
having to try to tear myself away. With Paul playing in his

first match, it was important that I should be there for him on the tee. Unfortunately, the elderly gentleman was not going to let me escape that easily. The minutes were ticking away and now he was bringing out his family photos. Would I like to see the grandchildren? I could hardly ignore the request and, sure enough, the children were delightful. It was just that this was not the time to be admiring them. By now, I had reached that point where nerves turn to giggles and that was the state in which I arrived at Paul's side. Goodness knows what he, Phil Mickelson and David Duval were thinking. They must have wondered if I had hit the bottle. With the referee right behind, I could not begin to explain myself at that point. Instead, I stifled the laughter as best I could and the match began.

Paul hit into the edge of the right rough.

'That's OK,' I said.

'What do you mean, OK?' he replied. 'It's brilliant.'

As we set off down the fairway, I explained why I had been late. At the same time, I ventured that we might have trouble with our referee.

The match was uneventful until we came to the seventh, a par three. There, Phil hit his shot big and right and Paul missed the green short and left. David then thinned the American second clean across the green, his ball finishing a good twenty feet past the chip that I was about to play. It was Phil to play by miles, yet here was our referee doing everything short of taking a tape to the different balls before decreeing, solemnly, 'America to play.' David looked at me and, at the end of the hole, we agreed that this fellow had to go. I put in a complaint over a radio and a replacement referee was delivered to the eighth tee. I hope they dealt with it tactfully but it was just not on to play a Ryder Cup match with a referee in whom neither side had any confidence.

Paul and I won by three and two before halving our foursomes with Davis Love and Justin Leonard. At the end of the day Europe had six points to America's two. The following morning's fourballs were shared, with Paul and I responsible for a loss to Hal Sutton and Jeff Maggert.

In our last game together, we played Tiger Woods and Steve Pate. It turned into one of the best putting afternoons of my life. The match was always close, but Paul put our tee shot stiff at the sixteenth to have us two up with two to play. After we had both hit the fairway down the next hole, Paul turned to me and said, 'Thanks.' He said there was ten times the pressure he had known in winning the Open and what he was implying was that I had helped him to feel at home. We halved the hole and won the match, two and one. You can make great friends amid the pressure of a Ryder Cup match and Paul and I have been close ever since.

The score was 10–6 on the Saturday night. All we needed were four and a half more points to win.

Jesper Parnevik was the first to scent danger. He was off at number seven, one match ahead of me in the singles, and we were having breakfast together.

'I don't like the look of this,' he said.

'What on earth do you mean?' I muttered.

'Where are the four and a half points coming from?' he challenged.

I did not answer him directly. It suddenly struck me that as one who spent most of his time playing the States, Parnevik knew what he was talking about.

You did not have to be out there long on the Sunday to recognise that the atmosphere had changed to something we have never known before in a Ryder Cup. I had been heckled on and off all week and shrugged it off. If anything, it had made me play better. Now, though, things were getting really ugly and some of the American players were making things a hundred times worse with the way they were inciting the crowd. The atmosphere was not too far removed from mass hysteria. When, for example, Andrew

Coltart lost his ball at the ninth, there was cruel laughter as a group of spectators encouraged him to look in the wrong place.

Though, as I mentioned earlier, Payne Stewart, my opponent, was trying hard to protect me from the crowd's excesses, there was a limit to what he could do. Almost certainly, he was no less shaken than I was by the events on the ninth tee when the spectator had to be ejected after his deliberate attempt to distract me (see p. 117). From my point of view, my father's presence at that moment was probably the worst thing about the whole incident. With the amount of time and money he had poured into my golf across the years, watching me play against this double US Open champion should have been a highlight of his golfing days. Instead, his love affair with the Ryder Cup was shattered.

Payne got back to square over the next two holes in a move that mirrored what was happening in most of the games ahead. Everything seemed to be going the Americans' way, and when Justin Leonard holed a great putt across the green of the seventeenth against José Maria Olazábal, the hosts thought, wrongly, that they were home and dry. Olazábal had a putt to keep the Ryder Cup alive and, in what added up to one of the most unsavoury scenes the competition has ever known, he had to ask some of the American players and their followers to desist from dancing on the green in order that he could tackle it. There are two opinions as to whether they were treading on his line, but they should never have been there at all. Olazábal missed and the celebrations continued, with the guilty parties largely unrepentant. 'Spur-of-the-moment stuff' was how they dismissed it.

Before too long, the crowds had converged on our game, in which, though it no longer mattered for the overall match, I was level after seventeen. There were 30,000 people stampeding down the eighteenth fairway, most of them waving US flags. I had a security man with me but we had lost Alastair, my caddie, and with him the putter I was going to need. Payne had knocked his ball into a greenside bunker, and as I was propelled down the fairway by the teeming hordes, I ended up stumbling into the trap as he was about to hit. 'I'm sorry,' I said. Payne played his third on to the green before picking up his ball and mine and giving me the match. After such a day, he clearly felt that golf as he knew it could never be quite the same again. 'That will do us,' he said, sadly.

A USPGA man made a speech at the prize-giving at which he talked of how wonderful it was that the match should have been played in such a fine spirit. That speech appalled me. But enough is enough. Plenty has been written of the thirty-third Ryder Cup, with nothing summing up that Sunday afternoon better than Michael Bonallack's description: he likened the goings-on in that madding crowd to a bear pit.

Two months after the Ryder Cup, I was in La Manga for the Lexus European Cup Final. Sky News was on the television and I heard how Payne Stewart was thought to be on a small plane that was out of control. It did not take long for the news to be confirmed.

Since the Ryder Cup had been his last big event, I received a host of calls from TV people and journalists wanting me to pay tribute to this great champion. I did not find that difficult.

He was colourful, courageous and a good friend. On his own admission, he had once bordered on the arrogant, but he had worked hard to reform and become a committed Christian. He was a good man through and through.

I carry a number of valued items in my business folder at all times. Pride of place among the pictures goes to one of Eimear and the children, but, tucked into the left-hand sleeve, there is a photo that was sent to me by the 1999

President of the USPGA. It is of myself and Payne on the last afternoon of the Ryder Cup. The letter accompanying it congratulated me on my play and suggested that I might like the picture as a memento of our game together. Every time I pull it out, I think back to the moment Payne gave me the match, and how fragile life can be.

2002

Just when I was beginning to wonder if my best golfing days lay in the past, I had the finest week of my life at the 2002 Ryder Cup. I was part of an extraordinary side which, under the captaincy of Sam Torrance, defeated the Americans by 15^1/$_2$–12^1/$_2$ at the Belfry.

It was team golf through and through but, on a personal basis, I played the golf of my dreams. Over the week, I would win four and a half points out of five, though it goes without saying that I could not have done that on my own. I had two great partners in Bernhard Langer, for the opening fourballs and both sets of foursomes, and Padraig Harrington for the Saturday-afternoon fourballs.

The match, as everyone knows, had been put back a year because of the events of 11 September 2001. Then, the Ryder Cup was only a couple of weeks away and the Americans were too shocked at what had happened to be in any mood to play a golf match in Britain. They wanted the security of home. Those of us who had found ourselves stranded in America at the Amex tournament at the time of the Twin Towers disaster could understand why. To a man, our reaction had been to return to our families as quickly as possible.

The twelve-month postponement involved no end of administrative work for the organisers. And it was not easy for the twelve men who had been selected for the European team, either. We had made the team because we were playing well in 2001 but, over the next twelve months, several members of the side would have to withstand all manner of attacks in the media about their form. There were constant references to how A, who was not in the team, was playing better than B, who was. Early on, there were calls for a fresh side to be selected, while another idea to be advanced was that the teams should be increased from twelve to fourteen in order that the match could take in some top players of the moment.

I never had any time for those suggestions. Since the officials had agreed at the outset that they would stay with the original twelve players, I felt that there was nothing more to say on the matter. It was a *fait accompli*. Phil Price and Lee Westwood, when they did their pre-match interviews in the week of the match, talked of how they had been surrounded by a sea of negativity for months. Lee said that people would ask him about his form in tones to suggest they were expecting bad tidings. So you can imagine the mood in the team when Lee won three of his four opening matches, and Price, in a result that he will remember all his days, defeated none other than Phil Mickelson in the singles.

Lee had started to turn the corner a week earlier, thanks not least to a practice round he had at the Belfry with Sam Torrance while most of the rest of us were playing in the Amex tournament in Ireland. He had been hitting the ball all over the place on the front nine and Sam had taken him to one side and reminded him that he was a class player and that even if form comes and goes, class lasts for ever. Lee started to play better on the back nine and his confidence grew in each of the next seven days.

My main problems in the 2002 season centred on my back. It was playing up on a pretty regular basis and I was making it worse with worry. Would I make it to the Belfry? As someone pointed out, I seemed to be nearing the end of my golfing tether. At the start of September, IMG convened a meeting at their headquarters in Chiswick involving all the people in my team: Hugh, my psychologist; Denis, my coach;

and Guy, my manager. The subject under debate was whether I was in any state to play in the match and whether I could play anything close to my best golf if I did. The alternatives were also discussed, with the most likely possibility being that I would take a break until the end of the year. At the end of that meeting, it was decided that I should wait until the week before the match, the Amex week, to make my final decision. When the time came, I played better in each round and, on the Sunday night, I rang Sam to confirm that I would be at the Belfry.

He did not say it to my face but he told everyone else that he always knew I would be there. He knew me well enough to recognise that I would not want to miss out on the Ryder Cup and he also appreciated that once I had made my decision, I would begin to unwind – and that is precisely what happened. At the Belfry, the stresses and strains melted away and I felt more relaxed than I have ever felt at a major event. What was very noticeable early on in this 2002 match, or 2001 match, as they still seemed to want to call it, was that the team spirit was brilliant. In the summer of 2001, Sam had rung Sir Alex Ferguson and asked how to get the best out of a team. Sir Alex had talked to him at length but there was one particular piece of advice which Sam saw as key. He said that there should be no stars on the team; everyone should be treated the same. The way Sam made that work was to make every one of us feel good about himself.

In my case, I think he did me a huge favour at the opening ceremony on the Thursday afternoon when he introduced me to the crowd as 'Monty'. For some reason, I had always felt close to spectators when playing in the Midlands. They have seen me in all my moods and know instinctively how to jolly me along. They laugh at me and with me, and, when it came to this Ryder Cup, they lifted me on to a new plane with their applause and vocal encouragement. 'Come on, Monty!' was the cry from behind the ropes. It was funny to hear them on the practice days when I was teamed with Bernhard, whose general stoicism and great play have earned him so much respect down the years. Whenever anyone wanted something signed, it would be, 'Mr Langer, can I have your autograph?' before they would turn to me and say, 'Monty, can I have yours?' It interested me enormously that when Curtis Strange was asked if he had learned anything about Ryder Cups from his captaincy at the Belfry, the first thing that came to his mind was the difference a home crowd can make.

The caddies came in for VIP treatment too. Tony Jacklin, the victorious captain of two European teams in the eighties, had always done everything possible to make the players feel on top of the world. Sam extended that thinking to the caddies, with whom he was, in any case, on the best of terms. Sam is everyone's friend on tour. He took note of the caddies' opinions, made sure that they had a good team room with eating arrangements on a par with our own and had them wearing similar uniforms to his players. The best was reserved till last in that they had cashmere sweaters for the Sunday, which was a lovely idea.

Players and caddies were wonderfully united with no one having any complaints. The atmosphere improved each day in the European camp at a time when the Americans were still having to cope with the fall-out from the Amex week, when Tiger had been asked if he would sooner win the Amex, with its status and million-dollar purse, or the Ryder Cup. Tiger is an honest soul and he opted for the Amex. Unfortunately, he added that there were 'a million reasons why' he favoured the Amex and people did not take the comment in the light-hearted manner in which it was intended. He was accused of being interested only in money.

One other aspect of Sam's captaincy worth mentioning at this stage concerns course preparation. It is the home captain's prerogative to set up the course as he wants, and Sam had paid particular attention to the area around the greens. The last thing he wanted was that layer of thick greenside rough they have in the States and from which a player like Mickelson is so lethal. With the grass cut short, the Europeans could play all the usual run-up shots while the Americans would be in two minds as to how best to get the ball up to the hole.

When it came to the Thursday night and Sam had to put his pairings to paper, he got them absolutely right. As he said himself, he had not tried to second-guess what the Americans would do with their pairings; he had simply chosen the players he felt would work best together and was sending them out in the order he sensed was correct. Thomas Björn and Darren Clarke were to go out first: two players with similar temperaments who, when they are good, can be very good indeed. In the second slot, he had Lee Westwood and Sergio Garcia – an inspired combination if ever there was one. If Lee's confidence was still a little fragile, Garcia had confidence to spare. In third place he had myself and Bernhard, which was equally well thought-out. Though the tension I had been feeling before the match had melted away, Sam recognised that if I did become fraught, Bernhard would be the fellow to keep me calm. He felt it was more likely that Bernhard's serenity would rub off on me than that Bernhard would pick up any of my more heated ways. Finally, Sam had linked Padraig Harrington and Niclas Fasth, which made equally good sense because one is as thorough as the other.

After the pairings sheets had been handed out to the press, each captain was asked what he thought about his prospects. Strange said that a lot of it would be down to luck in terms of who ended up playing whom but added that if his side played to its potential, he would feel confident.

When Torrance was asked what he would need to win he had a rather more succinct answer: 'Fourteen and a half points.'

Day One

What a first morning! With each of the top three pairs winning, we went into lunch with a heady 3–1 lead. I am always aware of what is happening everywhere else on a golf course and saw some great European shots ahead as Thomas and Darren, the latter of whom had opened with three birdies, had a better ball of 62 in defeating Tiger and Paul Azinger by one hole. At the same time, there was early evidence on the leaderboard to suggest that the partnership of Lee and Sergio was working out as intended as they moved steadily towards a four and three win over David Duval and Davis Love. The match following us was poised to go either way.

Bernhard and I played well and downed the putts to defeat the tenacious combination of Scott Hoch and Jim Furyk by four and three. As Mike Aitken wrote in the *Scotsman*, the adrenaline of the Ryder Cup had affected me 'like a handful of Prozac … There's something about golf's tightest event which frees the Scot; the harder the going gets, the easier his swing becomes.'

I cannot say it often enough: I deemed it a privilege to be playing with Bernhard. He is the best partner anyone could have, and, of course, when you get him, you get Peter Coleman, his caddie. As a team, they are rock solid, and, between them, they give you a wonderful sense of security. You feel you are in safe hands. What is more, Andy Prodger, whose first Ryder Cup this was with me, was a natural fourth member of the party. He is a man of few words but those you get are wise. He and Peter have always got on well and, as we played Hoch and Furyk, I had the feeling that everything that could have been right was right.

The Americans always had the edge in the fourth fourball. They were three up after twelve but, thanks to some powerful work on the greens, Niclas Fasth and Padraig Harrington cut that deficit to one coming up the last. The other members of both teams abandoned their lunches to witness a finish in which Padraig had a twenty-footer to save a half-point. He hit the putt to perfection and the crowd, to a man, had embarked on the beginnings of an almighty cheer when the ball spun round the back of the hole.

We knew that the Americans were going to be doubly dangerous in the afternoon foursomes and, up at the top, Hal Sutton and Scott Verplank came back from two down with six to play to defeat Darren Clarke and Thomas Björn. However, Sergio Garcia and Lee Westwood won the next match against Woods and Calcavecchia and it looked as if Bernhard and I were going to contribute a second point as we left the fourteenth green with a three-hole lead over Mickelson and David Toms. Instead, we lost three holes in a row – all to birdies – to find ourselves level coming up the last. I split the fairway with my tee shot and Bernhard hit a good second that finished just off the right edge of the green. Toms, for his part, left the American second on the lower tier of the green. You have to wonder what the greenkeeper was thinking as Mickelson proceeded to take his wedge to that prize putting surface. His shot, which was probably as good as he could have hoped for from where he was, ran two-putt distance past the flag. Now it was my turn to try to chip close. Alas, I gave the shot too much and, with neither side getting up and down, we ended up tying hole and match. Padraig Harrington and Paul McGinley had by then lost to some fine play from Stewart Cink and Jim Furyk.

Our 4½–3½ lead sounded good on paper but it could so easily have been 5–3 or even 6–2. I knew that that was not how I should be thinking and very soon put it about that we should not be feeling disappointed. Instead, we should be remembering that we had the lead.

As much as the heroics of the Europeans, spectators leaving the Belfry that night were discussing Tiger Woods's performance. That Tiger should have lost fourballs and four-somes to bring his Ryder Cup record to eight losses in twelve starts was something they could not comprehend. 'Tiger doesn't feel good right now and that's no bad thing,' said Curtis Strange. 'He probably feels that he let the team down but that makes you want to come back strongly.'

Though Tiger's day had hardly yielded the expected results, Strange could not have been more proud of the way his troops had rallied. He picked out Verplank and Sutton for coming back against Clarke and Björn, while he also had something to say of Mickelson and the thirty-yard wedge shot he played on the the last green. 'I said to Mickelson, "Not everyone would agree with your choice of club at the last but, my god, you've got balls!"' Meanwhile, in the European team room, the level of expectancy had risen markedly as we realised we had less to fear than we had thought. This was not any slight on our opponents, we were just playing better than we could have hoped. The putts were dropping and there was a general feeling of optimism.

Day Two

The Americans made a resounding start to the Saturday-morning foursomes when Toms holed from twenty-two feet for a birdie which put him and Mickelson ahead of Pierre Fulke and Phillip Price. There were encouraging signs for our players when Mickelson caught the water at both the third and sixth but then the world number two conjured up some magic shots, with pride of place surely going to the one I saw on the BBC's highlights in which he hit a wood to within a foot or so of the hole at the fifteenth to put the Americans two up. Sergio and Lee kept a steady supply of blue figures up on the leaderboard as they defeated Stewart Cink and Jim Furyk, while Bernhard and I did our stuff with a win over Scott Verplank and Scott Hoch.

Among the steps Sam had taken in preparing the course, he had had the greens cut to a length that was all right for us but very slow for the Americans. Like Bernhard, I had a great feel on these surfaces and, in this third match of ours, the early putt that probably meant the most was the ten-footer I sank at the tenth to put us two up. Verplank promptly holed from twenty-five feet at the eleventh and, when Hoch birdied the long fifteenth, the game was all square. Luckily we won the next as Hoch missed his eight-footer and I made mine, and we ended up winning at the last when I knocked a seventy-five-foot putt stone dead. I am sure that everyone would have been whispering that three-putts were on the cards and I have to say that the thought had struck me, too. I was hugely relieved when it settled so close to the hole.

What Curtis had said about Tiger being anxious to make up for his two losses the day before duly materialised as he and Davis Love won comfortably against Darren Clarke and Thomas Björn.

So we had had two wins and two losses for the score to be 6½–5½ going into the afternoon fourballs, which would prove our one poor series, as we collected only one and a half points.

In the first match, Mark Calcavecchia and David Duval dug themselves out of a hole to have the Americans drawing first blood. Jesper Parnevik, whose first outing this was, had made a thirty-footer at the seventh to take him and Niclas Fasth to three up but the tide turned when Duval drove the green at the tenth. Curtis and most of the rest of the Americans, including Tiger, had agreed that it was not worth going for that green off the tee, even in the fourballs. Curtis's reasoning was that players of the calibre of those doing duty at the Belfry had more of a chance of pinning down a birdie between them if they played short of the water off the tee and looked to get the ball close with their seconds. Duval, though, had never been totally convinced that that was right, and on that second afternoon the shot he hit could not have been more telling. Momentum was with them from that point and they ended up winning by a hole.

With Bernhard having asked to play only four matches out of the five, he took a break in the afternoon and I went out with Padraig Harrington against Phil Mickelson and David Toms. They were a sticky combination but Padraig and I started well – I think I made three birdies in the first eight holes – and kept the pressure on our illustrious opponents. We had some anxious moments at the seventeenth, where Phil had a chance to take the match down the last but, with the pace of the greens not suiting him any more than it did Toms, he missed and Padraig and I made what would be Europe's only full point of the afternoon.

Sergio and Lee had the chance of a memorable win over Tiger and Davis Love but, after putting in some great work over the afternoon, they missed a short putt apiece over the last couple of holes to end up losing. It was not too difficult to understand why they were so upset with themselves.

Paul McGinley was no less of a hero on the Saturday than he would be on the Sunday. Scott Hoch and Jim Furyk went one up on Paul and Darren Clarke as Hoch holed from thirty feet for a winning par at the seventeenth but Paul got down in two from thirty feet at the last to salvage the half we so badly needed. It meant that we would go into the last day with the score poised at 8–8.

Then, Sam played his masterstroke. He loaded the front order of his line-up in a very courageous manner. Rewards only come to those who risk. This was a risk and it paid off. People might imagine that we had the playing order all

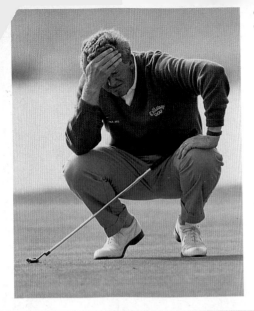

Golf . . . One day great, one day terrible. (Allsport)

Below The Open, 2002: a tough week – great on Friday; a different story on Saturday . . . (Allsport)

organised, but that was not the case. There were long discussions on Saturday evening but, with nothing decided, I was still in the dark when I went off for a back massage. As I was leaving Sam asked, 'Do you mind where you play?' I replied that I didn't care and Sam's reply was, 'Good, Monty, because I have a plan!' It was when I emerged from treatment at about 8 p.m. that Darren Clarke showed me a hand-written list of the Sunday pairings. I immediately looked at No. 7, 8 and 9 (my usual position) but couldn't find my name. Then I did what I usually do next, which is look for the longest name, and still couldn't find it. Finally, I looked at the No. 1 pairing, where the appropriate abbreviation 'Monty' was lined up against Scott Hoch. Looking down the order from myself to Sergio 2nd, Darren 3rd, Bernhard 4th and so on, Sam's plan was becoming clearer.

Sam had made it plain to those at the bottom that he was not throwing them to the lions. He has always had a theory that heroes emerge from the shadows and he would be proved right.

Curtis had done things very differently and was more than somewhat taken aback when he compared his list to ours. Having guessed that Sam would have put me and Sergio at the bottom, he had Phil Mickelson at eleven and Tiger at twelve. He was asked if he was worried in case the two of them might be redundant, but, if he did fear as much, he was hardly going to say so, because it would only have sent the wrong message to his team.

The line-up for the final day was as follows:

Montgomerie v Hoch
Garcia v Toms
Clarke v Duval
Langer v Sutton
Harrington v Calcavecchia

Björn v Cink
Westwood v Verplank
Fasth v Azinger
McGinley v Furyk
Fulke v Love
Price v Mickelson
Parnevik v Woods.

Day Three

One or two people said that from the moment they saw my antics on the practice range on the Sunday morning, they knew that I was going to be all right in my match with Scott Hoch. I had gone out to hit balls and, blanching at the sight of the bucketful that Andy had poured out in front of me, I gave someone in the stand the chance to hit a few for me. The chap who emerged, a big, cheerful man, had commented on how my first few wedge shots looked a little feeble and I asked if he could do better. The answer, as it turned out, was in the negative. It was rather a contrast to what happened on one of the practice days when a chap called Steve had noted that I had a 'crap' lie at the short twelfth and I let him have a go at the little approach shot before I did. He was obviously a bit of a golfer and, undaunted by crowd comments, he hit it to a foot, whereas I couldn't get any closer than eight feet. 'You're one up!' I told him.

Quite why I was feeling so good about playing Scott Hoch I do not know. There was some unfinished business between us after Seve had prematurely ended our match five years before by picking up Hoch's ball to give him half a point. I had had the toughest of matches against him on that last day at Valderrama in 1997 and, as Ernie Els said in the *Daily Telegraph*'s 2002 Ryder Cup supplement, this particular American does not go away. He's a very difficult player to escape.

The city boasts an old and learned college,
  Where you'd think the leading industry was Greek;
Even there the favoured instruments of knowledge
  Are a driver and a putter and a cleek.
R.F. Murray, 1885

St Andrews 2000. Seve Ballesteros and I follow in the footsteps of Bobby Jones, Jack Nicklaus and Gary Player in receiving honorary degrees in law from St Andrews University.

... but playing in Scotland, here at Loch Lomond,
on days like this is always good for the soul. (Allsport)

Top The birthday girl. Eimear, at her 30th birthday party with HRH Prince Andrew and Bernhard Gallacher's wife, Lesley.

Inset Eimear's 30th birthday party. Thank heavens I can give the microphone to someone who knows what he is doing – Mr Rory Bremner.

Above right With Guy Kinnings. Guy, a Senior International Vice President with IMG has managed my affairs for ten years and been a loyal friend. This picture catches me doing what I should have done more often – enjoying a relaxing evening in good company.

Right With the boss, Mark McCormack, before a Skins game in Palm Springs in October 1997. I have been a McCormack client since 1989.

Receiving the MBE from Her
Majesty Queen Elizabeth. A proud
day in my life.

Eimear with Phil Mickleson's wife,
Amy, at the opening ceremony of
the 1999 Ryder Cup at Brookline.

4 November 1998. Outside Buckingham
Palace with Eimear and Olivia after
receiving my MBE. (Photo: PA News)

Left 1999. Our three children contained long enough for the click of the camera. From left to right: Venetia, aged four, Cameron, aged one and Olivia, six. (Photo: Brian Aris)

Opposite page:

Top Masters 2001. I am not entirely sure what message Olivia, my daughter, was trying to convey to Freddie Couples' young stepson, when they both caddied for us at the Par 3 Competition, Augusta. (Photo: Getty Images)

Middle right At sea with my son, Cameron, in Barbados in January 2002.

Middle left First day at Feltonfleet school for Olivia, Venetia and Cameron in September 2001.

Above Ghyll Royd revisited. I enjoyed mingling with the boys on my return to my old preparatory school.

Below Our home in Oxshott, which we are very lucky and proud to own. (Photo: Brian Aris)

Ready for the gala dinner at the 1997 Ryder Cup at Valderrama.
(Photo: Getty Images)

The crowd were so noisy as our eleven-fifteen starting time approached that Ivor Robson, the starter, could not make himself heard when he wanted to announce my name. He did as he should have done by making a second attempt, but this time I was about to launch into my drive. I stood back and started over again, and suddenly I was horribly conscious of the weight of expectation. To be honest, it was appalling. I have unfurled more than my share of straight drives under extreme pressure and, thankfully, I did so again. I understand that some commentators felt that it might have been the longest drive down all week at that hole – it was all down to the adrenaline. When I had caught the green with my second, I holed from thirty-five feet to have the cheers rising and the first of the afternoon's blue figures going up on the board. That was what Sam had wanted, or, should I say, ordered.

In all four of my previous matches I had never at any stage been behind and the pattern continued. After that opening birdie on the Sunday, I went on to make six more on my way to defeating Hoch at the fourteenth. I was seven under par when I closed him out and I greatly appreciated what he said about never having seen anyone play better than I had in this Ryder Cup: 'I played Monty three times and I cannot believe that he putted as well as he did.'

When I arrived on the eighth green with a two-hole lead, the adjacent leaderboard showed that Europe were up in four of the first five matches and level in the other. The crowd were ecstatic and I imagine that there were people out there who will boast of having been at the 2002 match until their dying day.

It was on the homeward nine, when Sergio and Darren started to wobble a little, that our men at the bottom began to surface. Though Sam had been expecting a point or so from that region, the delighted exclamations from the crowd as Phillip Price started to draw away from Phil Mickelson and Jesper Parnevik clung to Tiger Woods suggested that this was not what they had anticipated. There was one theory doing the rounds that Price, as pale as a ghost on this last afternoon, had caused Mickelson to take fright. In fact, the Welshman was playing the golf of his life and the American would admit afterwards that he had felt under pressure from the start.

Bernhard Langer, an influence for the good from start to finish, was a four and three winner against Hal Sutton, while Padraig Harrington got his job done and defeated Mark Calcavecchia by a resounding five and four. Then came Thomas Björn, whose two and one win over Stewart Cink upped the European singles points to four and a half, with the half belonging to Darren Clarke. 'If ever there were a match which should have been halved that might have been it,' said David Duval, who had sportingly conceded a testing putt on the last.

Once Phil Price's result – he won by three and two – had come in, the expectation was that Niclas Fasth would tie things up for Europe as he came to the last with a one-hole lead over Paul Azinger. Instead, Azinger holed from a greenside bunker to finish all square. 'I knew I had to do something,' Azinger had said to the media men around the green.

People afterwards commented on how wide our victory margin was, particularly in the singles. But had Furyk, who was playing Paul McGinley, holed his bunker shot, as he very nearly did, it would have been down to the two remaining live matches and therefore Pierre Fulke or Jasper Parnevik to eke out the crucial half point to win. As it was, Furyk's bunker shot just slipped by and McGinley had his chance to provide the match-winning half. He had holed from ten feet to draw level at the seventeenth and now he holed from the same distance again in front of a crowd whose cheers will ring through his ears for evermore. The noise around the green was indescribable. Paul was jumping up and down, and even his pregnant wife, Alison, was to be seen leaping skywards before starting to cry. Paul will be forever fêted at home for adding to the list of Irishmen – Christy O'Connor Jr, Eamonn Darcy and Philip Walton – who have put the finishing touches to a European win. He had been two down against Furyk at the twelfth when I was among those to tell him, 'Come on, we need this point.' Furyk himself could not have been more generous at the end when he described Paul as 'a wonderful gentleman and a new friend'.

Sergio Garcia, who had lost to David Toms, at this point went rushing down the eighteenth fairway to celebrate with Pierre Fulke, who at the time was level with Davis Love. Though the two players had thought of calling it a day when they heard the noise from the green, Love thought they had best continue. However, once Garcia had dented what remained of their concentration, they entered into new negotiations. At first, Fulke, who had no intention of complaining about Garcia because he felt any young man of Sergio's age would have acted as he had done, offered to give Love the match. Love, though, thought a half was more in order.

That done, everyone waited for the denouement of the Woods–Parnevik match. Woods was one up after seventeen holes and an official had advised that the two should finish. But when Tiger three-putted the last green, he picked up the four-footer Jesper needed to square the match. 'Jesper's fought hard all day. I wouldn't have wanted to see him miss that,' said Tiger, demonstrating to the doubters that he fully understood what this Ryder Cup was all about.

The first congratulatory call for Sam came on his mobile phone shortly before Tiger had made that gesture. Had it come a moment or so later, Sam said he would have held up his mobile to the packed stands and told them, 'It's Seve!' They would have liked that.

Back on the eve of the contest, Bernhard and Malcolm

Mason, Sam's old caddie and the man who was caddying for Bernhard that day, had been chatting with me on the sixth tee about how emotional Sam would be on the Sunday night. Malcolm said that he would not cry if we lost but that he would never stop if we won. Spot on.

We had a hell of a party that evening with much jollity involving both sets of players. Sam, for his part, enjoyed nothing so much as when we all went into the Belfry's main bar where Lee Westwood, armed with microphone, took it upon himself to introduce each of us to the public. Eventually, he came to Phillip Price. You would have thought that Phillip would have been appalled. As it was, he was exhorting Westwood with the words, 'Remember to tell them who I beat.'

It was not until a couple of days later that I heard what Sam had done when he went back for the winning captain's press conference on the Monday morning. Having been taken down to the tenth green for a photo-shoot with the gleaming Ryder Cup trophy, he had asked to stop off on the tenth tee on the way back. He showed the trophy all around before asking one of the members if he could have a go with his driver. Then, with all the exuberance you would expect of one who had enjoyed the golfing week of his life, he crashed a drive 285 yards on to that notoriously elusive green.

The big question exercising all minds at that rather premature point was whether Sam should have a second crack at the captaincy in 2004. Both he and his wife, Suzanne, had been brilliant but I don't think Thomas Björn was too far out when he suggested that Sam would need to think about it very carefully. 'It would,' said Thomas, 'be a big shame for Sam if the next one was not quite so good. This one was perfect in every way.'

Sam had something good to say about everyone in the side, including the fact that each of the twelve had contributed at least half a point. He gave me a new label of 'King of the Castle', which made my children laugh, and he reiterated that if the Montgomerie he had seen at the Belfry could carry on as he was, there would be no stopping him.

That 2002 Ryder Cup, though, was the ultimate for me. Were I to win each of the Majors in turn, I doubt whether I could enjoy myself as much as I did in that September week.

Chapter 15

AFTER THE BALL

It was, as they say, the party to end all parties: Eimear's thirtieth on 27 October 1998. Birthdays are huge in Eimear's family. In fact, they are not so much birthdays as birthweeks.

Eimear has always liked ABBA and, back in the July of that year, it had occurred to me that I should throw a party for her with an ABBA theme. Without saying anything to her, I went to Guy Kinnings and the two of us agreed that we should try to hire Björn Again, the ABBA lookalikes, for the evening in question. Guy's brother, Max, has contacts in the theatrical world and he got in touch with the group's agents. Initially, there was disappointment. Björn Again had moved on to bigger things, like opening for the Spice Girls, and they did not do private parties any more. When we refused to take no for an answer, they asked if they could have a look at a prospective guest-list. That was encouraging. With names like Prince Andrew at the top, we felt we might be in luck and we were.

I have never been one for half measures, and once we had hired them I turned my thoughts to how we could warm up the guests between the meal and the dancing. A comedian, I thought. Why not a comedian? I had heard a few at various golf-related functions and the one who had appealed above the rest was Rory Bremner. 'We can't get him, can we?' I ventured, doubtfully. Guy, who was by then thinking along the same recklessly unrestrained lines, thought it was worth a try.

Bremner's charges are as cheerfully outrageous as you would think for one of his talents. However, we arrived at a compromise. I would have eighteen holes with him at Wisley and he would cut his usual fee in half.

By the end of September, when the Admirable Crichton marquee people wanted to come and measure up the garden, I had to tell Eimear. She was ecstatic. We initially wanted a marquee for a hundred, but as we started to compose the guest-list it grew and grew. What is more, in the spend, spend, spend mode which was maybe precipitated by the fact that I had just secured my sixth Order of Merit, I lapped up Admirable Crichton's suggestion that we should have water flowing between tables and cascading down the various levels of the marquee. At the same stage, I happily subscribed to the plan of an indoor rockery ablaze with Scottish heather.

Because we live in a cul-de-sac, security for Prince Andrew was seen as something of a problem. The security people came to the house beforehand and explained that the electric gates at the end of the drive would have to be kept open for the duration of the party in order that HRH, if the need arose, could make a quick getaway. They made a couple of other points, along with the warning that the Prince would not stay beyond midnight.

As it transpired, he danced until one-thirty.

My job was to host Table 2, which included several sets of parents from Bedales, where our daughters Olivia and Venetia used to be at school until we found the daily journey – forty miles each way – too much of a strain. I had Becs Kinnings (Guy's wife) on one side of me and Julia Maile, one of the mothers from Olivia's school, on the other.

Of my golfing friends, we had Sam Torrance, and his wife Suzanne, Andrew Coltart and Emma and Darren Clarke and

Heather. 'This is some party,' said Darren halfway through the evening. 'Don't tell me what it cost.'

I didn't.

I was one of seventeen kilted Scots, most of the rest having been good enough to come down from Scotland. Eimear wore a black dress and looked stunning. I cannot tell you how proud I felt of her.

Rory Bremner was a great hit. He took off a few politicians before moving over to the sports world, where he did Murray Walker, Nigel Mansell, Bill McLaren, Gavin Hastings and Peter Alliss. He also enjoyed himself at the expense of various American golf commentators, and when he had finished all that he threw in a few Prince Charles jokes. I noted that quite a few of our guests were doing as I did in taking a surreptitious look at Prince Andrew at that point. Thankfully, HRH took it in the best of spirits.

When Rory finished, a black curtain opened and there were Björn Again, starting off with 'Waterloo'. Most of the people seemed to think they were ABBA. I couldn't believe what I was seeing but almost instantaneously everyone wanted to dance and they scarcely paused for breath all evening. The children's nanny, Heather, had brought Olivia and Venetia down by this point. I persuaded Olivia on to the dance floor and the two children, who knew all the ABBA songs from hearing them on the school run, were transfixed.

All evening the waterfalls flowed prettily through the downstairs of the house and the marquee, and it was only when the party was coming to a close that we put two and two together as to why one loo after another was refusing to flush. When we turned the waterfalls off, the plumbing returned to normal.

Twenty-one people stayed in the house that night and when, in the morning, they looked out to see where the marquee had been in relation to where they were sleeping, there was no sign of it. In what added to the magic of the occasion, everything had been taken away in the dead of night.

It was a wonderful party and one that told its own story of how much I loved Eimear. Yet, if the truth be known, there were already problems in our relationship. There was very little communication between the two of us: if Eimear had a problem, I would brush it off with a suggestion that we deal with it later, maybe after the end of that week's tournament. And if there were something bothering me, I would keep it to myself. I loathed anything in the way of confrontation. Once that behaviour pattern takes hold, it can only worsen, and by the summer of 2000 we were scarcely talking at all. The more I had become wrapped up in the business of winning Orders of Merit, the less time I had for Eimear and the children.

I have to admit that I found it difficult to blame myself for any of our problems at that stage. I saw myself as a good husband: I was neither a womaniser nor a drinker, while I always hurried home at the end of every tournament. When press people asked why I did not have an elongated spell in America in order to boost my chances of winning a Major, I would explain that family came first. I said I was not prepared to uproot Eimear and the children and take them over there, and, by the same token, I was not prepared to go over there on my own for anything more than a couple of weeks at a time. Eimear, as I now know, reached the point where she felt like screaming when I said such things. As she would explain, I might have been home in person but I was never there in spirit. Mentally, I was a million miles away.

May 2000 was a bad month in our relationship, with things going downhill in a big way at the Benson and Hedges at the Belfry. I had been well placed to get within striking distance of Darren Clarke on the 2000 Order of Merit when

I signed off with a bogey. Instead of a top-three finish, I ended up in an anticlimactic fifth place. On that Sunday everyone's sympathy centred on Padraig Harrington, the tournament leader who was disqualified when it came to light that he had failed to sign his first-round scorecard. The trauma attached to my departure went entirely unnoticed. Though Eimear and the children had driven up for the final round, I was not to be consoled by any of them. They drove back in the car in which they had come and I went home alone.

The hurt Eimear felt was compounded when, the following week, I asked her to leave midway through the third round of the Volvo PGA Championship at Wentworth. Though not too many weeks before I had referred to her as an inspiration as I won in France, I was now saying that she was a distraction. That was hugely upsetting for her and it set her thinking further about the effect my attitude was having on the family as a whole. The then seven-year-old Olivia, for example, had started to concern herself with my scoring. She knew that the mood in our household was apt to mirror where I stood in relation to par.

Eimear has since talked of the pressures attached to having to come across as 'the perfect family' at this point: she said it was harder and harder to keep up. What got to her more than anything was that there were no periods of relief. Even if I won a tournament, I did not stop to celebrate. I merely started fretting about the next event on the calendar. Everyone was walking on eggshells and Eimear was becoming desperate, not least because of my growing tendency to snap at the children for nothing. She could not tolerate that.

Following the Wentworth incident she made a conscious decision to withdraw some of the support she had given so freely for so long. She travelled to fewer tournaments and stopped what had amounted to a twenty-four-hour telephone helpline service.

Things finally came to a head at the Open at St Andrews. We had been at the Scottish Open at Loch Lomond in the second week in July and, on the Sunday, we had gone as a family to the opening of the Colin Montgomerie Golf Academy at Turnberry. Everything on that trip had revolved around me, and, since we were going straight to St Andrews for the Open, that was not about to change.

The house on Market Street that IMG had booked for the family was very much a part of that picture, the perfect setting from which to tackle the oldest Major of them all. We were just finishing the unpacking when Eimear broke our silence to draw attention to a dinner invitation we had received from close friends at home. It was for the Tuesday after the Open and the time had come when she would have to reply. Did I think I would want to go?

I said that I was not prepared to think about it. 'I haven't got a clue,' I said, irritated. I was more interested in fixing a time to meet Alastair at the course the following morning.

A little later, when Eimear dared to broach the subject again and got a similarly unhelpful response, she snapped. Eyeing me with cold contempt, she announced that she had finally had enough. Golf, she pronounced, had taken over my life to the point where I would do better on my own. She was superfluous. The marriage might as well be over. In fact, it was over in her eyes. Having said as much, she walked from the room.

We both have short fuses but she had never spoken to me like that before. I knew at once that this was serious. My overriding feeling was one of fury. What was she doing on the eve of the Open – and not just any Open, but the Millennium Open? No one would forget the winner of this one. Half of me wanted to scream at her, but a house in Market Street, with the windows open and the town filled with golfing folk, was no place to get involved in a slanging match. Instead of retaliating, I put my head down and walked into the St Andrews night.

Open visitors were everywhere, meeting up with old friends on corners and spilling out from the bars, the restaurants and the fish and chip shops. I stormed past the lot of them and I think they must have recognised that this was no time to be asking for autographs. Before too long, I had left their hauntingly merry chatter behind. Having turned into South Street, I headed in the direction of the churchyard and the twin towers of St Rule and St Regulus. From there, I walked along the coast and ended up at the little harbour. This was the harbour to which Young Tom Morris had made his sad return in 1875. He had been across the Forth at North Berwick playing in an exhibition match with his father and Mungo Park, and, while he was there, he had received word that his young wife, who was expecting their first child, had been taken ill at their house in St Andrews. He hurried home and, on arrival in St Andrews, learned that he was too late. Six months later, he himself died of a broken heart. Although, at that stage, I was feeling wronged and self-righteous, I thought fleetingly of how I would feel if Eimear were not there for me. The prospect was appalling.

I rang Hugh Mantle and Guy Kinnings. I wanted to know what they thought of what had happened. I wanted their help in understanding Eimear, but, as much as that, I was seeking reassurance that they, like me, thought she was being thoroughly unreasonable. Hugh, though he could not have been more tactful, sensed at once what was going on. Back in 1996, he had been faced with the choice of working with British teams at the 1996 Olympics in Atlanta or staying at home with a wife who was clearly craving some attention. He chose the Olympics and it cost him his marriage. I asked if he could come up to St Andrews, but he said that our meeting could wait until after the Open. He then worked on calming me down. Some time afterwards, he would tell me that he had been less concerned about the longer term than the next five minutes. He did not, as he said, want me to do anything stupid. Gradually, he impressed on me that marriages do not go wrong overnight. He said it would have taken a long time to reach the situation we were in and that it would take a long time to sort things out.

Guy was as supportive as he always is. He listened to what I was saying, and, without taking sides, made it clear that he wanted the best for Eimear and for me. I got back to Market Street, where the door had been left open, and sank into the sofa for the night.

I practised on the Monday and again on the Tuesday before Eimear and I went to St Andrews University for a ceremony at which Seve Ballesteros and I were to receive honorary degrees. Both Seve and I saw this as a great honour, especially since the only other players to have been so honoured are Bobby Jones, Jack Nicklaus and Gary Player. Though people may have noticed that Eimear was quiet, she did not make it obvious that we were barely speaking.

When there is something wrong with a golfer's marriage, I can confidently report that the first place it shows is on the greens. Drives and long irons are not a problem because they are, relatively speaking, over in the proverbial flash. Putting, on the other hand, requires an elongated bout of concentration for which you are not equipped. Your mind wanders all over the place. I was never going to beat Tiger that year but, had I putted even half decently, I could have finished second. All it would have taken was an average of two putts per green.

After three rounds, all of which provided a welcome escape from the growing tension in Market Street, I was lying comfortably inside the top ten. I was taking aim on second place and was shaping up pretty well when, all of a sudden, events caught up with me. The fact that I had spotted Eimear and Heather, our nanny, in the crowd may or may not have had anything to do with it. Either way, I suddenly broke down in tears, with the defining moment when I hit a second-rate chip to the twelfth green. It was never going to take much to send me over the edge at that point and that chip, even though it would normally have rated nothing more than my usual slumped shoulders and angry glare, was enough. To this day, I don't know what my playing companion, Vijay Singh, made of what was going on, but all credit to him in the way he kept his thoughts to himself.

Until then, I had not confided in anyone other than Hugh and Guy. Now, when Alastair asked if I wanted to walk in, I shook my head. 'I need to talk,' I told him. 'Forget the yardages and let me tell you what's going on.' Alastair was always a great listener. That afternoon he handed me a club when the need arose but we never discussed what it was or what I should do with it. Nor, which was maybe just as well, did we give a moment's thought to the line of the putts. If I had waited at all, I would not have been able to see through the tears. I was on automatic pilot and stayed that way over the last six holes. When I got back to base and the little cluster of press people standing beyond the R&A's bay window started asking me what I had hit to the seventeenth green, it was as much as I could do not to yell at them, 'What the hell does it matter?'

The atmosphere between Eimear and myself was impossible as we drove home on the Monday. And so it went on over the coming weeks until it became clear that, for the sake of the children as much as anyone else, we would be better off apart while we considered our respective futures.

I moved up to the third floor of the family house and then I decided I must move out. But where was I to go? Without putting too much thought into it, I headed for the Hilton at Chelsea Harbour and asked for a room overlooking the water. I can remember going up in the elevator and finding my room. I can remember opening the door and I can remember shutting it. I can remember breaking down.

As I lay there, the success I had had in golf and such adulation as had come my way from crowds inside Europe and beyond suddenly seemed so meaningless. Six months or so before, I had said in an interview that I would have no interest in winning championships if it were a matter of taking the trophies back to an empty home. Now I was beginning to get an inkling of what it would mean and I was not sure I could cope.

There was no way I was going to sleep that night. Instead, I started tramping the streets of London. From Chelsea Harbour, I went up the King's Road, and from there round Sloane Square and up Sloane Street past Harrods before returning to the hotel in the small hours.

I had a week away for a Skins game in California, but aside from that I spent a month at the Hilton in which I left the hotel at about ten o'clock each night and would return foot-weary and heavy-hearted at three in the morning, or even later. One night I would head towards the West End and the next I would go to Putney and Stamford Bridge. All my golfing life I have had to fight a weight problem but now I was losing a couple of pounds a day. The misery diet is what I christened it.

Sometimes people would look at me with recognition in their faces but then they would think again. It couldn't be Colin Montgomerie, the golfer, walking the streets at this hour of the night. If there were people who stared at me, I did a bit of staring myself. I was disturbed by the sight of 'regular' families. Every time I saw one, maybe in McDonald's or one of the other restaurants I frequented, such as the Good Earth, I felt like going up to them and saying, 'Do you realise how lucky you are?'

By day, I spent a lot of time at IMG's office in Chiswick, either indulging my fetish for cleaning my car or talking to

Guy. I also went on daytime walks that were almost as long and lonely as the night-time trudging. Harrods was a favourite stopping point, simply because it is a good place to waste time. Should the need ever arise, I could get a job behind one of their information desks, for I got to know my way round the store like I know my way around the Rules of Golf.

Now we were into December, there was one department I avoided like the plague: the Christmas department. For one with a heavy heart such as mine, there was nothing more painful than the sound of Christmas carols and bells. What was going to happen to me when the holidays started properly?

Guy had taken on the role of Eimear's and my intermediary and I had heard through him that she wanted to go ahead with a version of a holiday we had booked to Barbados. Some months before, we had arranged to stay in a villa belonging to the former Davis Cup captain, David Lloyd. Eimear's adaptation involved the holiday being split down the middle: she would go out with the children on 23 December and come back on 3 January; I, in turn, would fly out to Barbados on the third and take over. I could not believe that that was what she wanted but, not wanting to upset her more than I seemed to have done already, I indicated that I would go along with whatever she suggested. If the truth be known, I was beginning to despair. The only thing that kept me going was the way in which all three of Guy, Hugh and Alastair continued to be positive. What they were saying was what I needed to hear.

The first glimmer of hope – and I have to admit that it was no more than the merest gleam – came after the Million Dollar tournament in Sun City. The tournament itself had been a nightmare for, great place though it is to be with your family, Sun City is no place to be on your own. I could not face being alone any more than I could face the social functions the players are supposed to attend. I lasted no longer than ten minutes at one party, while I had no appetite for the annual barbecue in the game park. It had been arranged – again through Guy – that I could have the children the following weekend and, once I had escaped Sun City, I set up shop in the IMG office and organised a weekend to remember. I did not want help from Heather or anyone else. It was important that I should organise everything from start to finish and, in the process, demonstrate to Eimear that I was entirely capable of looking after my own children.

By then, I had moved out of the Hilton and taken a three-bedroomed apartment on a three-month lease in a block called Hyde Park Residence, which lies between the Dorchester and Grosvenor House. It was the perfect base from which to run the children's weekend.

I drove out to Oxshott early on the Saturday morning to pick them up before stopping off to get the car washed. (This time for Cameron's benefit rather than mine.) After that, we headed for Regent's Park Zoo and from there it was on to the Rainforest Café for tea. Then we watched a video of *The Sound of Music* back at the flat before I put them to bed.

The next morning we went to the Millennium Dome, where I had asked the chief executive Pierre-Yves Gerbeau, whom I knew, to show us round. I was not looking for the VIP treatment for myself. I simply wanted to make the most of the experience as far as Olivia, Venetia and Cameron were concerned. Others may have poured scorn on the Dome but, not least because of the fun the children had that day, you won't hear me say a bad word about it.

After seeing everything there was to see, we had lunch at Harry Ramsden's before setting off for home. I stopped on the way so that Olivia could buy her mum chocolates, and as I let them out at the gates and drove off, I knew that I was delivering three happy children. At no time had I said to any

of them that they should tell their mother that they had
enjoyed themselves but, a couple of days later, Eimear sent
me a text message: 'Thanks for giving them a good time.'

The weekend had worked from another point of view. It
was not until I had the three of them to myself for those two
days that I began to understand the accusations that Eimear
had been levelling at me. I saw then that we had not been like
a normal family doing normal things. Eimear and the
children were a thriving little unit but my contribution was
nowhere near what it should have been. She was right in
what she had said about golf meaning too much to me. In
the nicest possible way Hugh, too, had noted that the
marriage had been a one-way affair in which I had not been
listening enough to Eimear to get any feedback. I had had my
job to do and I had taken it for granted that she would hold
the fort at home. As Hugh said, there are plenty of women
who will happily play that role to the exclusion of all else, but
the girl I married was not one of them. Much though she
loved her family, she longed to be a person in her own right
rather than just a kept woman. True, she had been happy for
me to be the one pursuing a career, but I had never really
thought about the extent to which she had had to write off
her own ambitions. I realised that Hugh was right when he
said I would have to learn to give my spouse her head a bit,
allow her room for personal development.

Hugh had also put me right on my theory that Eimear had
an easy time of it as I made the money. Though I had never
blinked at the cost of some of her designer clothes, largely
because no one could look better in them than she does, I
had failed to see the other side of the coin. Hugh wondered
if I appreciated just how well she had adjusted to our relative
wealth, with particular reference to bringing up the children
in a rich environment.

Eimear and I started to exchange regular text messages
after the children's weekend, but my spirits sagged when I

learned that the two-shift Barbados holiday was to go ahead. Eimear and the children would be leaving on the 23rd without me.

By way of an antidote to the pain I was feeling, I had a couple of schemes up my sleeve. First, I had decided to spend Christmas Day working with the homeless in London. Second, I had this wild idea of chartering a yacht in Antigua and mooring it outside the Lloyds' villa on 2 January, the day before I was meant to take over. It was to be a romantic gesture, a final thrust which, I hoped, might win over Eimear. Guy, perhaps by way of humouring me, said it was a brilliant idea.

Putting the finishing touches to the yacht arrangement kept me busy, but when it came to the 23rd all I could think of was Eimear and the children. Where were they? How could they be doing this to me?

I knew that their flight landed in Barbados at four o'clock and that at ten o'clock my time they would be moving into the villa and hopefully ringing to say they had arrived safely. The more the evening wore on, the more miserable I became. I ordered a pizza and watched football without even registering who was playing. At 10.10, the call came. There was then a long silence and a lot of crackles before Eimear got through. She confirmed that all was well before waxing lyrical about the villa. I asked about the children and then I asked about the weather, only to be interrupted.

'The children need a father and I need a husband. You'd better get out here,' she said.

Normally, I ask for seat 1A on a flight. That night, when BA told me their Christmas Eve flight was full, I told them that I would travel in the toilet as long as I got on. The following morning I learned that I was in luck. BA found me a seat. I got together a haphazard selection of clothes, tossed them in a suitcase, cancelled the yacht and got myself to Gatwick airport.

Eimear did not come and meet me at the other end. Instead, I took a cab to the house, walked through the unlocked door and found her and the children on the beach. It was some moment and the start of our new life together.

We had a wonderful Christmas, the best ever. Because there were babysitters to hand, Eimear and I were able to spend plenty of time together. We went out for dinners, we walked along the beach and we talked as we had never talked before, not even in our courting days.

Back home, the tabloid papers' interest in what was going on was reaching fever pitch. Guy was fielding a dozen or more calls a day from news reporters wanting to know what was happening in the marriage. Was it on, was it off? For months people had been tipping them off about our problems and now they were desperate for answers. So desperate that they were 'door-stepping' the house and even peering from a helicopter to ascertain whether we were together or apart. Though Guy's latest bulletin was that Eimear and I had enjoyed a holiday in Barbados and that the marriage was fine, the newspapermen still had their doubts.

By the end of January, all the indications were that at least one of the papers was planning an exclusive on the Montgomerie marriage. Though all our friends had been pretty discreet, it seems that there were enough snippets of information flying around for the newshounds to have pieced together a story of sorts. The broadsheets had an equally good idea of what was afoot, and, because there was no sign of their interest abating, Eimear and I decided to co-operate with the *Daily Telegraph* in giving our side of the story as to how my obsession with golf had come close to wrecking our lives together.

We were nervous on the night of Friday, 19 January. The article was to appear the next day and, as you would imagine, we were having second thoughts about whether we had done the right thing. It was with some trepidation that we opened the paper on the Saturday morning. There, sprawled right across the front of the Saturday sports section, was a picture of me looking out of sorts, along with a brief confession by way of a headline: 'Life can't be much fun for the wife of any top sportsman who becomes as ambitious, dedicated and blinkered as I was. I started to put golf ahead of my family.'

A lot of home truths came out in that piece, mostly because I had wanted to make a clean breast of everything for the sake of the woman I loved. 'The reality of the situation,' I told the *Telegraph*, 'is that money doesn't matter as much as I thought it did, neither does winning tournaments … I would sooner be married to Eimear and have my children around me than win any number of tournaments.'

There was also our joint vision of the future … From now on, we would not be papering over the cracks in our marriage but addressing problems as they arose. Golf would no longer be the only subject of conversation. There would be room for Eimear and the children as well as me to have problems. Towards the end of the article, I admitted to having learned 'a painful but vital lesson'.

Not long after we had nervously scanned the article, the phone started to ring. One friend got in touch, then another. They all said how much they admired us for having spoken out about our problems. A few admitted that their marriages were in much the same mess as ours had been and that our experiences had given them inspiration to sort things out. There were text messages wishing us luck and, over the next few days, there were letters from all over the world, including one from a lady in India with whom Eimear corresponds to this day. People would come up and shake me by the hand at tournaments.

I think Denis Pugh is right when he says that the way in which I made an honest breast of things was the start of people beginning to see me in a rather better light. Until then, they had thought of me as someone who had led a pretty gilded life, what with my seven Orders of Merit, my prize-money and my beautiful wife. Now they realised that I was not too different from the rest of them.

Chapter 16

TIGER WOODS

It is an old tale but one that has passed into the folklore of the game: Sandy Lyle's reaction in the early 1980s to the first time he heard of Tiger Woods. Someone asked, 'What do you think of Tiger Woods?' and Sandy replied, 'Sorry, I've never played there.'

I have to admit that I would have been similarly caught out at that juncture. I knew nothing of Tiger, and it is only in recent years that I have become aware of his extraordinary beginnings in the game: of how he would sit in his high chair and watch his father hit balls into a net before one day picking up a toy club and ball and reproducing his father's shots to perfection. Earl Woods called to his wife, Kultida, and said, 'We have a genius on our hands.'

I liked the story of what happened on the day when the toddler Tiger was asked to appear on the *Mike Douglas Show*. Bob Hope, who was appearing in the line-up of the same show, challenged Tiger to a putting contest. When Tiger missed three straight putts, he got angry, grabbed the ball and threw it in the cup before complaining to the host that his improvised green was a disaster: it was impossible to read. Apparently, Douglas laughed out loud at the very idea of a two-year-old attempting to read a green.

Rudy Doran, Tiger's first coach, has written a book, *In Every Kid There Lurks a Tiger*, which includes his first impressions when Kultida Woods brought her four-year-old son for a lesson at the Heartwell Golf Park in Long Beach, California. 'The three of us,' said Doran, 'walked to the range, where the boy pulled a sawed-off 21½-inch wood from his bag. I teed up a few balls and he hit them one after another. He was in perfect balance and he hit each ball 60 to 70 yards with a nice draw. Tiger's mannerisms were like those of a very experienced player, yet I knew he couldn't be very experienced because he was only four. After watching a few more swings, I was convinced that Tiger wasn't a typical junior golfer. It doesn't take long to identify genius.'

Doran went on to liken the four-year-old Tiger to the greatest golfer in history. 'If', he said, 'you could have taken Jack Nicklaus and shrunk him down to that size, that's what you would have had.'

It was as a four-year-old that Tiger arrived home one day with a pocket filled with quarters. When he said he had won them from other boys on the putting green, his father said he was not to play for quarters again. The next time, he came home with his pockets stuffed with dollar notes. It would seem to be pretty clear that Tiger knew precisely where he was headed. When, at six, he was invited to conduct an exhibition match with Sam Snead, the old champion gave Tiger his autograph at the end of the proceedings. Tiger coolly responded by giving his to Snead. At ten, Tiger announced that he would be studying accountancy at college. 'Why?' his father asked. 'So that I can manage the people who manage my money,' he explained.

At that period, as John Strege reveals in his excellent biography of Tiger, *Golf Digest* published a list of Jack Nicklaus's accomplishments and the age at which he had achieved them. Tiger cut out the relevant pages and pinned them to his bedroom wall. 'That was his guide and his goals were set by it,' said Earl. While Nicklaus broke 50 for nine holes for the first time at the age of nine, Tiger did as much at the age of three. While Nicklaus broke 80 at twelve, Woods achieved that feat at eight. And when it came to breaking 70, Nicklaus was thirteen to Woods's twelve.

Tiger would have seen me as a complete amateur as I hung around the children's course at Troon in my earliest years and finally broke 100 for the first time at Ilkley at the age of fourteen. I remember being given a can of Coke to celebrate.

The first time I became aware of Tiger would have been when he was twelve or thirteen years of age and was breaking every record in the junior game. If I gave a weary sigh and said I had heard it all before, I apologise. People are always eulogising over gifted youngsters, but how many of these kids ever come to anything? In any case, I was far too busy trying to beat players of the stature of Nick Faldo and Sandy Lyle to start worrying about a slip of a junior. Or so I thought.

Gradually we heard the name more and more. When he was fifteen, Tiger won the first of three successive US Junior Championships. When he was eighteen, the age at which I was striving to win the first of my Scottish youth caps, he won the first of three successive US Amateurs. That would take some doing in any circumstances but it was the way he won them that was so significant. In the 1993 championship, when he was playing Trip Kuehne, he was six down after thirteen holes of the thirty-six-hole final and still five down with twelve to play. He won at the last. He did much the same, if rather less spectacularly, to beat the forty-three-year-old George Marucci at the Newport Country Club the following year. The third win, at Pumpkin Ridge, had echoes of the first. This time, he was up against Steve Scott, a player who was a year younger than he was. Tiger was five down at lunch and furious with himself. He knew that if he had putted even half decently, he would have been no more than two behind. In a short practice session before the afternoon instalment, Butch Harmon pointed to his posture as the source of his problems, not just on his putting but on all his shots. Tiger made the necessary adjustment and went out and cut the deficit to one in the space of the first nine holes. He was back to two down playing the thirty-fourth and less experienced spectators than Scott's relatives might well have been tempted into counting their chickens. Instead, Tiger forced his way into a play-off and won at the second extra hole. His afternoon round that day had been the equivalent of a 65. He described it as the best round of his life.

I watched him on TV that day for half an hour or so and was flabbergasted by the way he seemed capable of coming up with the miraculous to order. I felt that he could not fail to take the professional world by storm.

He was nineteen and still an amateur when he played in the Masters for the first time. Then, all the talk in the locker room was of how far he hit the ball. I honestly don't think that the field as a whole had begun to understand how good he was. What is more, when he finished in a share of forty-first place, assorted pundits seemed to be tumbling over each other to prophesy that if he were going to come up to expectations, he would need to find some control to go with his length.

My next memory of Tiger at Augusta is of playing with him on the third day in 1997. He was three ahead of me and we were the last group. I was in the midst of my run of heading the Order of Merit and not short of confidence. However, when it came to hitting from the first tee, I was as nervous as I have ever been. Like it or not, I was in awe of the young man. Tiger had the honour and there was a chorus of amazed 'oohs!' as his ball flew the fairway bunker with miles to spare. I was expecting my effort to be puny by comparison but, as luck would have it, my ball cannoned off the back of the bunker and I ended up with the longer drive: not by much but it was Tiger to play first. We both hit wedges and both started with fours. As we left the green, I thought to myself, I can handle this.

Then came the 575-yard second and that was the last I saw of him. He hit a drive which, in my mind's eye, is still bounding down the fairway. Plenty of players arrive at the point he reached but they get there in two shots rather than one. He was 150 yards from the green and needed nothing more than a nine iron for his second. I realised then that the course was made for Tiger. Ordinary mortals can seldom go for the pins at Augusta, but he could. He did it time and again, and, after knocking a three wood and a sand-wedge to a foot at the eighteenth – Ian Woosnam needed a driver and an eight iron when he won in 1991 – he returned the easiest of 65s. His aggregate was 201, and he was nine shots clear of Costantino Rocca.

I, meantime, had shot a 74 in which the only thing wrong was that I had been mesmerised by seeing what I knew to be history in the making. At the end of that Saturday I was shell-shocked rather than angry as I sat in the vast media auditorium. The first question the press had for me was whether I thought that Tiger would go on to win. 'Of course he'll win,' I said. 'What's more, he'll win by more than nine shots.'

'How can you be so sure?' they pressed.

'Because Tiger's not Greg Norman and Rocca's not Faldo,' I returned, in a reference to how Norman had been six shots ahead of Faldo in 1996 but ended up losing. There was no disrespect intended towards either Norman or Rocca. It was simply that Tiger, with his length, was not playing the same course as the rest of us, and Rocca did not have the experience to do a Faldo.

I went on to explain that I had just had a close-up of what Tiger was really like. I had studied the way he worked with his caddie and I had seen the look in his eyes as he stood over a putt. He stared the ball into the hole in a way that went fathoms deeper than anything I had seen before. I also went back to the question of his length. He was forty yards longer than I was and presumably most others were. That had to make a huge difference to him; it would do to anyone.

Sure enough, Tiger went on to win by twelve. We were all humbled by his performance. I remember wondering if anyone else would ever get a look in at the Masters in Tiger's time, but then, of course, we had three different winners – Mark O'Meara, José Maria Olazábal and Vijay Singh – before he won again in 2001 and 2002.

He may have had a slight lull before the 2002 instalment, but, as I wrote in my newspaper column at the start of Masters week, he was still by tenfold the best player. We have had other world number ones whose skills in the different areas, when you put them together, were just enough to have them ahead of the next person. Tiger, though, has got to the top by being the best in all departments.

At the 2002 Deutsche Bank SAP Open at St Leon-Rot, where I would lose to Tiger on the third play-off hole, one of the journalists had asked how you should think when going head-to-head with him. I replied that since he did everything so much better than the next man, you could only think about scoring better than him on the day. Simple in theory, but not so simple when it comes to putting it into practice.

For Tiger, of course, ordinary tournaments are no more than ordinary tournaments. He is playing with the Majors in mind. Nothing is ever for sure in this game but, if things go according to Tiger's 'Major' plan, he will always be there or thereabouts on the Friday before making his move at the weekend. The third day always seems to be Tiger day. A lot of people lose Majors in the third round but he doesn't. However, as people will be quick to note, that did not apply in the 2002 Open at Muirfield where he amassed an 81 through the wind-lashed downpours on the Saturday.

Because of the round I had alongside Tiger at the 1997 Masters, I was probably as quick as any of the players to face up to the truth about him. That day, as he played a game so far beyond my ken, I looked at him not just as a fellow player but, with the business background I had had at Houston

Baptist coming to the fore, in the marketing sense. I thought that he would turn the game upside down and that prize-money in the States and elsewhere would shoot through the roof. Seven men have changed the course of world golf. My list would start with Arnold Palmer and it would take in Mark McCormack, who turned Palmer into the sort of star the game had never known. After those two, I would put Jack Nicklaus and Gary Player. Then came Greg Norman and Seve Ballesteros before coming to Tiger.

No one knocks him any more. Such jealousy as there was has mostly given way to wide-eyed admiration, with special reference to the manner in which he handles his success. But there is no question that he pays a high price for it. There are all sorts of things in everyday life that he cannot begin to do.

Mark O'Meara gave a good illustration when he told of the day he and his wife Alicia decided that Tiger was becoming too much of a hermit and that they would take him out to Wendy's, or some such place, for his supper. The outing was fine for the first five minutes but, all of a sudden, a waitress cottoned on to who was in the room and started to scream. At this point, an American journalist, just in case the audience needed such help, interrupted the story with a bright enquiry as to how Mark knew they weren't screaming for him. Any-how, the upshot of it all was that O'Meara and party had to make a quick exit. The outing had failed, dismally.

I think it was Lee Westwood who, along with his wife Laurae, suggested that Tiger and his girlfriend of the time might like to go with them to the cinema. Woods simply explained, quietly, that it could not work.

I have played with Tiger on several occasions now and, apart from demanding a first-hand account of some of the shots he has played, people want to hear about Tiger the person. What did he talk about during the course of those rounds? The answer is the same every time: cars, women and where he went to supper the night before.

As everyone knows, he is a great sport and a generous rival. I have always been amazed at his depth of knowledge concerning other players, and not just those on the US Tour. There have been several times when I have heard him refer to some unsung player's record.

That Tiger has always embraced the larger golfing world is something for which we should all be grateful. The last thing you would want is to have a player in his position who was only interested in lining his own pockets.

Chapter 17

WAYS OF LEARNING

At the 2002 Smurfit European Open, someone showed me a couple of press handouts in which Padraig Harrington and Michael Campbell had talked about my 'low-maintenance' swing. Harrington, after being asked about how hard he worked on his game, began by saying that he envied those who did not have to work as hard as he does. 'I look around me at guys on tour and the ones that make me jealous are those with low-maintenance golf swings. Monty's action is a classic instance. It doesn't matter if he hasn't played for three months. He doesn't have to go looking for his swing because it's there and that's a great situation to be in.' Campbell gave me a mention when he was talking of how he was trying to get rid of the swing thoughts swirling round in his head. Sometimes he had as many as five on the go in the course of a single swing. 'Monty,' he said, 'is a feel player, someone who doesn't need swing thoughts in his mind. He just goes out there and plays.'

I was flattered by what I read. My interpretation of what they were saying is that my swing has two dimensions to it rather than three. There is a back motion and a forward motion and I don't have to worry about taking the club round my body, like an Ian Woosnam, any more than I need to know where my hands are halfway up the backswing.

It was only when I came a bit unstuck after my seven years at the top that I began to appreciate the extent to which others have to graft at this game. When Denis Pugh tried to get me back into my habitual groove and asked me to pay attention to a couple of small points, I was really struggling to accommodate them. Until then, just about my only thoughts concerned course management. When people ask where I got my swing, the answer I give them is that it came from Troon. As a child, I would have seen my father and everyone else swinging golf clubs every day because Troon, as everyone knows, is like St Andrews in being given over to golf. My interpretation of how these men and women were playing the game is what you see today: my action remains unchanged and, as I mentioned earlier, there are plenty of pictures to prove the point. My father would make the odd suggestion when he saw me departing from what I usually did but, to all intents and purposes, my action was ninety-nine per cent natural. To me, the game was – and still is – simple rather than scientific.

What Bill Ferguson got so right when I first went to him for lessons was to leave well alone. He would have realised that my swing was a bit different from the norm but he recognised that it would be madness to introduce change. Though he kept half an eye on my basics, Bill taught me most by giving me the opportunity to caddie for him in local professional events. He was making me 'streetwise' in the golfing sense. He also came up with one brilliant piece of advice that is worth passing on to anyone who is about to embark on a professional career: 'Wear earplugs when you go to the practice range.' There are lots of professionals who would say I am too busy chatting out there to listen to anything, but there have been plenty of times when I have practised next to someone who is taking a lesson that I have had to make a deliberate effort to tune out from what is being said. The moment you hear a coach telling someone that his hands are too high/too low or that his wrists are not pronating properly, you immediately start asking yourself,

'Where are my hands? What about my wrists?' It is because I have listened to Bill Ferguson on this score – I always listened to Bill – that I have not incorporated too much of anyone else's game into my own.

If there were one player who has influenced me above the rest it would be Nick Faldo. Through playing alongside him in the Ryder Cup, I picked up all manner of little tips about 'big-time' golf. For instance, when the pressure was really on, he would advocate a count to three by way of a prelude to taking the putter back. It was easier than taking it back from scratch. I was also influenced by his confidence. Talking about getting a hole-in-one on a particular hole, and then doing it the following day as he did in the 1993 Ryder Cup, is the ultimate. Another thing I noticed as Nick and I worked in tandem in the Ryder Cup was that his preparation was on a different plane to everyone else's. He was physically fit at a time when fitness was still seen as something of an optional extra, while he also concerned himself with matters to which the rest of us would never have given a second thought. It was not enough for his golf-glove to fit well: it had to fit to perfection and the same applied to everything else he wore. I marvelled at what he was doing but, as Nick would be the first to say, his preparations paled in comparison with those of Tiger Woods today. He has raised the bar as never before. Nick Faldo, who has often said that he wished he had had access to the same knowledge as Woods when he was his age, was amazed when he worked out alongside Tiger in the gym for the first time. He could not believe his upper-body strength, with particular reference to his bulging biceps.

Where Woods is unique is in his metronomic daily preparation. Though a lot of us would be tempted to do the bare minimum before, say, a seven-thirty starting time, he will get up at four o'clock in order to do everything as per usual. He will go for a three- or four-mile run before moving on to his usual quota of stretches in the gym. That done, he will put in precisely the same solid stint on the practice ground as he would before a mid-morning start. I doubt whether I could ever go to such lengths, even though it has become increasingly apparent that I cannot afford to be slack about the physical fitness side of things if I am to keep the wear and tear on my back in check. Unless I diet and work on building up my core muscles to help take the strain, I can only expect more of the problems that have surfaced in the last couple of years.

The truth is that all of us on tour who like our food have been made to think. Darren Clarke and Lee Westwood are two more in the same mould as I am, in that their weight tends to go up and down. But, just when you think that there is no future for anyone less than svelte, you see the comfortably contoured Craig Parry cleaning up in the 2002 NEC in Seattle. I have to admit, it was a reassuring sight.

Seve Ballesteros, though he may not know it, was another of my teachers. I played with him for the first time in the 1990 Swiss Masters and was feeling more than a little apprehensive because he was such a big star as far as the rest of us were concerned. We shook hands on the first tee and, two minutes later, we were shaking hands again after I had holed my second for an albatross. (I bagged all three of albatross, eagle and birdie in that round, which has to be a pretty rare feat.) Having shown Seve that I could play a bit with that opening two, I relaxed and was better placed to digest the way he played. I found myself almost wanting him to miss greens in order that I could see him getting up and down. I remember saying to myself, 'He can't get up and down from there, can he?' and the answer, invariably, was that he could.

Who could forget the 1991 Volvo PGA Championship at Wentworth when he hit a buggy off the tee? He was left with 216 yards to the green and everyone was shaking his head at his sad demise when he drew a five iron round the trees and left it next to the hole to win the tournament with a three to my four.

In the 1989 European Masters at Crans, he was in rough and just short of a wall with his drive before making his escape en route to an unlikely four. That particular piece of golfing legerdemain is recalled on a plaque, though you might struggle to find it because it is so far removed from the beaten track. Another instance of his pulling off the impossible came when he won the 1983 Masters. Having duffed his first chip, he blithely holed out with his next attempt.

Being exposed to Seve's brilliance changed my whole perspective on what was possible. But there was something concrete to be learned as well. For all his more spectacular shots, his swing was slow and his head kept well down. When the rest of us tackle difficult shots, the temptation is there to look up as you hit the ball and sometimes even earlier. Seve never did.

The amount he cared about his golf took me aback. He kept it welled up inside him until suddenly it was there for all to see as we lost the 1993 Ryder Cup. José Maria Olazábal is another to care to the same degree, and, had I been a caddie, I would have wanted to work for one of them because neither ever gives up. Just look at Seve today and you will see that he remains convinced that he is going to win again.

Greg Norman is another to have left his stamp on the way I play. You cannot win at this game all the time, and, though I have a pretty good strike rate in having won once in every ten or so attempts, you have to be able to accept failure. As Gary Player has always said, golf is one game where even the best player loses more often than he wins. If not on so public a stage, everyone has days such as the one Norman had at the 1996 Masters when he was six ahead but ended up losing to Nick Faldo. I felt terrible for him, but what made a deeper impression on me that Sunday afternoon was the press conference he gave immediately after he had lost. He took his disappointment so well, and, as a result, everything else in his life remained unscathed. At Augusta, they used to have a dinner for international players on the Monday night. Those members of the 'international set' who had won the Masters would be on the top table in their green jackets, and I will never forget studying Norman in 1997, twelve months after his horrific last-day experience. He was wearing his own fawn jacket and you could almost see him thinking back to how close he had come to graduating to the top table.

Last but by no means least among the players who have influenced the Montgomerie game would be Freddie Couples. Like me, Freddie is a traditionalist, and it was intriguing for me to see such a strait-laced golfer using a belly putter in the Williams Challenge at the end of the 2001 season. He had had a 65 in the first round to my 74 and we happened to be starting out at the same time on the second day, Freddie from the first tee and me from the tenth. It was when we converged on the putting green that I asked him, 'What's that putter like?'

'It's the difference between night and day but more so,' he answered.

Since it was well known that Freddie had been starting to miss the five-footers before he made the switch, I began to think that it might work for me. Freddie could see how my mind was working. 'I've got a couple of spares,' he said. 'I'll give you one after the round.' He could see that I was backing off a bit and it did not take a moment for him to recognise that half of me did not want to be seen dead with a belly putter. 'Hey,' he said, 'we're not trying to paint pictures here. It's about getting the ball in the hole, isn't it?'

He said that when I was getting my own particular putter made up by Callaway I should pay particular attention to the length of the club. It had to be just right, sitting in the belly button without being too tight. Every time I lose a bit of weight, the club has to grow a little longer. I added half an inch midway through the 2002 season and I was expecting to add another inch by the end of the year.

When I won my seven Orders of Merit, I don't think I was ever higher than fortieth in the putting stats. At the time of the 2002 Smurfit European Open, I was up to two, with Michael Campbell, that week's winner, the only player ahead of me. My improvement was all down to the change of putter, but I cannot think how we are being allowed to use these longer implements. Long putters, be they anchored to the chin, the chest or the belly, all give the player the three pivotal points of two hands and body rather than just the two hands. You would never be allowed to have a brace that helped to keep your right arm on target when throwing a dart. Nor would you be allowed anything to steady the moving arm in snooker. It is extraordinary, to me, that golf officialdom has not acted on this score. Though it is hardly in my interests to say so, I think that all long putters – yes, all of them – should be declared illegal.

Chapter 18

EASY DOES IT

There were journalists at the 1997 Ryder Cup at Valderrama who could not believe what they were seeing.

When the teams were practising, each of the players had a set slot on the practice ground. Name-boards went up behind them in order that spectators could see, at a glance, who was who. Where, within a day or so, most of the others, with particular reference to José Maria Olazábal and Darren Clarke, had worn their areas bare, mine caught the eye for rather different reasons. Save for about ten or twelve divots, it was otherwise in pristine condition. Had those same journalists been regulars at the Dutch Open, they would have been still more taken aback. In 1996 I contrived to finish fourth in a week when I had done nothing more than hit a few balls into a handily placed practice net at the start of each day.

On to Congressional and the US Open of 1997, when I came so close to capturing the trophy. Having had a tiring week at Slaley Hall, which was compounded by that endless drive home on the Sunday night after I had won, I was anxious not to overdo things when I got to America. Hence the reason why I played only nine holes on the Tuesday and nine holes on the Wednesday. I was hitting the ball as well as I have ever hit it and all I needed was to stay in the groove.

When it came to the Thursday morning, I arranged to meet my caddie Alastair on the practice ground an hour ahead of my starting time. It was only as I emerged from the locker room that I realised I did not have a clue where the practice ground was. It hit me equally forcibly that, at this late stage, I would need to be careful whom I asked for instructions. There are one or two more mischievous players who would love to have passed that kind of information round Congressional.

I didn't practise that morning other than on the practice putting green, but handed in a 65 on my way to finishing the tournament in second place, a shot behind Ernie Els. Even now, there will almost certainly be readers who are saying, 'Well, it serves him right that he didn't win if he didn't practise.' But who can say whether it would have made any difference either way?

The one thing I know for sure is that I am not one of those to go along with Gary Player's 'The more I practise, the luckier I get' comment. Having said that, I must admit to a huge admiration for Gary and the effort he has put into the game on so many different fronts. He is a living legend who, in his later sixties, is still adding to his list of honours.

If you were to run through the top fifty on the world rankings, you would be right in picking out Vijay Singh as the player who works the hardest at a tournament. And myself, though I have been rather more conscientious in the last couple of seasons, as the player who spends the fewest hours on the practice ground. I do not, mind you, want to do Carlos Franco an injustice. He might argue that he should be considered for that bottom billing.

There was a time when I would spend long hours on a tournament practice ground simply because I did not want to be the odd one out. If, say, I were playing in the old-style Dunhill Championship – then a team event – or a Ryder Cup, I never wanted to lay myself open to anyone saying that

I was not giving it my best shot. It was for much the same reason that I headed for the range sixty minutes ahead of time on the last morning of the 2001 Open at Lytham when I was still seen as a possible winner. I did not want people saying, 'Where the hell is Monty? Why isn't he on the practice ground?' Once I got there, I spent a good fifteen minutes sitting in the caravan eating a burger before I started hitting balls.

The truth is that I have learned over the years that I am more likely to have a successful day when I limit myself to what I feel like doing. That way, I can be fresh when I get to the first tee. Also, as one who remains convinced that the new clubs and balls have at least as much as practice to do with improved standards, I genuinely believe that a lot of the work being done at tournament ranges around the world is not particularly productive. It may have something to do with a natural inclination to try to turn negatives into positives but, when I see a row of players working their tails off, I don't feel a pang of conscience. Instead, I tell myself that it is a good thing they are out there. To no small extent, some of them will be ingraining faults. Even if they are working feverishly on the right thing and have a coach looking over their shoulder, that is not to say that it will all come good on the course. I do not set much store by too many of the more clichéd golf sayings, but I definitely adhere to that old theory, 'If you haven't brought it with you, you won't find it here.'

I suspect that there are a number of players who would say that they are not too different from me, only their consciences probably dictate that they make a more sustained effort to come across as fiendishly hard-working. There are others who, if they were ruthlessly honest with themselves, would admit that a lot of the balls they hit are down to boredom. With not too much else to do on a tournament day away from home, they will hit balls to the point where they become addicted to hitting them. They could not stop if they wanted to, and that, as they will tell you in the tour's physiotherapy van, is not good news.

At the start of the 1999 English Open at Hanbury Manor, when Ian Woosnam had shut his fingers in a door and there were several bad backs making themselves felt, everyone seemed to be talking about injury problems. Guy Delacave, the Tour's head physiotherapist, said it was no coincidence that I had been relatively injury-free up to that point. Though I had always put it down to a combination of being lucky and relatively sensible – I would never, for example, follow the rest of the family in taking to the ski slopes – Delacave had other ideas. He maintained that my good attendance at tournaments owed most to the fact that I did not hit as many practice balls as the rest. He thought that one of the benefits from the lack of wear and tear on my joints was that I would enjoy a longer span on tour than most. 'I honestly think that there is a limit to the number of movements – swings and impacts – a body can take,' he said. However, as I would discover at the end of the 2001 season, I was not immune to back problems, though I have no doubt that they would have been worse if I had spent more time on the practice ground.

Apparently, Delacave suggested to Olazábal that it would be no bad idea if all the professionals were to follow my example. Olazábal, by all accounts, had looked at him a little quizzically and said that that was hardly possible. 'I would love to do the same as Monty, but the rest of us have to work,' he explained.

At the 1999 European Tour dinner at Wentworth, Olazábal gave a speech that created great merriment as he referred to his and my very different preparations for the last round of that year's Benson and Hedges International Open at the Oxfordshire. He said that things started with him hitting a big bucketful of balls and me hitting no more than ten or twelve shots. Then, as he moved on to put in some last-minute work on his short game, I sat down for a bacon roll with the caddies. After that, we had headed for the course where, as he said, with feigned fury at the injustice of it all, 'Monty left me for dead.'

During a tournament, practising, to me, should be about warming up, about hitting just enough balls to get yourself in the swing of things. That much is essential and, at this point, it is maybe worth recommending that any handicap golfer who is not in the habit of warming up before the off should take a look at the pattern of his or her scores. If he or she scores better on the homeward half, that would suggest to me that it would pay the player to hit a dozen balls before setting out.

In fairness to myself, when I am on the practice ground I will hit my handful of balls – let us say twenty-five at the maximum – as I mean to hit them on the course. True, I will do a lot of chatting between shots, but that is because I have always seen the practice ground as somewhere to relax rather than to get wound up about the round ahead. The last thing you want is to arrive on the first tee in a state of agitation.

Sometimes my fellow professionals are not too keen to chat. If the truth be told, there are quite a few of them who dread being anywhere near me on the range because they know it will not be too many minutes before I start talking. No one has ever told me to go away, though I must confess that there have been occasions when I have had to peer into their golf bags and pass comment on, say, their latest driver to get a conversation started.

At my Links Academy at Turnberry, I have asked that there should be no more than twenty-six balls in each of the warm-up bags. While that would not appeal to Vijay Singh, who likes to hit balls by the barrel, it is all the average man needs. It allows him two shots with every club in the bag.

While I have enjoyed my reputation as someone who can

usually turn up and carry on where he has left off, it would be entirely wrong to suggest that I have got away with murder all my life. There have been plenty of times when I have practised extremely hard. Not 'Vijay Singh' hard perhaps, or 'Swedish' hard, but inordinately hard for me. The first time I really applied myself was in teenage days when I was on holiday from Strathallan. Every morning I would go to the range at Ilkley, which, to me, is as inviting a practice ground as I have ever seen in all my golfing days. I would set forth with a drink and a picnic made up by my mother. I would also have a radio tuned in to Radio 2 and that would be me for the day. My signal to go home was when the midges came out in the evening.

Bill Ferguson was coaching me at the time, and every now and then he would wander across to the practice ground and say, 'Where the hell do you think you're aiming?' When I tired of hitting straightforward shots, I would experiment, seeing how the ball would react if, say, I put my hands forward or back. One way and another it all helped me to reach the point I am at now where I have the feeling that I know my own swing inside out. Even at the start of 2000, when I was struggling, I did not have too much of a correction to make. Denis Pugh, who is the professional at Wisley, where I play and practise, showed me a video of how I was swinging when I finished second to Ernie Els in the 1997 US Open. Then, I was keeping the club-face square for a good foot through the hitting area and that was something I had recently stopped doing. My swing had become too rounded.

I often thank my lucky stars that I never went in for the kind of wholesale changes adopted by some of my fellow professionals. I am sure, for example, that if Seve Ballesteros had remained with what worked for him in his earlier years and had not become fouled up in the mechanics of the game, he would have found things easier for longer.

In October 2001, when I was giving a clinic at my Turnberry academy to Europe's leading youngsters at the Lexus Under-21 Championships, I stressed the point that they should be wary of reinventing themselves if and when they turned professional. I said that there were far too many players whose first move was to embark on a sea of changes. They change their clubs because they are being offered money and they change their golf ball for the same reason. They then look at a change of coach and a change of swing, simply because people will have told them that they will have to do these things when they leave the amateur game. When I turned professional, I gave myself two years to make it with the swing that I had and, to my relief, it came up with the goods within that time-frame. The purists might say that it is too long and that it is not as per the textbook but, against that, it is a fluid action which repeats.

Schoolboy days apart, I practised hard during my time at university in Houston. We would finish classes at twelve-thirty and arrive at the golf club an hour later. Then we would play eighteen holes before spending half an hour chipping and maybe as much as an hour on the putting green. At weekends, when we were not away at a tournament, I would put in a good four to five hours' practice per day.

Nowadays, I practise as much as I need to practise to put something right. Quite often, I will be up at Wisley for an hour or an hour and a half on a Saturday morning. That is usually enough time to install a correction in the memory bank.

A number of professionals have a green or a bunker in their back garden. I have an Astroturf green that would run at a manageable ten on the stimpmeter. Cameron probably plays around on it more than I do, but I am out there if I have new putters to test or if I have a problem with my alignment.

It goes without saying that it's not just physical practice

that can make a difference to how you play on a given day. You have to be in a positive frame of mind when you arrive on the first tee. If you are not, you are wasting your time. At the Lexus Championship I mentioned earlier, a Spanish brother and sister, Rafael and Emma Cabrera, asked what to do when your last practice round before a competition has been a bad one. What they said took me aback because I had just been looking at their records and they had won everything there was to win in Spain and beyond. In fact, Emma, at fifteen, was the Spanish champion at Under-16, Under-18, Under-21 *and* Women's level. I told them that with golfing CVs like they had, they scarcely needed to be worrying about their last practice round. They knew that they were good and they should embark on every round brimful of confidence.

One point I did make was that they should never try a shot in a tournament context that they had never tried in practice. Nick Faldo taught me that there is a right way to play a hole and a wrong way. In 1993, when we were playing together in the Ryder Cup and we came to a hole where there was the possibility of cutting a corner, I said to Nick, 'Let's go for it.' 'No,' he replied. 'We'll do it the way we know.'

Initially, when a player turns professional, he will still be boasting of how well he did to reach such-and-such a green with, say, a drive and a wedge. After a year or so, he learns that that is not how the better players talk. The top men are not remotely interested in what clubs they took. They are only interested in the figures that go down on the scorecard. When you set out on a round, you have to be determined to waste as few shots as possible, and I probably wasted fewer than anyone in my first twelve years on tour.

Not too long ago, I made the mistake of saying that if any ten or twelve handicap golfer were to take me on as a caddie during his monthly medal, I believed I could save him up to four shots. The reason why it was a mistake was that I was promptly inundated with e-mails and letters offering me caddying assignments all over the country. I half expected to receive an angry call from Martin Rowley, secretary of the Caddies' Association. My thoughts when I made that somewhat rash offer were that I would help the player to think better. I would advise on the lines of putts and on clubbing; on when to go for a shot and when to play the percentages. I would also be exhorting him to hit to that side of the green where the consequences would be less dire if he were to miss. On top of all that, I would tell the player what my caddie tells me: that I should leave my mistakes on the hole where I made them.

Apart from making sure I never have to rush to a first tee, I am not too different from most golfers in adhering to a couple of superstitions. In the first place, I would not dream of teeing up with anything other than a white tee. In my mind, red and yellow tees connote water hazards and, as such, are bad news. I know that white is associated with out of bounds, but at my stage of life I feel reasonably confident that I can keep a ball somewhere on the course. If, say, someone had made off with my supply of white tees and there were only yellow and red to be had, I would be forced to hit my three wood off the deck. My other little idiosyncrasy concerns the end of my stint on the practice putting green. When the time has come for me to move to the first tee, I like to miss three putts in a row before I go. Why? Because I am telling myself that, by the law of averages, I am bound to make the next one.

Chapter 19

RIGHT-HAND MEN

It was Martin Rowley, secretary of the Caddies' Association, who reminded me of a story about one of the first caddies I ever had on tour. Most caddies know their stuff inside out, but this man, who shall remain nameless, was not quite up to the usual high standard. The idea was that he and I would compare notes on yardages over our first practice round together. At the first, I looked at my book and told him I had 126 yards to the green. He looked at his book and gave a satisfied nod. His figure was identical. When it came to the next, I gave 130 yards as my distance and he put his at 129. OK, that one-yard difference might have upset Bernhard Langer, who wants to know things down to the last millimetre, but I was impressed.

I continued to be impressed until we came to the fifth, when it suddenly struck me that this was too good to be true. After I had arrived at my ball and given the relevant distance at 177 yards and he had indicated that I was spot on, I asked if I could have a look at his notebook. It was empty.

Alastair McLean was my longest-serving caddie on tour. He and I met at the 1991 German Open, where he was working for Mark Mouland. Ever since the caddie-with-the-blank-book incident, I had set great store by a caddie's notes, and when Mark and I were paired together over the first two rounds I sneaked a look at the entries in Alastair's book. I was bowled over by what I saw: there were notes about the direction of the wind, where shots had pitched and how far they had run once they had landed. Nothing was left to chance.

The fact that Alastair was Scottish was another big plus. We chatted easily – we are both great football fans – and I was convinced that I had hit on the caddie I had been looking for since the day I turned professional.

Mark was not playing particularly well at the time, and when I had a word with him after the first two days and asked if he would consider releasing Alastair, he could not have been more generous. 'Yeah,' he said. 'Go on. You might as well.' Alastair started the following week.

Although there were obviously those who said Alastair should have been making rather better use of his academic qualifications – he had a degree in history from Dundee University – we were as ambitious as each other. It was because he had spent eighteen months searching in vain for a suitable job that he thought he would use his golfing qualifications – he had a one handicap at Lundin Links – to try for a caddying post.

Alastair was first class with our children and first class with me, a soothing influence, if you like. When we parted company in May 2002 we were still as good a team as the European Tour has known. But, after so long together, we probably each knew in our heart of hearts that we needed a change. There is an energy you feel at the start of a caddie–player relationship (which I am sure Alastair is now enjoying with Adam Scott) that simply isn't there after ten years. The exception that proves the rule is Bernhard Langer and Pete Coleman.

Alastair's finest hour, or couple of hours, came in the last round of the Volvo Masters at Valderrama in 1995. That year, as I mentioned earlier, the Order of Merit race was between myself and Sam Torrance and, when it came to the last day, Sam had posted an early 68 and I had to finish first or second

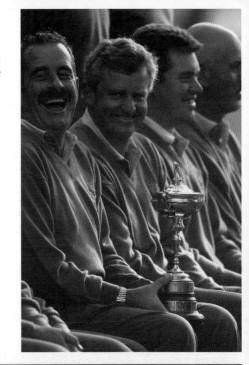

Ryder Cup 2002: (*right*) The team spirit was great, right from the off; (*below*) with Sam Torrance and Lee Westwood during the first practice round.

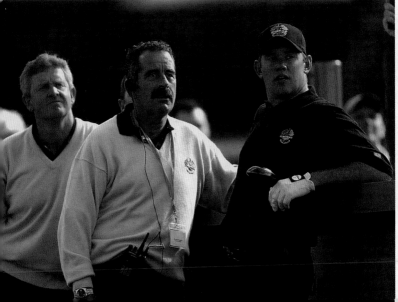

Right Enjoying, as ever, talking to the gentlemen of the press.

Relaxed scenes in the run-up to the tournament all helped towards the strong start in the first morning fourball matches, where, on the second, I holed a 32-footer and it all began to happen (*bottom right*).

Right Whilst Bernhard and I were an almost unstoppable team, we did experience some pressure in the foursomes at the 18th on the Friday night.

Left This might look like it was a team effort but Bernhard knew the line anyway!

Eighth tee, morning foursome, second day.

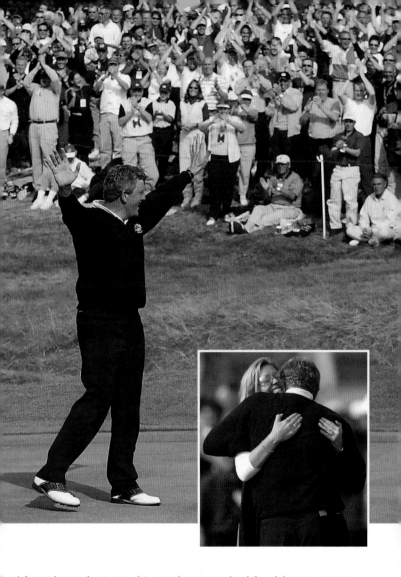

Top left I wish I made Eimear this proud every week; (*left*) celebrating victory with Padraig Harrington in the Saturday afternoon fourball matches; (*this page*) winning the singles at the 14th on the Sunday. It was one of those rare putts where I knew it was in the moment I hit it, giving us the first singles points on the board. The roar as the putt went in was deafening.

A very special moment as the trophy is passed down the line.

if I were to beat him. Alastair and I worked our way round to perfection that afternoon. It was almost as if we were playing snooker in the way that I was hitting one shot with the next and even the one after that in mind. We aimed to finish one under and that is precisely what we did. It was as good a player-and-caddie performance as you will ever see.

The role of the caddie is obviously so much more than merely bag carrier. In my earliest years on tour, I had a caddie who shook more under pressure than any player you would care to name, and that was a problem. It is vital that someone in the caddie's position should give out positive vibes and never more so than when the pressure is mounting. At the same time, he has to be vigilant, checking that his player is not doing anything amid the gathering tension that he would not normally do. Is he hurrying his pre-shot routine? Is he swinging a little quicker than usual? Alastair was good at all of that while, when it came to the 2000 Open at St Andrews, he slipped seamlessly into the role of counsellor as I broke down over the last nine because of my marital problems.

After all that had gone before, splitting from Alastair – it happened on the Sunday night after we had flown home from the 2002 French Open – was not easy. It was difficult to raise the subject because we were so close. But, after a good heart-to-heart, we ended up wishing each other all the best and, hopefully, our friendship will remain intact.

As wise a member of the caddying fraternity as Dave Musgrove, who used to work for Sandy Lyle, noted that the parting of the ways could be a good move for me. 'This is the time when players can win,' he said. By way of illustrating his point, he recalled how, when Alastair was off with a bad back in 1998, I had promptly won the Volvo PGA Championship with Andy Prodger.

Intriguingly, there had been a moment in that championship that had made both Andy and myself realise that if ever the occasion were right, we would make a good team. I was in danger of missing the cut and made matters worse at the fifteenth by knocking the ball into the ditch. 'I'll be lucky to get away with anything less than a six,' I said, disconsolately. There was no sympathy in Andy's voice. He had no intention of allowing me to indulge in any self-pity. He simply announced, matter-of-factly, that we needed a five. I managed to comply and we went on to finish birdie, birdie, eagle to sweep through the cut on our way to winning the tournament.

Andy, who is in his early fifties (ten or so years older than Alastair), was born in London and was first introduced to golf when he found regular holiday work picking up practice balls on a Hertfordshire driving range. He hit a lot of balls himself during those stints and eventually landed a job working for Bernard Hunt, of 1970s Ryder Cup fame, and his brother Geoffrey in the shop at Hartsbourne Country Club. Not least because of the Hunts' influence, Andy was soon playing to a handicap of two. By way of a next step, he played in local assistants' tournaments while, in 1973, he had the chance he craved of trying to qualify for that year's Open at my home course, Troon. It was then that an incident occurred to change his career. After the first round of pre-qualifying, he and his caddie were involved in a car accident and had to go home.

The next five years were littered with further disappointments. He carried on playing for a while but when he kept missing cuts, often by no more than a shot or two, he left the Hunts and sought other employment. He tried everything – engineering and factory work – before deciding that whatever job he chose, it had to be conducted in the fresh air.

In 1980 the caddie with whom he had had the accident – Stan Francourt – suggested he accompany him to Italy where he was going to caddie for Craig Defoy. Andy didn't get a bag immediately but suddenly noticed that Nick Faldo was pulling his own trolley. 'I found out,' he said, 'that he'd fired his caddie, John Moorhouse, and then he'd tried a German lad, but he'd only lasted the practice round. Everyone seemed to be avoiding Nick. To tell the truth, I think they were all a bit scared of him. I might have been too if I wasn't so new to the caddying game. I approached him and asked about caddying for him and he said yes.' They finished in fourth place and that was the start of a two-year relationship. They then parted for four years – usual reasons, communications not so good – before getting back together in July 1986. It was in this next period that they would win the 1987 Open at Muirfield and the 1989 Masters at Augusta.

I rang Andy on the Monday after the 2002 French Open and told him that I had just split from Alastair. Though I knew he was working for Phillip Price, I asked if there were any chance of his caddying for me again. He replied that he would love to have the chance and we agreed on a trial run until the US Open at Bethpage State Park, though I added that it would almost certainly be a permanent appointment. Andy said that he would speak to Phillip on the Sunday once the Benson and Hedges tournament had finished and that it would be no bad thing if I were to say something to him later that night. That seemed to be the best way of tackling what is always a potentially awkward situation.

The week at the Belfry was not easy. I had to walk past Phillip and Andy on the practice range one day, and though all three of us said, 'Good morning,' I felt an absolute cad. I would imagine that Andy was not very comfortable either.

The press had wasted no time in speculating who would get my bag and, hardly surprisingly, they did not take long to list Andy among the favourites. The rumours continued and all sorts of players were asking their caddies if they were about to leave. Darren Clarke asked Billy Foster if he were about to disappear; Paul Lawrie asked Colin Byrne.

It was on the Friday evening, after Phillip had signed off

for the night at three under, that his wife Sandra said to Andy, 'You're not off to caddie for Monty, are you?'

Andy is among the most endearingly open and honest men that I have ever met and this put him in a difficult position. He was not going to lie. 'Actually, I am,' he returned.

When he arrived at the club on the Saturday morning, a member of Phillip's management group was waiting for him. He said that his services were no longer required. Phillip, who used Pierre Fulke's caddie that day, left a message on my phone that morning which I did not receive until the evening. He wanted to discuss the situation and we agreed to meet for breakfast the following morning. He was not happy with what had happened behind his back, but he was very professional. I apologised profusely and, hurt though he was, he accepted that I had set out to do things in the right way.

Only when we arrived in Germany for the Deutsche Bank SAP Open did Andy and I feel free to look forward rather than back. No sooner had we got on to the course than we discovered we were as excited as each other. We both felt that winning the event was not too far-fetched, even with Tiger in the field. That day, I told the journalists who were there that I hoped it would prove possible to take the best of what I had with Alastair and combine it with the best of what Andy had to offer. I noted that we both seemed to see the game in the same way and that the emphasis would be on course management.

Andy, for his part, said that the most important thing as far as he was concerned was that I should keep my spirits up. He was going to do his utmost to stop me from having 'those crazy five minutes' which, as he has since wryly noted, can last for two or three holes. He appreciated that there could be problems in the States when the hecklers were going about their business, but said that he would be doing his best to make me ignore them.

Andy knew a bit about abuse himself. When he was caddying

for Nick Faldo as he lost to Curtis Strange in a play-off for the US Open in 1988 at Brookline, the crowd had given him hell. 'I couldn't put a divot back before they were running me over,' he said.

Our first round together in Germany, where I eventually finished second behind Tiger, was a 66, which left us two shots behind Alex Cejka. It reminded me of the occasion when I switched from Wilson clubs to Callaway in 1995 and began 68, 63. People are always waiting to say that you should have kept things as they were and there is no better way to shut them up than to get off on the right foot.

One particularly interesting aspect of Andy's caddying is that he only ever feeds me one yardage. As a rule, caddies will give you the actual distance and then tell you what distance the shot is playing. Andy, or Prodge, as I tend to call him, does all his calculations before giving me the distance I have to hit. It is all I want to know and it saves having a couple of conflicting figures going through my head.

On the one hand, he is ahead of the game and, on the other, he is full to overflowing with good, old-fashioned virtues. It came as no surprise to discover that he was still contentedly pouring coins into old-style telephone boxes when the rest of the caddies were up and running with their mobile phones. However, with the US Open coming up, I decided that it might be easier to get him up to date on this front because I am always wanting to check starting times, practice-round times and the rest. Andy did not seem to take long to get the hang of it and it seemed that any communication problems were over. On about the third day, though, we lost contact, and when I saw him I asked if there was anything wrong with the phone. He said that it was brilliant but added that it had run out of power. 'Have you tried charging it?' I asked. At that, he brought the manual out of his pocket. 'Give us a chance,' he said. 'I haven't got to that page yet.'

As we set out for the 2002 US Open, I was wondering which was the more improbable: me with the new belly putter I had been using since the start of the season or Prodge with his mobile?

Chapter 20

FLIGHT FRIGHT

Though I have become infinitely more relaxed about air travel in the last couple of years, I spent the first thirteen years of my professional career living in fear and dread of my next flight, which was usually two days later. And not without reason. Back in 1969, my father decided to take the family on a package holiday to Ibiza. I was six at the time and, like my older brother Douglas, I could not have been more excited at the prospect. We travelled on a 707 on the earliest of early morning flights out of Luton airport. I sat next to my father and Douglas was in the row behind with my mother. The first half of the flight was fine but, with no feedback from other aircraft, our pilot was not prepared for the extent of the turbulence over the Pyrenees. When he ran into it there were a few bounces before the plane began to keel over. A 707 can bank thirty-five degrees without any repercussions. In this instance, we were banking a good eighty degrees. The string slings running along either side of the ceiling were nowhere near as secure as the luggage bins they have today, and coats, bags and cases were flying all over the place. Meanwhile, some of those passengers who were not properly strapped in flew against the windows. One man was felled by a flying food trolley. The emergency lasted for no more than seventeen seconds, but it certainly sowed a seed of doubt about flying in my mind at an early age.

Mind you, my ordeal was nothing compared to the one

and a half hours of suffering that the British Ryder Cup side
endured ten years earlier when they were on their way to the
1959 competition in California. The team had done the first
leg of the journey – Southampton to New York – on the
Queen Elizabeth, the idea of the voyage being that it would
help to foster team spirit rather better than a transatlantic
flight. As it turned out, the sea was heaving and the players
spent much of their time being violently sick. The flight from
New York to Los Angeles came as a welcome relief and left
but a short hop – forty minutes at most – across the San
Jacinto Mountains to Palm Springs, where the match was to
be held at the Eldorado County Club.

It turned into a nightmare as the plane encountered rough
weather that was the tail-end of a hurricane which had
devastated much of Mexico. To quote from the article that
Ron Heager, the *Express*'s golf correspondent, lived to write,
'The plane began to toss like a cork as we met the storm that
lit up the vivid purple skies. The bumps were mild at first but
sufficient to turn bronzed golfers ashen. Heads ducked down
between knees. Collars were loosened. In the eye of the
storm, the jolts increased in frequency and violence. We were
trapped in a big lift racing up and down berserk … there was
a sickening, downward plunge. We were a stone dropped in
a well as we fell from our flying height of 13,000 feet to
9,000. It was the Big Dipper without the laughs. Anything
not strapped down took off and floated to the roof of the
plane.'

They eventually flew back to Los Angeles where Dai
Rees, the British captain, turned down the offer of a later
flight for them all and instead commandeered a Greyhound
bus.

Just as surely as that Ryder Cup party thought the end was
nigh, so my mother, father and everyone else on our flight to
Ibiza thought they were breathing their last. Fire engines and
ambulances were lined up on the runway as we landed.

Some of the passengers were seriously injured, with one man, possibly the poor chap who had been in collision with the food trolley, having sustained a broken neck.

My parents probably assumed that Douglas and I had got over the incident pretty quickly: from what I have gathered, we barely mentioned it after the first couple of days of our holiday. It was only years later that the latent terror started to manifest itself. Obviously, the thuds and the screams were still somewhere in the far reaches of my mind. Whenever I was due to travel somewhere, I would embark on some obsessive checking of the weather forecast, almost as if I were due to fly the aircraft myself.

I never missed a tournament because of it, but there were several occasions when I would change flights from morning to afternoon and from one day to another. And if there were no sign of the weather improving, I would hop in a car and drive if it were at all possible. On one occasion I did a round trip from home to Stuttgart, to Crans-Montana and home again. It might have been a manageable way of negotiating the tour for Neil Coles, who decided to conduct his career from ground level following a panic attack on a plane to Scotland, but it was hardly the way ahead for the modern globe-trotting professional.

Pilots who heard that I was a nervous wreck would from time to time invite me into the cockpit. Indeed, I remember one wind-tossed journey from Singapore to London when I stayed in the cockpit through the journey. The two shifts of pilots did seven hours apiece but I sat there staring at the controls for all fourteen hours.

Oddly enough, I never had a problem with take-offs and landings, the moments when air travel is at its most risky. It was the bouncing around between which did for me. I could not begin to eat a meal on a plane, and that still applies. All I do is drink water and watch films or weather charts. There were times when I would step off a plane feeling absolutely shattered, and quite how I ever settled to play tournament golf I will never know.

Since I never found a pill that could quash my anxiety, I looked at other options. About three or four years ago I was taken to a flight-deck simulator a couple of times and put through a bit of makeshift turbulence. I also had a handful of flying lessons. They thought it might help my cause were I to get my pilot's licence, but when they presented me with the manual I realised that it was something which would have to wait until I had finished my tournament-playing career.

For a while, I used to jump at any chance to fly privately, because when there was just me and the pilots I somehow felt more in charge of my own destiny. It was also a good way of getting to spend extra hours at home. But it does not take long for hiring planes to become akin to calling taxis. The more you use them, the more necessary they seem. I was taking too many, and when, at the start of 2002, I had to pull out of the Johnnie Walker Classic in Perth and then missed the cut in Dubai, it opened my eyes to what it is like to have money going out but none coming in.

That made me think, I can tell you. I called in my accountant and studied what private flying was costing me. The answer was too much.

The other reason why I cut back was that my flying phobia suddenly evaporated – and that in spite of Payne Stewart's fatal accident of 25 October 1999, in which he and five friends were flying in a Lear jet from Orlando to Dallas which lost pressure, possibly down to a faulty door or window seal. It was reported that the occupants would not have suffered as they would have died instantly, but the plane, on autopilot, kept flying macabrely until it ran out of fuel.

I don't think there was any tournament-playing professional anywhere who did not think how easily what had happened to Payne could have happened to them. We all spend far too much time in the air. Naturally, I thought that that event would increase my phobia. Instead, probably the very next time I was in a plane that started to shake about in turbulence, I found myself totally unperturbed. I have no idea why.

There is a sequel to the mid-air incident that was the root cause of my fear of flying. In 1996, the year in which my father had had his triple heart bypass, he and I went out to Sun City. The Sun City event organisers always invite you to take a family member and my father was the obvious candidate, especially after everything he had been through in the previous months. We were on a BA flight and, not long into the journey, the pilot invited us both up on to the flight deck. My father and the pilot got talking and before too long, Dad mentioned that day in 1969.

The pilot's ears pricked up. 'Was that a British Airtours flight you're talking about?' he asked.

'Yes,' returned my father.

'Was it out of Luton?' he pressed.

My father nodded.

'First thing in the morning?'

Dad nodded again.

'You're not going to believe this,' said the pilot, 'but I was the co-pilot that day.'

He added that it had been the worst experience of his career. That 707, he said, had never flown again.

Chapter 21

US TOUR

Even before I embarked on my stretch of seven Orders of Merit, everyone from press to public said that I would never know how good I could be if I did not give the USPGA Tour a proper go. They made out that if I were based over there, I would be that much more likely to win Majors. By way of persuading me, they would cite players like Peter Thomson, Gary Player, Greg Norman and Tony Jacklin, great international players who had all raised their games to a new level through playing in the States.

In 1991, at a stage when I had done nothing more than win the 1989 Portuguese Open and record six second-place finishes, I thought seriously of going to the American Qualifying School of that year and playing on the US Tour in 1992. 'I've made progress every year as a professional and I now feel it is time to go over there and give it a try,' I said in the September 1991 edition of *Golf Monthly*. 'With no Ryder Cup next year and no family as yet, next season is definitely the right time. If I don't go then, I may never have another chance.' I suggested that, thanks to my four years at Houston Baptist, it would not take long for me to readjust to the American lifestyle.

'If we do go,' I added, speaking as a married man, for Eimear and I had been married the year before, 'I'll do it properly. I'll go to qualifying school this season and then spend the whole of next year in the States. Even if I don't make it through the school, I will stay and play on the mini-tour. I turned professional because I felt I couldn't get any further as an amateur. To try my hand in America would be another step forward.'

We had second thoughts, and what I had said about how, if I didn't go in 1992 I might never go, turned out to be true. That year, I moved up to third place on the Order of Merit, and the following year was brilliant as Eimear gave birth to Olivia and I went into the number-one position on the European Tour.

When I started to win the Order of Merit on a regular basis the pro-America brigade became still more persistent, arguing that I was no longer being stretched at home. Here, I would explain that I was certainly not winning every week. At best, I was winning one week in every five or six – a statistic that still left plenty of room for improvement in my own backyard. Had I felt the need to conquer fresh fields, things might have been different. As it was, the urge to win in Europe remained as pressing as it ever was. It became more satisfying rather than less. Still more importantly, I enjoyed Europe, and all the more so because I felt appreciated. There was a faction of the press good enough to say, albeit with a twinkle, that the Tour would be a duller place without me, while Ken Schofield, the chief executive, insisted that I was playing a key role in the Tour's success. In fact, when I lost my Order of Merit title in 2000, he sent me a letter to that effect. I am not one for storing old correspondence but I kept this letter because it really means something to me. In the letter, Ken described my Order of Merit sequence as 'phenomenal' and went on to write, 'Moreover you have inspired and motivated a new generation of Europeans to endeavour to reach the standard you have set – that standard being of the very highest worldwide. The mantle of European Number One you have handled with integrity, dignity and a passion for competition which every player who follows will do well to try to emulate.'

There were family considerations, too, contributing to why Eimear and I felt we should stay where we were. On those days when the call of the US circuit was at its strongest – and there were a few of them, especially when the USPGA started offering me a player's card on a yearly basis – we would soon come down to earth as we thought about how it might affect Olivia, Venetia and Cameron. We are British through and through and, besides, we wanted our children to be educated on this side of the Atlantic. In 1996 and 1997, I considered a halfway-house arrangement of dipping into both Tours and playing just enough over there to keep my card, but fifteen tournaments per year is some commitment and one which would have kept me away from home, Eimear and the children for too long.

When, today, people debate whether I made the wrong decision, I point them in the direction of the list of European Tour players – Sandy Lyle, Nick Faldo, Seve Ballesteros, Bernhard Langer, Ian Woosnam and José Maria Olazábal – who won American Majors in the 1980s and 1990s while based at home. I also remind them of the extent to which the European Tour is improving and expanding all the time. Some players dislike having to trek halfway around the world for the opening tournaments in Australia and the Far and Middle East, but there's no doubt that the 'European' Tour is now a global phenomenon, and that has to be a good thing.

America, I have to say, was not the only move the Montgomerie family considered. In 1997, when we were worried – unnecessarily, as it turned out – about what Tony Blair was going to do, we thought about basing ourselves in Monaco, the Isle of Man, the Channel Islands or Switzerland. As plenty of others will have discovered before us, merely looking at these options reinforced our belief that we were happy where we were. Of all the possibilities, Switzerland seemed the most inviting. Eimear and I both love the country. Apart from having been to Crans-sur-Sierre for a series of

Canon European Masters, we have spent a couple of Christmas holidays in that town, with everyone but me enjoying the winter sports. (I know there are golfers who ski, but never having done any skiing as a child, I feel I am that much more susceptible to accidents.) Yet, fabulous winter wonderland and peaceful place though Switzerland is, I doubt whether we would have been happy living there on a permanent basis. The education would have been first class, with the children probably finishing up bilingual or even trilingual, besides skiing like the natives. In many ways, it would have suited me, too, in that it would not have made any great impact on my travelling lifestyle. But it would not have been right for Eimear. She would have hated being left alone in a strange country for so many weeks at a time.

Where we live at the moment, she has lots of friends, along with a never-ending stream of engagements: lunches, meetings with the charities in which she is involved and so on. She often goes up to London for the day and knows the city better than the average taxi-driver. Once I escaped the Order of Merit treadmill we also started to enjoy a bit of London nightlife – something I had never embraced before. We are members of several clubs – Annabel's, Crockfords and Harry's Bar, to name but three. None of them serves up the sausage and bacon sandwiches I so enjoy in the Caddyshack restaurant on the practice ground, but I have to admit that I am not averse to a bit of fine dining.

Almost certainly, I could have made more money had I gone to America, but whether you are worth five, ten, fifteen, twenty or fifty million would not seem to me to make a whole lot of difference. We have enough money for what we want to do and we have enough money to pay the British taxes. I have had a seven-figure tax bill every year for the last six years but, in keeping with what my father has always said of how no one should go bleating to him about a high tax bill, I am not looking for sympathy. We have no desire to buy planes and boats. If we wanted a holiday on a boat, we would hire one. In truth, a spot of family fishing on Loch Lomond, which is what we did in the week before the 2002 US Open in New York, represents the height of my seafaring ambitions, though Eimear and I did enjoy the cruise we took off the Italian coast in the week after the 2002 Open. That was precisely the kind of holiday I needed in that my mobile phone did not work and I, myself, had to switch off.

Having said all of this, I would hate anyone to think that I have anything against America. I loved my years at college in Houston, and I always jump at the opportunity to take the children on holiday to the States, especially to Disney World. My one and only complaint about the country is that it is all too far from home.

What I have omitted to mention is that we did end up making a move of sorts in 1997. We moved from one side of Oxshott to the other, and that was far enough for me.

Chapter 22

THE CHANGING GAME

We are all taught to think 'one shot at a time', but when the PGA European Tour and the PGA are already talking about where the Ryder Cup will be in the year 2030, it has the effect of making everyone look rather further ahead than the next eighteen holes.

Though the R&A and the USGA have jointly decided that drivers boasting too much of the so-called springboard effect will be banned for the professionals from 2003, the influence of modern technology still strikes me as a cause for concern, particularly with regard to our great seaside courses. Our links have been stretched further and further over the last few years, almost as if our coastline itself were elastic. Though Muirfield only had to add distance to a couple of short holes for the 2002 Open, Royal St George's has introduced as many as six new tees for 2003. They were lucky to have the space, because there has to come a time when there are no more bushes and linksland scrub that can be removed to create new back tees.

My hope is that people will suddenly tumble to the value of our links and start seeing them as sacred grounds, developing the game more around them rather than the latest big-headed drivers. They are a part of our heritage and those who continue to ignore the fact do so at their peril. Never mind how splendid a modern course might be; it will always lack that dimension of history that means much more in our game than so many seem to think.

Tiger Woods appreciates better than anyone that golf is a mix of past and present. He was quick to acknowledge that there was something very special about winning the 2000 Open at St Andrews, the so-called Home of Golf. And he was just as quick to enjoy the comparisons everyone has been making between him and players like Bobby Jones, Ben Hogan and Jack Nicklaus. 'The mere fact that people are making these comparisons means that I've done all right for myself,' he has said.

When the R&A and the USGA came to the club compromise at the start of 2002, Tim Finchem, the chief executive of the PGA Tour, accompanied his congratulations with the suggestions that the two bodies should act at once 'to cap the allowable golf ball distance at current levels'. Tiger, whose opinion counts for so much, was happy with that idea but totally against the suggestion that came from Hootie Johnson, the chairman of the Masters. A month or so before the USGA announced their compromise, Johnson had said that the Masters' championship committee had made all the alterations they could to Augusta and that if the players continued to hit further, they would have to consider introducing a special Masters ball. Anyone who wanted to play in the event would have no option but to use it.

Personally, I think that Johnson's views made a lot of sense. I am convinced that the time has come when there should be more of a standard-issue ball for the top players. If you think about it, golf is the only sport in which the competitor comes to the course with his own choice of balls. If you are playing at Wimbledon, standard balls are handed out, and the same applies in snooker, rugby and football. You name it.

Phil Mickelson was not wrong when he complained that Johnson's standard Masters ball might not complement his play as it might someone else's, but the answer here is that the balls could still be made for the individual, just so long as they came off the club-face at eighty per cent, or eighty-five per cent at most, of their present velocity. Apart from anything else, the adjustment would help to offset any future developments in the realm of aerodynamics and refined paint-work. It would take a few weeks for players and spectators to adjust, but, at the end of the day, Tiger would still be the longest and everyone would wonder what all the fuss had been about.

The same applies to the public, who are even now begin-ning to bemoan the fact that they will not be allowed to use the springboard-effect clubs after January 2008. Though I can see that the switch will be hard on the over-sixties and -seventies, for whom ten to fifteen yards more can turn back the years, they, too, would soon accommodate the changes.

Even the architects of modern courses cannot afford to be too complacent where the technological advance is con-cerned. When, for instance, Dave Thomas designed the excellent new course at St Leon-Rot four years ago, he thought he was ahead of the clock. As it turned out, much of the bunkering was already redundant when we played the Deutsche Bank SAP Open there in May 2002. At the time when Thomas would have been drawing up the plans you could not make a 250-yard carry with a driver. By 2002 you could make that distance with a three wood.

A by-product of constantly putting tees back is that the distance between greens and tees is always growing. In the beginning of golf the next tee would be alongside the last green. Indeed, when the 'Articles and Laws in Playing the Golf' first appeared in 1744, the first of the thirteen regula-tions read, 'You must tee your ball within a club length of the hole.' Even when I started out as a professional in the late 1980s you would seldom have to walk more than twenty yards to the next tee. Today, you might have to walk eighty yards, and that is bordering on the ridiculous.

I know there are tournament courses – admittedly not

Open venues – where they get round the problem by ferrying the players from green to tee in buggies, but that was never how it was meant to be. There is a flow to this game that that kind of thing can only disrupt, quite apart from other considerations such as the number of volunteers needed to drive the buggies back and forth.

The PGA European Tour is going from strength to strength. Ken Schofield and his team silenced the so-called Gang of Four – Seve Ballesteros, Bernhard Langer, José Maria Olazábal and Nick Faldo – when they voiced criticisms of the way things were run a couple of years ago. Halfway through 2002, at a time when so many other industries were struggling, the Tour was still announcing prize-money increases for events in the second half of the season.

People are forever asking me about the money and whether there is too much of it. I have been to tournaments where each day sees a still more handsome gift being left in the bedroom. There have been African bronzes so big that they have had to be shipped back to Britain, Arabian carpets of such quality that you half expect to be able to fly home on them. I know that if I were hosting a tournament in Scotland, I would be handing out the gifts. Competitive animal that I am, I would want my tournament to be bigger and better than the rest and I would want everyone to go away with happy memories. If the event were at Troon, I might give them a replica of Culzean Castle, a favourite Ayrshire landmark and one where, though it is hardly pertinent, Eimear and I thought about having our wedding reception. If the tournament were at Loch Lomond, I would be looking at a model of the clubhouse. In other words, I would be shamelessly contributing to the spoiling process.

Golf itself is an antidote to the spoiling. No sooner do you think that you've cracked golf and are feeling a bit cocky than the game comes back and hurts you in a hurry. No one can say they have conquered it. Tiger has come closest but, as I have said many times before, no one has ever played the perfect round of golf and no one ever will.

Chapter 23

THE WAY AHEAD

I have said many times that I will not play the Senior Tour. Eimear, who probably knows me better than I know myself, is no less emphatic when she says that I will. She maintains that I would be incapable of sitting at home while everyone else was out there. It will be interesting to see which of us is right.

In the shorter term, I believe I have another five or six years' good golf left in me on the regular Tour. I have said that I do not play this game to finish halfway down the field, and when the day comes when I am no longer capable of winning, I will know to stop.

For the moment, there are still elements of my game I can improve. During my seven years at the top of the Order of Merit, the area in which I improved the most was course management: I learned when to attack and when to be patient. And to accept that if you are going to miss a green, you have to miss it on the 'right' side. To give an example away from the obvious, you have to try to leave yourself with a chip into the wind rather than downwind.

Driving was my forte during those years and it still is, but when we turned into the 2000s I felt that I was costing myself a bit of length through not getting the right trajectory and roll. As Denis Pugh pointed out, my swing had become too rounded through the ball. I was not hitting out after the shot as I used to when I was winning Orders of Merit. It was something I worked on a lot in 2001 and early 2002, while I also redoubled my efforts to become a more consistent putter. I started using the belly putter at the start of 2002 and was putting a much better stroke on the ball as a result. As I said earlier, it took a lot of gall for a traditionalist such as myself to start using such a club. Mercifully, the early results helped to cancel out the embarrassment. I was taking two putts fewer per round.

My temperament, in terms of my boiling point, is better than it was and is still improving. The 2001 Open was something of a turning point. As I have said before, my joint thirteenth place was hardly what I had been anticipating when I reached the halfway stage with a one-shot lead, but it was the first time that I had had the feeling that the crowd and I were conspiring to win this thing together. Because of it, I believe I will make a far better showing in future than I have in previous ones, though I would be the first to admit that I wasted the chance I had at Muirfield in 2002.

If I am going to win Majors, I have to accept that I will not be able to shoot four perfect rounds. Hugh Mantle thinks that I have to be more relaxed going into Majors. He would like me sticking to a pre-Major routine instead of chopping and changing with regard to when I travel to the event and how many practice rounds I have. He reckons that the ideal for me would be to reach the point where I stopped putting pressure on myself and stopped taking on board the pressures others put upon me. As he has pointed out, very few of the top players are at their best when they are feeling pressure. Though everyone will be talking about how well a man shaping to win is handling the pressure, it is more likely that much of his good golf is down to the fact that he is not feeling any at all. He will be having one of those days when he sees his tee shots bisecting the fairway and visualises every putt dropping.

Aside from my quest to win Majors, I should love to be a

Ryder Cup captain. Everyone in golf knows as much. To date, I have been honoured to captain two GB and Ireland teams in the Seve Trophy match. Each time, I found it a fascinating exercise. In the first match I played in all five games and it confirmed what I have always thought about how you could never again have a playing captain of the Ryder Cup. A captain is far too concerned with the team situation to be able to concentrate on his own input. There are all sorts of things to consider when you are captain. Take the 2002 Seve Trophy, when Irish Television wanted Padraig Harrington to take part in a half-hour chat show at the end of the first day's play. Padraig came to me with the request and he and I talked it over with the rest of the team before deciding that the answer was in the negative. My feeling was that you cannot afford to have individuals doing their own thing in a team situation.

From experience, coupled with the talks I have had with Hugh Mantle, I know that when you have a team meeting, everyone must go away happy. The last thing you want is a couple of disillusioned players joining forces outside the door and discussing how they are the odd ones out. All the senior players should be involved in the decision-making process and senior and junior players alike must realise that, to a man, they are crucial to proceedings.

I see my business interests expanding over the next few years, with pride of place going to course design. There is something addictive about design work. Ever since I was first asked if I would be interested in helping plan a course, I have found myself thinking 'design' in every practice round I play. I do all my usual reconnaissance work but, at the same time, I make a series of mental notes. I have no formal qualifications in this field, but when you are playing all the time at a mix of top-class and lesser venues all over the world, you very quickly learn to sort out good points from bad. It is this experience, coupled with the opportunities I have had over the last few years to work with some of the finest golf-course architects in the business, which has contributed to my development.

My philosophy is that a course should be capable of stretching run-of-the-mill amateurs and crack professionals alike. In other words, it should be fun and reasonably thought-provoking for the handicap contingent but a test for the best once the pin positions are in their championship locations. And I think all the hazards – bunkers and water – should be where they are for a very good reason, rather than merely for scenic effect. All too often, when you play in the States, getting up and down from sand is almost too easy. That is why I like links golf, where a bunkered ball is often the equivalent of half a penalty shot. Look at the bunkers we had at Muirfield in 2002. In my opinion, they do the job they are meant to do.

One of my favourite design projects so far has been the Emirates Hills eighteen-hole project in Dubai, now named The Montgomerie. Everything turned out as well if not better than I had expected as I worked with Desmond Muirhead, and the chances are that it will play host to a European Tour event within the next couple of years.

I have projects on the go in China, Malaysia, Korea, Ireland and Scotland, all of which are at various stages of development. It is thrilling to keep tabs on their progress, with particular reference to the small course I have been working on in Glasgow for children who cannot afford to join a regular club. Though there are players who can lend their names to this or that course without tossing and turning at night over whether the bunker at the fourth should be ten yards further left or whatever, I find it impossible not to get immersed. My first design in China will open at the end of 2002 and my project at Carton House in Dublin will open in 2003.

When my playing days are over, and if I have spare time

when not designing new courses, I like the idea of television commentary. Watching the 2001 Wimbledon interested me enormously in that John McEnroe was doing a grand job in the commentary box after a career in which he behaved so notoriously. Because of his obvious love of tennis and the extent to which he cares about Wimbledon, people listen to him and give him a lot of respect.

People are very forgiving and I am noticing that they increasingly respect my opinions. That, I have to say, is no less gratifying in its own way than any number of lucrative contracts.

Eimear's ideas for the future are interwoven with mine but, at the same time, she has plans of her own which I am keen to see her fulfil. Since we sorted things out between us in 2000, I am more than happy for her to be herself. As a schoolgirl, she was always very keen on the arts. She was a good enough pianist to have reached Grade Six and also had a promising voice, taking the lead in many of the Marr College Christmas productions. Now she has not only gone back to the piano lessons but is taking classes from an opera singer who visits the house on a weekly basis.

She does not travel with me as much as she did because it does not make sense for her to be away as much as she was. I needed to become more self-sufficient instead of leaning on her all the time. At the same time, the children are at an age when they need one parent at home if they are to grow up to be happy and well adjusted. Because of the nature of my work, Eimear is the prime parent, though I happily took over at the start of 2002 when she wanted to fulfil an old ambition to visit India. The children and I moved into the same bedroom, watched DVDs and had midnight feasts which, for my benefit as much as for theirs, took place at nine-thirty. We are already making plans with regard to Eimear's next adventure.

At the same time as I have learned to be a less selfish

husband, I think I can fairly claim that I have become more of a 'team player'. Not in the Ryder Cup or Seve Trophy sense, but when it comes to other players and life on tour. Easy though it is to concern yourself with nothing beyond your own golf, you have a certain moral duty to pull your weight off the course. On the eve of a tournament, when you are itching to crawl into bed and get a good night's sleep before the first round, you will almost certainly be expected to turn up at a pro-am dinner or some other function. I used to try to escape them but, the more I have soaked up the workings of the Tour, the more cheerfully accommodating I have become of what has to be done. The sponsors have to get their money's worth out of an event or why else would they want to be involved?

I am probably not the only older hand to have discovered that you generally get out of these social occasions what you put into them. At the 2001 Dunhill Links Championship, for instance, I found myself sitting between Michael Douglas and Boris Becker. Douglas was fascinating on the subject of how much he wants to become a good player, while Boris and I had an intriguing conversation about the pressures of our respective sports. When I asked him what was the equivalent of the two-foot putt, he told me it was the service toss. He said it was easy to throw the ball up to the required height at the start of a match but that it becomes tougher and tougher to release the ball when you are getting towards the end of a closely contested fifth set.

I am as star-struck as the next person when I meet a Michael Douglas or a Boris Becker, but the truth is that I have always admired anyone who excels at anything, whatever he or she does. What intrigues me about my own job is how all these people I meet – film stars, sportsmen, royalty, you name it – all have an ambition to become a good golfer. There may still be those in the private golf-club sector who will look out of the clubhouse window and say dismissively of me, 'He's a professional,' but most people feel envy. Not a day goes by when someone does not tell me that he would happily swap his lot for mine. It is simultaneously flattering and bizarre, and there are times, as I get ushered to the finest suite in the hotel or the best seat on the plane, that I have to pinch myself.

All this, for heaven's sake, because I play golf.

CAREER RECORD

COLIN MONTGOMERIE

Year	EUROPEAN TOUR Volvo Order of Merit Position	Euro	WORLDWIDE World Ranking	Total Prize Money Position	$
2001	5	1,578,676	14	28	1,912,941
2000	6	1,740,917	6	15	2,328,358
1999	1	1,822,879	3	4	2,988,543
1998	1	1,390,308	7	8	2,206,532
1997	1	1,118,527	7	1	3,366,900
1996	1	1,225,204	3	1	3,071,442
1995	1	1,169,073	6	3	2,153,211
1994	1	1,067,807	8	8	1,739,349
1993	1	859,156	14	15	1,219,710
1992	3	622,598	20	16	1,098,732
1991	4	481,006	36	25	827,938
1990	14	244,793	81	85	356,700
1989	25	152,718	162	184	178,951
1988	52	54,881	308	-	105,164
1987	164	2,731	-	-	3,941
TOTALS	Total (Euro) No.1 (1987 to 2001)	13,531,276	World Career Total ($) No.5 (1987 to 2001)		23,558,412

Progressive improvement year by year in Volvo Order of Merit, World Ranking and Worldwide Earnings from 1987 to 1996

COLIN MONTGOMERIE – Ryder Cup Record

Singles: 6 Played: 4 Won, 2 Halved, None Lost

1991	Halved	v Mark Calcavecchia
1993	Won (I hole)	v Lee Janzen
1995	Won (3&1)	v Ben Crenshaw
1997	Halved	v Scott Hoch
1999	Won (1 hole)	v Payne Stewart
2002	Won (5&4)	v Scott Hoch

Foursomes: 11 Played: 7 Won, 1 Halved, 3 Lost

1991	Lost (4&2)	(with David Gilford) v Lanny Wadkins & Hale Irwin
1993	Won (4&3)	(with Nick Faldo) v Ray Floyd & Fred Couples
	Won (3&2)	(with Nick Faldo) v Lanny Wadkins & Corey Pavin
1995	Lost (1 hole)	(with Nick Faldo) v Corey Pavin & Tom Lehman
	Won (4&2)	(with Nick Faldo) v Curtis Strange & Jay Haas
1997	Won (5&3)	(with Bernhard Langer) v Tiger Woods & Mark O'Meara
	Won (1 hole)	(with Bernhard Langer) v Lee Janzen & Jim Furyk
1999	Won (3&2)	(with Paul Lawrie) v David Duval & Phil Mickelson
	Lost (1 hole)	(with Paul Lawrie) v Hal Sutton & Jeff Maggert
2002	Halved	(with Bernhard Langer) v Phil Mickelson & David Toms
	Won (1 hole)	(with Bernhard Langer) v Scott Verplank & Scott Hoch

Fourballs: 11 Played: 5 Won, 2 Halved, 4 Lost

1991	Won (2&1)	(with Bernhard Langer) v Steve Pate & Corey Pavin
1993	Halved	(with Nick Faldo) v Paul Azinger & Fred Couples
	Lost (2 holes)	(with Nick Faldo) v John Cook & Chip Beck
1995	Lost (3&2)	(with Nick Faldo) v Fred Couples & Davis Love III
	Lost (4&2)	(with Sam Torrance) v Brad Faxon & Fred Couples
1997	Lost (3&2)	(with Bernhard Langer) v Tiger Woods & Mark O'Meara
	Won (1 hole)	(with Darren Clarke) v Fred Couples & Davis Love III
1999	Halved	(with Paul Lawrie) v Davis Love III & Justin Leonard
	Won (2&1)	(with Paul Lawrie) v Steve Pate & Tiger Woods
2002	Won (4&3)	(with Bernhard Langer) v Scott Hoch & Jim Furyk
	Won (2&1)	(with Padraig Harrington) v Phil Mickelson & David Toms

Results overall: 28 Played: 16 Won, 5 Halved, 7 Lost

1993

1993 Volvo Order of Merit Final Placings

1	COLIN MONTGOMERIE
2	Nick Faldo
3	Ian Woosnam
4	Bernhard Langer
5	Sam Torrance
6	Costantino Rocca
7	Peter Baker
8	Darren Clarke
9	Gordon Brand Jnr
10	Barry Lane

Event	Montgomerie	Faldo	Woosnam	Langer	Torrance	Rocca	Baker	Clarke	Brand Jnr	Lane
Madeira Island Open	17t			13t	38t	20t	12t	13t	32t	6t
Dubai Desert Classic	2	26t	14t	mc	38t	12t	61	41	91	17t
Johnnie Walker Classic		14t		20t	mc	60t	mc	16	25t	9t
Turespana Iberia Open de Canarias	20t			12t	20t	12t	29t	71	53t	20t
Moroccan Open	12t			13t	12t	13t	54t	3	13t	13t
Turespana Masters Open de Andalucia	13t			11t	13t	41t	62t	1	12t	21t
Turespana Open Mediterrania	13t				211	16	mc	mc	72t	mc
Turespana Open Baleares	11t						41t	3	47t	20t
Portuguese Open								1	21t	2t
Kronenbourg Open						71	mc	3	mc	mc
Open V33 du Grand Lyon						3	mc	1	13t	13t
Roma Masters						mc	24t	3	63t	28t
MASTERS TOURNAMENT ##	52t	39t	17t	8t					45t	2t
Heineken Open Catalonia	36t				1				12t	5t
Cannes Open	7t	mc			6	2t	36t	39t	25t	12t
Benson & Hedges International Open	mc					4t	13t	12t	24t	8t
Peugeot Open de Espana							74	44t	26t	mc
Lancia Martini Italian Open							81	mc	121	41
Volvo PGA Championship	2t	10t	33t		mc		38t	34t	mc	12t
Dunhill British Masters	10t				21t		15t	1	33t	26t
Honda Open							5t	2t	16t	8t
Jersey European Airways Open							81		mc	mc
US OPEN ##	33t	72t	52t	mc			29t			16t
Peugeot Open de France		52t			1		34t	1	50t	22t
Carroll's Irish Open	23t	1			11	5t	34t	161	mc	50t
Bells Scottish Open	50t	5		14t	24t	50t	21t	24t	mc	30t
OPEN CHAMPIONSHIP	mc	2		501	50t	411	33t	38t	mc	13
Heineken Dutch Open	1				3	4	1	mc	mc	47t
Scandinavian Masters	7t				411		33t	171	14t	14t
BMW International Open					3t		1	9t	2	mc
US PGA CHAMPIONSHIP ##	mc	3	22t		511		3t	2	3	71t
Hohe Brucke Austrian Open								52t	mc	
Murphy's English Open	4t	8t	21t	211	121		2	1	16t	16t
Volvo German Open	8t	40t		21	21		1	41	41t	41t
Canon European Masters	21t	6t	61	81	wd			8t	59t	121
GA European Open	14t		40t	1	10	2	30t	25t	1	1
Trophee Lancome	mc	3t	6t	1	2	161	141	15t	mc	3t
Mercedes German Masters	37t	9	41		161	591	161	mc	mc	38t
Alfred Dunhill Open		16t	41t	mc	121	mc	mc	2	10t	9
Madrid Open		10t	mc	mc	35t	mc	81	2	161	16t
Volvo Masters	1	15t	15l	15t	15l	20l	8t	23t	25t	5

COLIN MONTGOMERIE

Other World events in 1993

USA Buick Classic 44t

Eur Toyota World Match Play Champ. 4
Eur Johnnie Walker World Champ. 4

Alfred Dunhill Cup (Scotland)
Ryder Cup (Europe)
World Cup (Scotland)

Note: Masters Tournament, US Open, US Open & US PGA Championship not Volvo Order of Merit events in 1993

1994

COLIN MONTGOMERIE

	1994 Volvo Order of Merit Final Placings
1	COLIN MONTGOMERIE
2	Bernhard Langer
3	Seve Ballesteros
4	Jose Maria Olazabal
5	Miguel Angel Jimenez
6	Vijay Singh
7	David Gilford
8	Nick Faldo
9	Mark Roe
10	Ernie Els

Tournament placings

Tournament	Montgomerie	Langer	Ballesteros	Olazabal	Jimenez	Singh	Gilford	Faldo	Roe	Els
Madeira Island Open						67t				
Moroccan Open		26t	3							
Dubai Desert Classic	6t	15t								
Johnnie Walker Classic	17t	11t	26t			65t	22t	18t	5t	9t
Turespana Open de Tenerife	1	16t		mc				43t	9t	
Open de Extremadura										
Turespana Masters Open de Andalucia	mc	18t		mc	2	1	18t	mc		
Turespana Open Mediterrania		15t	74	33t		10t	14t	7t		
Turespana Open Baleares										
Portuguese Open					2t	6t	7t			
Open V33										
MASTERS TOURNAMENT ##	mc	24t	18t	27t		13t				8t
Heineken Open Catalonia			82	27t						
Air France Cannes Open	2	14t	5	3t	5t					
Benson & Hedges International Open	14t	1						mc	2	
Peugeot Open de Espana	1		34t	8t	21t	58t	57t			
Tisettanta Italian Open				mc	4					
Volvo PGA Championship	37t	37t	19t	20t						
Alfred Dunhill Open	3t	3t	5t	4	mc	2				
Honda Open		2t	1	21t	17t	mc	16t			
Jersey European Airways Open	20t	2t								
US OPEN ##	2t	23t	18t	mc	mc	1				
Peugeot Open de France		24t	33t	4t		11t				
Murphy's Irish Open	24t	4				8t				
Bells Scottish Open	4	8t			16t	mc	1	36t		
OPEN CHAMPIONSHIP	8t	4t		38t	26t	12t	67t	24t	7t	
Heineken Dutch Open	12t			41	49t	1				
Scandinavian Masters					1	36t				
BMW International Open	9	3		1						
US PGA CHAMPIONSHIP ##	36t		mc	44t	4t	7t	25t			
Hohe Brucke Open										
Murphy's English Open	1	1	mc	35t	20t	20t	66t	6t	mc	39t
Volvo German Open	1	1	2	8t						
Canon European Masters	1	mc	4	20t	8t		mc	6t	20t	
European Open Championship	mc			2	3	1	16t	31t		
Dunhill British Masters	4	3t	24t	34t	33t	3t	2	13t	13t	20t
Trophee Lancome	3t	1	34t	3	1	5t	71	7t	53t	
Mercedes German Masters	mc		33t	10t	61t	41	6t	2	4t	
Chemapol Trophy Czech Open			1	2	8t			11t	13t	
Volvo Masters	4t			22t				21		4t

COLIN MONTGOMERIE

Other world events in 1994

USA Nestle Invitational mc
USA Players Championship 9t

Asa Philippine Open 3rd
Asa Kent Hong Kong Open mc
Eur Toyota World Match Play Champ. 2nd
Aus Alfred Dunhill Masters 4t
SAI Nedbank $Million 10t
Eur Johnnie Walker World Champ. 10t

Alfred Dunhill Cup (Scotland)

Note: Masters Tournament, US Open & US PGA Championship not Volvo Order of Merit events in 1994

1995 Volvo Order of Merit Final Placings

1995 — COLIN MONTGOMERIE

1	COLIN MONTGOMERIE
2	Sam Torrance
3	Bernhard Langer
4	Costantino Rocca
5	Michael Campbell
6	Alexander Cejka
7	Mark James
8	Barry Lane
9	Anders Forsbrand
10	Peter O'Malley

Tournament	Colin Montgomerie	Sam Torrance	Bernhard Langer	Costantino Rocca	Michael Campbell	Alexander Cejka	Mark James	Barry Lane	Anders Forsbrand	Peter O'Malley
Dubai Desert Classic	2	mc	16t	11t	3t	16t	34t	42t	51t	28t
Johnnie Walker Classic	7	23t	23t	23t	4t	33t				
Madeira Island Open										
Turespana Open Canarias										
Lexington S A PGA										
Turespana Open Mediterrania		2t	35t	5t	mc					
Turespana Open Aldalucia		14t	2	24t	10t	2				
Moroccan Open		46t	16t	37t	1	4				
Portuguese Open		10t	14t	1	37t	21t				
Turespana Open Baleares		44t	8t	50t	28t	4t				
MASTERS TOURNAMENT ##	17t		31t							
Open Catalonia Turespana Series				7	35t	mc	25t	15t		
Air France Cannes Open	13t			3t	1	19t	mc	19t	mc	
Conte of Florence Italian Open				2t	25t	2t	24t	24t	25t	41t
Benson & Hedges International Open	4t			1	15t	37t	7t	7t	4	mc
Peugeot Open de Espana	15t			25t	27t	mc	48t	5t		34t
Volvo PGA Championship	9t			56t		64t	mc			
Murphy's English Open	2				17t	mc	47t	5t		
Deutsche Bank Open – TPC of Europe	20t									
DHL Jersey Open										
US OPEN ##	28t		36t			44	22t			
Peugeot Open de France				1	21t	10t	11t	2t		
BMW International Oipen	4t			20t	38t		25t	20t		
Murphy's Irish Open	3			mc	12t	17t	33t	42t	mc	7t
The Scottish Open	3			11t	25t	13t	35t	10t	4	34t
OPEN CHAMPIONSHIP	mc			2t	24t	3t	20t	47t		
Heineken Dutch Open	7t				60t				53t	25t
Scandinavian Masters	2			23t	13t		17t	14t	63t	25t
US PGA CHAMPIONSHIP ##	2				16t	mc	mc		17t	
Hohe Brucke Open						mc				
Chemapol Trophy Czech Open				1	19t	mc	25t	7t	63t	
Volvo German Open	1			13t	21t	9t	37t		13t	22t
Canon European Masters	11t			2t	9	5	19t	17t	34t	
Trophee Lancome	1			5			26t	11t	14t	64t
Collingtree British Masters	7t			24t	33t	3t			61t	2
Smurfit European Open	3t			5	12t	mc	1	42t	57t	
Mercedes German Masters	wd			1	2	5t	mc	1	28t	16t
Volvo Masters	2			24t	41t	24t	45t	5t	28t	1

COLIN MONTGOMERIE

Other world events in 1995

USA Doral Ryder Open 17t
USA, Honda Classic 53t
USA Nestle Invitational 42T
USA Players Championship 14t

Eur Toyota World Match Play Champ. 5t
Jpn Visa Taiheyo Masters 4th
Saf Nedbank $Million 11th
Eur Johnnie Walker World Champ 16t

Alfred Dunhill Cup (Scotland – Winners)
Ryder Cup (Europe – Winners)

Note: Masters Tournament, US Open & US PGA Championship not Volvo Order of Merit events in 1995

1996 Volvo Order of Merit Final Placings

1996 — COLIN MONTGOMERIE

1	COLIN MONTGOMERIE
2	Ian Woosnam
3	Robert Allenby
4	Costantino Rocca
5	Mark McNulty
6	Lee Westwood
7	Andrew Coltart
8	Darren Clarke
9	Paul Broadhurst
10	Thomas Björn

Tournament	1 Montgomerie	2 Woosnam	3 Allenby	4 Rocca	5 McNulty	6 Westwood	7 Coltart	8 Clarke	9 Broadhurst	10 Björn
Johnnie Walker Classic	1									
Heineken Classic	1									
Dimension Data Pro-Am	14t									
Alfred Dunhill S A PGA Champ		53t	44t							
FNB Players Championship			1							
Open Catalonia		8t	4t							
Moroccan Open			8t							
Dubai Desert Classic	1	5t	7t		52t					
Portuguese Open										
Madeira Island Open										
MASTERS TOURNAMENT ##	39t	29t			mc					
Air France Cannes Open										
Turespana Masters		8t	5t	11t	20t					
Conte of Florence Italian Open										
Peugeot Open de Espana	wd									
Benson & Hedges International Open	9t	18t	54t	7t	1					
Volvo PGA Championship	7t		mc	1	18t					
Deutsche Bank Open - TPC of Europe	2		41t	40t						
Alamo English Open	2t	55t	mc	25t						
Slaley Hall Northumberland Challenge	10t	17t								
US OPEN ##		79t		67t						
BMW International Oipen		52t	21t	17t	1	mc				
Peugeot Open de France	mc	31t	21t	1	7t	31t				
Murphy's Irish Open	16t	12t	45t			mc				
The Scottish Open	mc	37t	25t	2	mc	63t				
OPEN CHAMPIONSHIP	12t	43t	mc	18t	11t	18t				
Sun Dutch Open		7t	54t	16t	26t	33t	2			
Volvo Scandinavian Masters		29t	36t	111	1					
US PGA CHAMPIONSHIP ##		mc	52t		mc					
Hohe Brucke Open										
Chemapol Trophy Czech Open		24t		5t	20t	mc				
Volvo German Open	9t		1	5	24t	53t	58t			
One 2 One British Masters	1	611	3	mc	mc	mc				
Canon European Masters	2	13t	mc	41	29t	7t	45t	7t	mc	
Trophee Lancôme	4t	244		8t	16t	24t	37t			
Loch Lomond World Invitational	244		8t	261	3t	18t				
Smurfit European Open	4	2	13t	241	3	1				
Linde German Masters		43t	10t	54t	61	24t	1			
Oki Pro-Am		7t	10t	mc	61	3	8t			
Volvo Masters	29t	25t	66	43t	1	21	341	25t	13t	20t

COLIN MONTGOMERY

Other world events in 1996

USA Players Championship 21
USA BellSouth Classic 23t
USA MCI Classic 8t

Eur Toyota World Match Play Champ. 5t
Aus. Alfred Dunhill Masters 39t
SA? Nedbank $Million 1st
USA Andersen Consulting WC of G 5t

Alfred Dunhill Cup (Scotland)

Note: Masters Tournament, US Open & US PGA Championship not Volvo Order of Merit events in 1996

1997 Volvo Order of Merit Final Placings

1997

Final Placings

1	COLIN MONTGOMERIE
2	Bernhard Langer
3	Lee Westwood
4	Darren Clarke
5	Ian Woosnam
6	Ignacio Garrido
7	Retief Goosen
8	Padraig Harrington
9	Jose Maria Olazabal
10	Robert Karlsson

Tournament	1	2	3	4	5	6	7	8	9	10
Johnnie Walker Classic	15t	7t	mc	45t	14	20	6	27t		mc
Heineken Classic	22t		45t	25t	6t	58t	17t	11t		mc
South African Open						15t	4	27t		40t
Dimension Data Pro-Am						mc		41		
Alfred Dunhill S A PGA Champ				11t				54t		
Dubai Desert Classic	6t	4		mc	7t	2		4	28t	6t
Moroccan Open				mc					38t	
Portuguese Open						4t			mc	
Turespana Masters - Open de Canarias			2	mc				30t	mc	
Madeira Island Open					39t	8t	37t	9t		12t
MASTERS TOURNAMENT ##	30t	7t	24t							
Cannes Open		36t	1	mc	26t	46t	29t	56t	36t	mc
Peugeot Open de Espana		16t	6t	23t	mc	17t	mc	mc	32t	11t
Conte of Florence Italian Open			2	7t		29t	17t	17t	4	2
Benson & Hedges International Open	59t	12t	5	22t	9	mc	mc	32t	60t	5t
Alamo English Open	12t		37t	4t	2	50t	53t	18t		22t
Volvo PGA Championship	5				2			26t		19t
Deutsche Bank Open - TPC of Europe		mc			3t	mc				65t
Compaq European Grand Prix	1	2			4		19t			
US OPEN ##	2	1			mc	43			16t	
Volvo German Open				4t		18t	3t		29t	mc
Peugeot Open de France	1	67				2	15t	41	mc	29t
Murphy's Irish Open	1			mc		9	25t	mc		
Loch Lomond World Invitational	10t		67	3t		39t	24t	3	6	
OPEN CHAMPIONSHIP	24t		10t	1	24t	mc	10t	7t	57t	43t
Sun Microsystems Dutch Open			13t					5t	mc	mc
Volvo Scandinavian Masters	8	14t		1		20t	mc	10t	2	17t
Chemapol Trophy Czech Open		7t	23t			20t		2	21	38t
US PGA CHAMPIONSHIP ##	13t	29t			mc	mc	27t		411	mc
Smurfit Euroipaen Open	22t		611	6t		32t	mc	50t	31t	38t
BMW International Open	3							mc	31t	mc
Canon European Masters	10t	12t	mc	2t	6t			43t	25t	63
Trophee Lancome	22t					321		13t	15t	
One 2 One British Masters	2	13t			8t	mc	361	59t	15t	211
Linde German Masters	2	1			mc	mc		30t	271	18t
Oki Pro-Am						30t		41	18t	3
Volvo Masters	8	15t	1		9t	21t		30t	571	4

COLIN MONTGOMERIE — Other world events in 1997

USA Doral Ryder Open 20t
USA Honda Classic 4
USA Bay Hill Invitational 19t
USA Players Championship 7t
USA MCI Classic 20t

Eur Toyota World Match Play Champ. 5t
Afr Hassan II Trophy 1st
SAf Nedbank $Million 7t
USA Andersen Consulting WC of G 1st

Alfred Dunhill Cup (Scotland)
Ryder Cup (Europe – Winners)
World Cup (Scotland)
(Won World Cup Individual Competition)

Note: Masters Tournament, US Open & US PGA Championship not Volvo Order of Merit events in 1997

1998 Volvo Order of Merit Final Placings

COLIN MONTGOMERIE — 1998

1	COLIN MONTGOMERIE
2	Darren Clarke
3	Lee Westwood
4	Miguel Angel Jimenez
5	Patrik Sjoland
6	Thomas Bjorn
7	Jose Maria Olazabal
8	Ernie Els
9	Andrew Coltart
10	Mathias Gronberg

Tournament	Montgomerie	Clarke	Westwood	Jimenez	Sjoland	Bjorn	Olazabal	Els	Coltart	Gronberg
Johnnie Walker Classic	4t			37t	mc			4t		mc
Heineken Classic				mc	1			15t		mc
South African Open				72t	mc					
Alfred Dunhill S A PGA Champ				2t	mc					
Dubai Desert Classic	10t	13t	mc	34t	35t	16t	12t	20t	mc	mc
Qatar Masters		9t	13t			3t		1		mc
Moroccan Open			14t	3					9	mc
Portuguese Open		6t	55t							3
MASTERS TOURNAMENT ##	8t	21t								
Cannes Open			9	27t	49t	44t	12t	32t	16t	
Peugeot Open de Espana		8t	44t	26t	26t			7t		
Fiat & Fila Italian Open					1			43t		
Turespana Masters Open Balleares	5t	6t		3t	11t	21				
Benson & Hedges International Open	1			2t	16t	2t		23t		
Volvo PGA Championship	10t		1	2t	27t					
Deutsche Bank - SAP Open TPC of Europe	4	29t	65t	1				5t	41t	
National Car Rental English Open		2	16t	1	7t	25t	9t	13t		
Madeira Island Open				1	21t		32t	41t		
US OPEN ##	18t	43t								
Peugeot Open de France	23t		7t	24t	18t					
Murphy's Irish Open	2			mc	21t	25t	49t			
The Standard Life Loch Lomond	7t	15	23t	mc	mc	9t				
OPEN CHAMPIONSHIP	mc	62t	16t	mc	mc	32t				
TNT Dutch Open		24t	24t	57t	33t	8t				
Volvo Scandinavian Masters	16t	3t	mc	42t	28t	14t				
German Open			9t	18t		55t				
US PGA CHAMPIONSHIP ##	44t	2	21t	17t	11t	mc	69			
Smurfit European Open	mc	2	3t	54t	7t				4	mc
BMW International Open	mc			mc			21t	67	13t	2
Canon European Masters	12t		6t				mc	21t	3	
One 2 One British Masters	1	6t	18t				37t	6t	19t	
Trophee Lancome	11t	12t	52t				18t	30t	1	mc
Linde German Masters	1	71t	mc				21t		33t	7t
Belgacom Open		6t					34t	61t	57t	35t
Volvo Masters	3	1	8t	2	16t				2	48t

COLIN MONTGOMERIE

Other world events in 1998

USA Doral Ryder Open	mc
USA Honda Classic	3rd
USA Bay Hill Invitational	8th
USA Players Championship	mc

Eur Cisco World Match Play Champ	5t
SAf Nedbank $Million	10th

Alfred Dunhill Cup (Scotland)	
World Cup (Scotland)	

Note: Masters Tournament, US Open & US PGA Championship not Volvo Order of Merit events in 1998

1999 Volvo Order of Merit Final Placings

1999 — COLIN MONTGOMERIE

Final placings 1–10:

1. **Colin Montgomerie**
2. Lee Westwood
3. Sergio Garcia
4. Miguel Angel Jimenez
5. Retief Goosen
6. Paul Lawrie
7. Padraig Harrington
8. Darren Clarke
9. Jarmo Sandelin
10. Angel Cabrera

Tournament	Montgomerie	Westwood	Garcia	Jimenez	Goosen	Lawrie	Harrington	Clarke	Sandelin	Cabrera
Alfred Dunhill S A PGA	5t		mc 2				5t1	mc	mc	mc 26t
Mercedes Benz – Vodacom S A Open			31t				4t	mc	7t	71
Heineken Classic							211	62t	211	211
Benson & Hedges Malaysian Open								24t	15t	43t
Dubai Desert Classic	33t		mc 2	8t	mc 33t	32t 1	24t	33t		25t
Qatar Masters	33t		331	20t	66t	41	91		16t	40t
WGC Anderson Consulting Match Play				mc	mc 41	mc 25t	49t		29t	
Algarve Portuguese Open						91	41			
Turespana Masters – Open Andalucia	11t		6t	mc	4t	25t		mc		
Madeira Island Open			38t	mc	71	41				
MASTERS TOURNAMENT ##				mc 2	21	2	54t			
Estoril Open			12t	461	61	1	2			
Peugeot Open de Espana			24t	6t	mc	mc 1	311	221		
Fiat and Fila Italian Open	20t		77t		71	43t	26t	261	21	
Novotel Perrier Open de France	1		56t	mc	41	28t	20t	71	10t	
Benson & Hedges International Open	1		20t	19t	2	2	471	131	mc	
Deutsche Bank – SAP Open TPC of Europe	5t				171	6t				
Volvo PGA Championship	1		5t	mc	mc 5	71	18t			
The Compass Group English Open	5t		23t	21	21t	29t	mc			
German Open		mc	2	mc 2	44t	59t=	1			
Moroccan Open			1							
US OPEN	15t		10t	111	111	mc	211	59n=		
Compaq European Grand Prix				mc 2	2	211	29t	mc		
Murphy's Irish Open	71	1	18t	430	300	29t				
The Standard Life Loch Lomond	1	15t	mc	2	15t	411	651			
OPEN CHAMPIONSHIP	15t		mc	5t	81	6t				
TNT Dutch Open			70t	1	1					
Smurfit European Open	15t	1	49t	1	1					
Volvo Scandinavian Masters	6t		24t	59t	301	211				
US PGA CHAMPIONSHIP			10t	34t	mc	411				
West of Ireland Golf Classic	1									
BMW International Open	30t		561	271	2	2				
WGC NEC Invitational	30t		211	121	33t	71				
Scottish PGA Championship										
Canon European Masters	4t	1	mc	10t	121					
Victor Chandler British Masters	2	41		10t	15t	71	28t	381	10t	
Trophee Lancome	3t		18t	2						
Linde German Masters	9t		69		461	5t	20t			
The Sarazan World Open										
Belgacom Open	16t	21	141	301	41					
Volvo Masters	20t	21	301	5t	371					
WGC American Express Championship	20t	25t	421	25t						

COLIN MONTGOMERIE

Other world events in 1999:

USA Honda Classic	38t
USA Bay Hill Invitational	60t
USA Players Championship	23t
USA BellSouth Classic	61
USA MCI Classic	60t

Eur Cisco World Match Play Champ. 1st
Aust Holden Australian Open 4th
SA? Nedbank $Million 2nd

Ryder Cup (Europe)
World Cup (Scotland)

Note: Masters Tournament not a Volvo Order of Merit event in 1999

INDEX